PRAISE FOR OTHER LOCH JOHNSON TITLES

The Making of International Agreements: Congress Confronts the Executive

". . . a useful analytical study [and] a valuable reference . . ."

—Gaddis Smith
Foreign Affairs

". . . fine book . . . comprehensively detailed . . . seasoned judgment . . ."

—Michael J. Glennon
American Journal of International Law

A Season of Inquiry: The Senate Intelligence Investigation

". . . brings a realism to a congressional probe rarely offered by authors of legislative case studies . . . a rare insight into the many variables that contribute to congressional investigative behavior."

—Harry Howe Ransom
American Political Science Review

". . . provides important insights into the real world of Capitol Hill . . . engaging . . ."

—Sanford J. Ungar
New York Times Book Review

America's Secret Power: The CIA in a Democratic Society

". . . imbued throughout with good sense about how secret intelligence and democratic society can be made to coexist."

—Gregory F. Treverton
Foreign Affairs

". . . a magisterial study . . . balanced judgment and meticulous documentation . . . the standard work on the Central Intelligence Agency . . ."

—Kevin V. Mulcahy
International Journal of Intelligence and Counterintelligence

Secret Agencies

". . . Johnson's concise and clear book is the best single-volume introduction to the nature of intelligence I have ever read."

—Robin W. Winks
Author of *Cloak and Gown*

"A remarkable, dispassionate, and informed analysis by an experienced insider . . ."

—Thomas F. Troy
Author of *Wild Bill and Intrepid*

Bombs, Bugs, Drugs, and Thugs

"An outstanding book, clearly the best recent, up-to-date survey of the American intelligence community, ranking with the top half-dozen ever."

—H. Bradford Westerfield
Yale University

". . . highly readable and provocative study . . ."

—Walter F. Mondale
Former Vice President

Other Books by Loch K. Johnson

Who's Watching the Spies? Establishing Intelligence Service Accountability, edited with Hans Born and Ian Leigh

American Foreign Policy: History, Politics, and Policy, with John Endicott and Daniel S. Papp

Fateful Decisions: Inside the National Security Council, edited with Karl F. Inderfurth

Strategic Intelligence: Windows into a Secret World, edited with James J. Wirtz

Bombs, Bugs, Drugs, and Thugs: Intelligence and America's Quest for Security; German edition: *Bomben, Wanzen und Intrigen: Amerikas Geheimdienste*

Secret Agencies: U.S. Intelligence in a Hostile World

America as a World Power: Foreign Policy in a Constitutional Framework

Runoff Elections in the United States, with Charles S. Bullock III

America's Secret Power: The CIA in a Democratic Society

Decisions of the Highest Order: Perspectives on the National Security Council, edited with Karl F. Inderfurth

Through the Straits of Armageddon: Arms Control Issues and Prospects, edited with Paul F. Diehl

A Season of Inquiry: The Senate Intelligence Investigation

The Making of International Agreements: Congress Confronts the Executive

GREAT QUESTIONS IN POLITICS SERIES

Seven Sins of American Foreign Policy

LOCH K. JOHNSON

SCHOOL OF PUBLIC AND INTERNATIONAL AFFAIRS

UNIVERSITY OF GEORGIA

New York   San Francisco   Boston
London   Toronto   Sydney   Tokyo   Singapore   Madrid
Mexico City   Munich   Paris   Cape Town   Hong Kong   Montreal

Editor in Chief: Eric Stano
Series Editor: George C. Edwards III
Senior Marketing Manager: Elizabeth Fogerty
Production Manager: Ellen MacElree
Project Coordination, Text Design, and Electronic Page Makeup: Stratford
Publishing Services
Cover Design Manager: Nancy Danahy
Cover Designer: Base Art Co.
Senior Manufacturing Buyer: Alfred C. Dorsey
Printer and Binder: Courier Corporation/Westford
Cover Printer: Coral Graphic Services

Library of Congress Cataloging-in-Publication Data
Johnson, Loch K.
    Seven sins of American foreign policy / Loch K. Johnson
    p. cm.— (Great question in politics series)
    Includes bibliographical references and index.
    Contents: Introduction: a heritage of ambivalence toward the world —
Ignorance — Executive branch dominance — Excessive emphasis on the military —
Unilateralism — Isolationism — Lack of empathy — Arrogance —
Conclusion: toward a more worthy foreign policy.
    ISBN 0-321-41585-X
    1. United States—Foreign relations—2001–   2. United States—Foreign public opinion.
3. United States—Foreign relations—Philosophy.   I. Title.   II. Series.
E902.J65 2006
327.73009'0511—dc22   2006011192

Visit us at www.ablongman.com

ISBN 0-321-41585-X (College version)

        0-321-39794-0 (Trade version)

1 2 3 4 5 6 7 8 9 10—CRW—08 07 06

For

Kristin and Leena

Contents

Preface

THE SEPTEMBER TERRORISTS

September 11, 2001—"9/11," as the day has been seared into the national memory—is a watershed moment in American history. Not since the War of 1812, when British redcoats invaded the nation's capital, have civilian targets in the United States been so savagely attacked by foreigners. The torching of the White House and the Capitol by the Royal Navy's Sir Admiral George Cockburn did not begin to approach the degree of carnage inflicted by the 9/11 terrorists on the World Trade Center in New York City; the Pentagon in Arlington, Virginia; and Flight 93 over Pennsylvania. Even the Japanese surprise attack at Pearl Harbor, directed against a military target, now seems less shocking than the murder of nearly 3,000 people, mainly civilians, during the first major terrorist event of the twenty-first century.[1]

Most of the world reacted to the 9/11 attacks with sympathy and support for the United States. This response was short-lived, however, replaced by a widespread disillusionment about—even marked hostility toward—America. As British historian Sir Michael Howard observed in 2002, "A year after September 11, the United

States finds itself more unpopular than perhaps it has ever been in its history."[2] In France, a foreign policy expert concluded in October 2002: ". . . no president since Nixon, and perhaps not even then, has been so unpopular here [as the incumbent President George W. Bush]."[3] In our own hemisphere, public opinion polls show the second President Bush to be "the most unpopular American president ever among Latin Americans."[4]

Hostility toward the Bush administration has hardly been isolated to France or Latin America. Anti-Americanism, not just anti-Bushism, has been rampant throughout Europe and runs deeper still in the Islamic world. According to pollster Daniel Yankelovich, in 2004, only 12 percent of Muslims believed that Americans respect Islamic values; 7 percent thought the West understands Muslim culture; and 11 percent approved of President Bush. Just 13 percent of Egyptians, 6 percent of Jordanians, and 3 percent of Saudi Arabians held a favorable opinion of the United States. An astounding 74 percent of Indonesians feared a U.S. military attack against their nation, as did 72 percent of the public in Nigeria, 72 percent in Pakistan, and 71 percent in Turkey. A majority of the populace in Germany, France, Italy, Greece, the Netherlands, and Pakistan expressed an unfavorable view of the United States to pollsters.[5]

Even most citizens in Great Britain, the main partner of the United States in the war against Iraq initiated in 2003, expressed a belief that Americans typically act out of their own interest, without regard for the interests of allies (73 percent), and that the United States represented a threat to world peace (55 percent).[6] If there was ever a friend of the United States, it would have to be Australia. Americans and Australians have had a long-standing favorable view of one another. Yet polling in 2005 indicated that Australians now have a more positive opinion of China, France, the United Nations, and seven other countries, regions, or groups than they do of the United States. Indeed, the poll results divided evenly on the question of whether the greatest danger to the world came from Islamic fundamentalism or American foreign policy.[7]

Soon after September 11, 2001, American and Northern Alliance forces swept through Afghanistan in search of the Al Qaeda terrorists who had ordered the attacks against the United States. Targeted, too, were members of the Taliban regime that had ruled Afghanistan and provided a safe haven for Osama bin Laden and other Al Qaeda leaders. The U.S.-led forces captured hundreds of prisoners and sent many of them to America's naval base at Guantánamo, on the southern edge of Cuba's main island. The prisoners are being held indefinitely, without formal charges or legal counsel.

Parliamentarians, scholars, and journalists around the world have raised troubling questions about possible human rights violations of the prisoners. In Europe, for example, participants attending a Norwegian conference on security issues in 2003 expressed dismay over media reports about America's poor treatment of prisoners held at Guantánamo.[8] In 2004, the release of photographs by a Pentagon whistle-blower depicting the torture of prisoners by U.S. military intelligence officers at the Abu Ghraib prison in Iraq further inflamed worldwide criticism of the United States. "The photographs shattered our reputation as the world's most admired champion of freedom and justice," observed Philip Gordon of the Brookings Institution in Washington, DC. "That is grave, because without the world's trust, America cannot flourish."[9]

Adding to the dismay expressed by America's allies abroad was the news in 2005 that the CIA had established a network of secret prisons around the world to detain and interrogate prisoners in the struggle against terrorism, including sites in Thailand and Eastern Europe.[10] Exactly how extreme the interrogations in these prisons have been is unclear, but the revelation did nothing to bolster the standing of the United States in the world; nor did the Bush administration's pursuit of an exemption from the rules of the Geneva Conventions for CIA interrogation methods. An American traveling in Amsterdam wrote home: "It was instructive to be an American visiting the Netherlands this week when the news broke that my country is operating a secret prison in Eastern Europe. As a middle-aged Dutchman said to me: 'What has happened to the America I grew up admiring? This is something the Communists would do.'"[11]

DEEPER CURRENTS OF ENMITY

A central theme of this book is that the pervasive negative attitudes toward the United States around the world today have a wellspring that runs deeper than the events surrounding the nation's response to the September 11th attacks. I argue that, through the years, seven major shortcomings or "sins"—a provocative word meant to suggest a cluster of questionable features of American foreign policy—have cost this nation the friendship and support of many allies abroad and, as a result, have impaired the ability of the United States to advance its own international interests.

The sins include an appalling ignorance of the culture and history of other countries; an institutional bias toward the dominance of presidential power in foreign affairs, leading to foreign policy by executive fiat; an inclination to seek a military solution to problems overseas, as if the world's most pressing challenges could be resolved through the use of precision bombs, missiles, paramilitary operations, and "special forces"; a go-it-alone attitude that downgrades working with other nations and international organizations in the search for common solutions to global problems; an isolationist instinct that drives some Americans back into a shell of disinterest, disregard, and even disdain for foreigners; a lack of empathy for the wrenching poverty and disease that haunts so many people in other lands; and an attitude of arrogance that is more in the spirit of the Roman Caesars than a trusted and respected world leader.

No doubt the United States has attracted a certain amount of enmity from other countries simply by virtue of envy of and resentment toward its great wealth and military might—an alienation generated by the nation's imposing power, regardless of what policy choices it might adopt. While attitudes of this nature are perhaps inevitable, the seven sins have added substantially to the hostility felt toward the United States from around the globe.

The critique presented in these pages grew out of a concern, in the aftermath of the 9/11 attacks, about why support for the United States in its time of tragedy rapidly dissolved into widespread expressions of antipathy toward Americans, even by many of our closest allies. The heartfelt sympathy of erstwhile friends turned to ashes; dampened cheeks gave way to scornful frowns; condolences dissolved into condemnations. What was eating at those who now went out of their way to pillory the United States, almost as if Americans had been the perpetrators of violence on September 11th, rather than its victims? Why did the world suddenly seem to hate us, even as we mourned the loss of lives from the cruel attacks? The search for answers led far beyond a decline in foreign sympathy toward the United States in the immediate aftermath of the terrorist attacks. The international skepticism—and sometimes fear—expressed by foreigners about the uses of American power in the world clearly had a much longer history.

The sins of American foreign policy have roots that extend more deeply than just the controversial decisions of the second Bush administration. Indeed, President George W. Bush has done much good in the world, such as his efforts to increase funding for antipoverty programs in Africa. These roots run through parties and administrations across the decades. In my efforts to trace them, the guiding questions have been: When has the United States excelled in its relations with the rest of the world? When has it stumbled? When has the rest of the world admired—or cringed at—America's global leadership? The sympathies expressed toward the United States during its time of suffering in 2001 masked, only briefly, a profound fault line of animosity regarding its conduct of foreign affairs. Fortunately, Americans have always had many friends abroad, too. However, the rising tide of suspicion and enmity toward the United States around the world is, or at least should be, cause for great concern.

Because not every reader will have a strong background in U.S. foreign policy, I begin with a brief historical sketch. This introduction reviews the ups and downs of America's involvement in world affairs and underscores the nation's persistent feelings of ambivalence toward the wisdom of foreign "entanglements."[12] It sets the stage for an examination of the "sins" of American foreign policy in the next seven chapters. A final chapter focuses on an evaluation of this nation's major foreign policy initiatives since the end of the Second World War—a "motorcycle ride through the art gallery," to borrow a phrase from Admiral William O. Studeman.

A foreign policy initiative is considered questionable ("sinful") if it is based on a false or sharply limited understanding of the region of the world it purports to address; if it violates the bedrock constitutional tenet of power-sharing between the legislative and executive branches of government; if it too quickly and unnecessarily resorts to the use of force in the resolution of global disputes; if it runs counter to established norms of contemporary international behavior accepted by the world's democracies; if it signals a withdrawal from the international community; if it exhibits a lack of concern for the basic human needs of other nations or projects a haughtiness in world affairs indicative of an imperious attitude toward others. It is unlikely that these sins are uniquely American, but this book is about U.S. foreign policy not the policies of other nations.

This list of sins has surfaced in my thinking as I have examined American foreign policy with legions of students over the past four decades, as well as in discussions with colleagues in academe and during my periodic stints in government, and with people I have met in frequent travels abroad and on the lecture circuit in the United States. Many will have a different list; some will disagree altogether with my choices. Others, overlooking the fact that we live on this side of heaven, may declare American foreign policy free of sin. An exchange of differing opinions is exactly what should occur in a democracy. The cause for concern is not differences of opinion about foreign policy goals, but the absence of a broader public discussion and debate about the proper course for the United States in the world today.

With respect to the ordering of my particular list of sins, I begin with ignorance. A greater understanding of global affairs would stimulate debate at home and improve the quality of foreign policy decisions, including greater attention to the other six sins. Public ignorance allows the executive branch to conduct foreign policy in a vacuum, without the need to justify its commitment of America's finite resources abroad. Further, dominance by the executive branch over foreign policy permits the president to embrace—prematurely and often in secret—military "solutions" to international disputes that, with patience, might be more safely addressed through diplomatic initiatives. In this regard, the first three sins have an affinity: ignorance spawns excessive executive discretion and overreliance on the military.

The next two sins, unilateralism and isolationism, also have close ties and often blend together, since unilateralism is often (though not always) a manifestation of a detachment from the international community. The final two sins, a lack of empathy and arrogance, also spring from a common source: a disregard for the views of other nations. I place no particular significance to the sequencing; each of the sins is important, and each warrants the attention of reformers.

What consequences flow from the effects of the seven sins? Have they contributed to the debit side of America's relations in the world? The specific metrics are elusive but my extensive discussions with experts and laymen alike, here and abroad, suggest the existence of real costs. Ignorance about the activities of Al Qaeda in early 2001 and about the absence of weapons of mass destruction (WMDs) in Iraq in 2002–03 led to substantial costs for the United States. Executive dominance over foreign policy, and the secrecy that attends it, has carried with it the heavy surcharge of limited debate in this country—an abandonment of the very anchor of democracy, as a poorly informed public and an inattentive Congress defer to the judgment of "experts" in the White House. Public opinion polls indicate, as well, that nations throughout the world are increasingly wary about the presence of U.S. military bases around the globe and America's perceived disregard for the views of others. Alienation toward the United States leads to the costs of declining cooperation with Americans in such matters as trade and the signing of international agreements, even a potential "ganging up" against America by other nations who fear—however incorrectly—that Washington, DC, aspires to the imperial status of ancient Rome.

Disconcerting for other nations, too, is the sense that the U.S. government believes in the maxim that what is good for America is good for the rest of the world. As historian John Lewis Gaddis notes, there is a distinct "whiff of grandiosity about the insistence that one nation's security is coterminous with that of everyone else."[13] When the young reporters Carl Bernstein and Bob Woodward of the *Washington Post* achieved fame for their disclosure of the Watergate scandal in the 1970s, the paper's wise owner Katherine Graham cautioned them to "beware of the demon Pomposity."[14] In a similar fashion and with the same result of estranging themselves from others, nations that don the mantle of superpower must beware of slipping into the trap of arrogance. The best remedy against the seventh sin is a sense of humility.

Honest and legitimate differences can exist between various schools of thought on the proper conduct of U.S. foreign policy and, honoring the canons of scholarship, this analysis presents a range of perspectives on the subject. Still, as the title indicates, this book does have a point of view, namely, that serious mistakes have been made in the relationships between the United States and the rest of the world and these mistakes have had harmful consequences for the national interest. The seven sins examined here have handicapped the nation's ability to achieve its foreign policy objectives, from the quest for peace and prosperity to the pursuit of global human rights and a better quality of life for Americans and everyone else.

Although at times quite critical, the book is not a diatribe against the United States or any particular administration. On the contrary, as is often the case with immigrants, the author (a New Zealander who arrived in San Francisco as a child in 1946) has an abiding love for this nation and a strong devotion to its political principles. Whether immigrant or natural born, most Americans would readily agree that the nation has had many great achievements. Still, we can do better.

With its demands on a reader's time and wallet, every book ought to have a good reason for existence. I offer this one: these pages seek to stimulate readers to think more critically about American foreign policy. The hope is that, through further public debate, we can find ways to improve the capabilities of the United States as a respected world leader, for our own sake and for the sake of others on this increasingly small and interwoven planet. Let me note, too, what the book is not. It is neither a traditional textbook nor a comprehensive historical treatment of American foreign policy. It does not offer an exhaustive inquiry into each of the seven sins, or systematically apply each of them to every major foreign policy initiative. It provides only some examples of the harmful influence of the sins, mainly from recent years, rather than attempting to comb the full record since the nation's earliest days. I have wanted this to be a little book—only the beginnings of a deeper exploration.

NOTES

1. For a detailed and dramatic narrative of the events of September 11, 2001, see the final report of the National Commission on Terrorist Attacks upon the United States (the Kean Commission, led by the Republican former governor of New Jersey Thomas H. Kean), entitled *The 9/11 Commission Report* (New York: Norton, 2004).
2. Michael Howard, "Smoke on the Horizon," *London Financial Times* (September 7, 2002), p. 1.
3. Alexandre Adler, quoted by Roger Cohen, David E. Sanger, and Steven R. Weisman, "Challenging the Rest of the World with a New Order," *New York Times* (October 12, 2004), p. A20.
4. Larry Rohter, "Bush Faces Tough Time in South America," *New York Times* (November 2, 2005), p. A12.
5. The Yankelovich figures are from Daniel Schorr, "Washington Notebook," *The New Leader* 81 (September/October 2004), p. 5. In the eighteen-month period from the summer of 2002 to the spring of 2004, America's favorability rating dropped from 63 percent to 37 percent in France and from 61 percent to 37 percent in Germany. See William J. Holstein, "Erasing the Image of the Ugly American," *New York Times* (October 23, 2005), p. C9.
6. See Schorr, ibid., and the compatible findings from the Pew Global Attitudes Project, summarized in "What Just Happened?" *New York Times* (December 26, 2004), p. E10.
7. Raymond Bonner, "U.S. Image Sags in Australian Poll," *New York Times* (March 29, 2005), p. A8.
8. Author's discussions with participants, Conference on "Making Intelligence Accountable: Executive and Legislative Oversight of Intelligence Services," Oslo, Norway, September 18–20, 2003.
9. Quoted in Cohen, Sanger, and Weisman, "Challenging the Rest of the World," p. A20.
10. See Dana Priest, "CIA Holds Terror Suspects in Secret Prisons," *Washington Post* (November 2, 2005), p. A1.
11. Gary Belis, letter to the editor, *New York Times* (November 4, 2005), p. A26.
12. In his famous Farewell Address (1796), President George Washington asked, "Why, by interweaving our destiny with that of any part of Europe,

entangle our peace and prosperity in the toils of European ambition, rival-
ship, interest, humor, or caprice?"

13. John Lewis Gaddis, *Surprise, Security, and the American Experience* (Cambridge, MA: Harvard University Press, 2004), p. 110.

14. Bob Woodward, remarks, Yale University, New Haven, Connecticut (October 25, 2005).

Acknowledgments

O ver the years I have had the opportunity to discuss American foreign policy in depth with a number of knowledgeable individuals, including Representative Les Aspin, Gary Bertsch, Representative Jonathan Bingham, Günter Bischof, Kiki Caruson, Senator Frank Church, Paul F. Diehl, John E. Endicott, Senator Wyche Fowler, John J. Glennon, Ambassador Martin J. Hillenbrand, Ambassador Karl F. Inderfurth, Edward J. Larson, David S. McLellan, Vice President Walter Mondale, Daniel S. Papp, Han Park, Jeffrey Pugh, Vernon Puryear, Harry Howe Ransom, Secretary of State Dean Rusk, Harold L. Sims, Robert H. Swansbrough, Gregory F. Treverton, Arthur C. Turner, Garry V. Wenske, H. Bradford Westerfield, Howard J. Wiarda, James J. Wirtz, and Amos Yoder. Moreover, my students at the University of Georgia have been sounding boards and sources of insight and inspiration. None of these good people should be blamed for any conclusions or errors of fact that appear in this book, but I would like to thank them for sharing their perspectives with me.

During the final work on this book, I was anchored in a most pleasant harbor: the Yale Center for International and Area Studies, where I was the Coca-Cola World Fund Distinguished Visiting Professor in the fall term of 2005. While at Yale University, I took part in the celebrated Grand Strategy seminar taught by Professors John Lewis Gaddis, Charles Hill, and Paul Kennedy. Filled with bright students and masterfully led by this trio of experienced hands, the seminar was just the place to be while writing a book on American foreign policy. Again, no one associated with that seminar is responsible for the results in this volume, but I am grateful for the chance to be a part of the seminar's wide-ranging discussion of strategy and America's role in the world. I thank each of the participants, especially Professors Gaddis, Hill, and Kennedy, for their warm welcome and their willingness to make me a full participant.

I have benefited as well from the insights of several reviewers who kindly read earlier drafts of the book and offered valuable guidance: Linda Adams, Baylor University; Christopher L. Ball, Iowa State University; Derrick Frazier, University of Illinois at Urbana-Champaign; Aaron Karp, Old Dominion University; Richard J. Kilroy, East Carolina University; B. David Meyer, University of North Carolina, Greensboro; and Richard Nolan, University of Florida. Of course, they are not responsible for the conclusions I have reached. Acquisitions editor Ed Costello suggested I write this book with Pearson Longman and the experience has been a good one, with excellent copy editing by Simone Payment and cheerful, sure-handed guidance from executive editor Eric Stano. My research assistants and doctoral students at the University of Georgia, Stacey Gibson-Mitchell and Larry Lamanna, along with undergraduate Rachel Lee Stewart, helped to check footnotes and facts with unwavering enthusiasm and thoroughness. At Yale University, I had the good help of Philip Brower on computer problems large and small, as well as the opportunity to discuss world affairs with undergraduate and graduate students in my class on "Intelligence and National Security."

I am indebted beyond mere words to Leena S. Johnson, in-house editor, adviser, wife, and indispensable partner in all things for the past thirty-seven years, who carefully read the drafts, kept the tea coming, and tolerated the solitary life of an academic; and to my daughter, Kristin E. Johnson, whose questions about the United States and the world have always been thoughtful and challenging, and whose own insights have been of enormous value to me.

About the Author

LOCH K. JOHNSON is Regents Professor of Public and International Affairs at the University of Georgia, senior editor of the journal *Intelligence and National Security*, and the author of several books and more than one hundred articles on U.S. national security. His most recent book is *Who's Watching the Spies?* (co-edited). He has won the Certificate of Distinction from the National Intelligence Study Center, the Studies in Intelligence Award from the Center for the Study of Intelligence, and the V.O. Key Prize from the Southern Political Science Association. He was an American Political Science Association Congressional Fellow, and he has served as secretary of the American Political Science Association and president of the International Studies Association, South. Johnson was special assistant to the chair of the Senate Select Committee on Intelligence in 1975–76, staff director of the House Subcommittee on Intelligence Oversight in 1977–79, and special assistant to the chair of the Aspin-Brown Commission on Intelligence in 1995.

Born in Auckland, New Zealand, Professor Johnson received his Ph.D. in political science from the University of California, Riverside. At the University of Georgia, he has won the Josiah Meigs Prize, the University's highest teaching honor, as well as the

Owens Award, its highest research honor. He led the founding of the new School of Public and International Affairs, established at the University in 2001. He has been a Visiting Fellow at Oxford University (2003), and the Coca-Cola World Fund Distinguished Visiting Professor at Yale University (2005).

INTRODUCTION

A Heritage of Ambivalence Toward the World

SPLENDID ISOLATION

Frank Church (D-ID), a prominent member of the Senate Foreign Relations Committee during the 1970s, maintained that America's "belief in freedom and popular government once made us a beacon of hope for the downtrodden and oppressed throughout the world." He urged the nation to embrace again a foreign policy that, "whether openly or secretly pursued, conformed once more to our historic ideals."[1] These remarks, delivered passionately by one of the Senate's most accomplished orators, sound reasonable enough—even noble. But what are America's "historic ideals"? How do they relate to the rest of the world?

Keeping Europe at a Distance

In the nation's earliest days, most citizens and certainly their leaders had no interest whatsoever in being a beacon of hope for anyone overseas, however downtrodden or oppressed. Militarily weak, groping for an identity, facing an uncertain future, they were concerned mainly about protecting the fragile tendrils of the new republic. Survival was their foremost objective. The goal was to distance themselves from the ever-present military dangers posed by bellicose European powers, with their mighty armies, warships that boasted 28-guns firing three broadsides in ninety seconds, and legendary warriors such as Napoleon, Nelson, and Wellington.

The Revolutionary War against Great Britain had been exhausting enough, in blood and treasure; the fledgling nation did not need further embroilment in the perilous machinations of the Europeans. What America did need was rest, a breathing space, time to put its house in order. It also needed time to sort out its unique rules of governance, so starkly different from other regimes of the time, with an emphasis on free and open elections (blacks and women excluded, a stain on the ledger that would take many decades to remove); the dispersal of powers among three departments of government (the executive, legislative, and judicial); freedom of speech and religion; and a constitutional framework that promised to ensure and protect the preeminence of the people over their rulers. In self-preservation, and with the self-absorption of youth, the new nation struck an aloof posture, at least to the extent it could as avaricious powers in Europe eyed the riches of the Western Hemisphere.

In this hope of separation from "all the wrangling world" (Thomas Paine's quaint phrase), the United States in its beginning was blessed by good fortune. The foremost advantage was geographic: the protection afforded by the wide moats of the Atlantic and Pacific oceans, what one wag at the time referred to as "America's greatest liquid assets."[2] The European powers were six weeks away by even the fastest of warships, and potential Asian adversaries farther still. Happily, too, no strong rivals existed within the Western Hemisphere, although a number of nations in Europe held disquieting footholds in the New World. English explorers and well-armed adventurers prowled Canada and the northwest territory; France had recently repossessed New Orleans, formerly a French colony, and the rest of the Louisiana territory (by treaty with Spain in 1800); Spain considered Florida part of its domain; and Russians peered longingly across the Bering Strait into Alaska and the northwest. Still, despite these looming threats, those who lived among the warring powers of Europe and the Far East looked upon America's relatively isolated and tranquil setting with great envy. "North and south, you have weak neighbors," sighed a French diplomat. "East and west, you have fish!"[3]

Fortuitous as well was an important historical circumstance: the reigning powers of Europe remained distracted by troubles on their own continent and had little time or inclination to deal with the upstart regime in North America. A nation's leaders are driven by a survival instinct, the fundamental law of man and nature; they are threat oriented. They want to know how many divisions and how many warships an opponent has. To what extent does another nation or terrorist organization imperil one's territorial integrity and right to exist, free of foreign control? In this regard, George Washington and his ragtag army, though victorious over the British in the Revolutionary War, paled as a threat to Europeans when compared to the great political and military upheavals that lacerated their lands in the late eighteenth century. America also had no navy to speak of, but did have the good fortune of an alliance with the French and their considerable armada. France, though, would soon have its own domestic problems to confront. Revolution ripped asunder the feudal social and political order in France, sending the French king and queen to the guillotine as traitors in 1783. Soon Napoleon's armies were on the march against the British, the Germans, and the Russians, while British ships under Lord Nelson's able and audacious command hunted the French and Spanish navies on the high seas of the Atlantic and the Mediterranean.

America aggressively sought commercial opportunities with the contentious Europeans, but tried to avoid political and military entanglements abroad. As Washington put it memorably in his Farewell Address:

> Europe has a set of primary interests, which to us have none, or a very remote relation. Hence, she must be engaged in frequent controversies, the causes of which are essentially foreign to our concerns. Hence, therefore, it must be unwise in us to implicate ourselves by artificial ties, in the ordinary combinations and collisions of her friendships or enmities.[4]

This policy of an arm's-length distance from Europe's political and military turmoil was followed unevenly, though, even by those in the American colonies who basically agreed with Washington's sentiments. As general of the rebellious forces, Washington himself had wooed France into an alliance against England during America's Revolutionary War; French troops, and especially the French navy, played an indispensable role in helping the colonialists defeat the numerically superior British forces. Following the war, Washington—now president—pushed the French away and issued a Proclamation of Neutrality in 1793 to avoid being caught up in the latest maelstrom gathering on the European continent. Near the end of his presidency, Washington signed the Jay Treaty of 1794, deftly restoring commercial ties with America's erstwhile bitter enemy, the British. As wars raged on in Europe, merchants in the new nation profited by selling goods to both the French and the British.

Although Washington further advised in his Farewell Address that the United States should "hold an equal and impartial hand" in its relations with other nations, Francophiles in America bitterly resented what they perceived as the president's ungrateful tilt away from France—the very nation that had assisted the colonists in securing their freedom from the British monarch, George III. Anglophiles, in turn, applauded Washington's efforts at rapprochement with London. As much as the new republic might have wished to seal itself off from entanglements overseas, foreign policy even at this early stage had demonstrated a capacity to inflame domestic constituencies and rile the best attempts at steering a course between warring factions abroad. In the wake of the Jay Treaty, an undeclared war broke out between the United States and France, beginning with the French navy's practice of halting American merchant vessels and roughing up their sailors.

John Adams followed Washington as president and, in 1797, he sent a diplomatic envoy to Paris in hopes of calming relations with the French. A beautiful woman and three gentlemen, identified only as Messieurs "X," "Y," and "Z," approached the envoy. Evidently secretly backed by the French foreign minister, Talleyrand, the mysterious quartet tried to extort a cash payment from the American envoy in return for a negotiated resolution of hostilities between the two governments. Outraged, President Adams publicly disclosed the French covert operation (the "XYZ affair," as it came to be known), further stirring American public opinion against France.

The splendid isolation Americans had both sought and been blessed with naturally proved to be neither splendid nor isolated. The new nation required commercial markets abroad to prosper and grow; yet, attempts to establish trading partnerships seemed to lead ineluctably into political and even military snares, however much Washington and other early leaders of the republic tried to keep them separate. The evolving prescription for America's nascent relations with the rest of the world seemed to be isolationism except when a timely military alliance might benefit the nation, as with the French during the War of Independence, or when commercial opportunities overseas might help entrepreneurs in Boston, New York, and Savannah sell their furs, fish, grain, tobacco, and textiles, and thereby aid the nation's embryonic economy. America's leaders continued their efforts, however quixotic, to keep commercial interests somehow neatly set apart from the stickier domains of political and military intrigue.

In his inaugural address, the nation's third president, the cerebral Thomas Jefferson, spoke in a spirit reminiscent of George Washington's Farewell Address. Jefferson advocated "peace, commerce and honest friendship with all nations, entangling alliances with none." Yet he was no more of a purist on the idea of keeping America separate from the rest of the world than Washington had been. Even though Jefferson was personally something of a Francophile, he was entirely prepared to join England in a war against France if Napoleon Bonaparte refused to sell New Orleans to the United States. In Jefferson's calculations, America's febrile aspirations for westward expansion trumped even the considerable attractions of French wine, women, and culture.

Far from turning away from the world, Jefferson displayed a penchant as well for the aggressive use of secret agents to achieve America's foreign policy objectives. In a scheme to overthrow the Bashaw of Tripoli, who had from time to time disrupted American commercial shipping in the Mediterranean, Jefferson authorized the shipment of a few artillery pieces and one thousand small arms to the Bashaw's older brother, who promised to assume the role of head of state and treat the Americans more favorably.[5] Thus was launched America's first significant covert action—an early and secret use of the preventive war doctrine adopted by the second Bush administration in 2001 under the misnomer of "preemption" (a term more accurately reserved for a quick attack against an adversary considered likely to strike first and at any moment). Like many covert actions to follow into the modern era, this one failed when the Bashaw's troops managed to capture and exile the would-be ruler.

From the start, the new republic followed the two most essential rules of foreign policy: first and foremost, protect oneself against military threats from abroad; and, second, seek out commercial opportunities to strengthen the economic might of the nation and the prosperity of its citizens. These basic tenets have guided the United States throughout its history, regardless of the nation's oscillation between isolationist and international instincts. Beginning in the twentieth century, the tenets were augmented by a growing interest in global democracy and human rights, followed by a concern for such quality of life issues as environmental protection and the eradication of disease. In the early days of the republic, however, the nation had to be cautious. Its military strength was negligible and its diplomats inexperienced. As a result, Washington, Adams, and Jefferson tried to keep the nation's profile low and distant from the great power confrontations in Europe. America did not have its head in the sand, though, and was bold and far-sighted enough to resist attempts by the European powers to seek a dominant role in the affairs of Latin America and Canada.

Expansionist Stirrings

The first attempt to throw Europeans out of the Western Hemisphere—America's War of Independence—had succeeded. The second attempt was a success as well, and was accomplished without shedding a single drop of blood. In 1803, Jefferson simply placed $15 million on the barrel head and bought out the French interests in New Orleans and the Louisiana Territory. Fortunately, Napoleon preferred to take the money and run, concentrating his efforts on vanquishing Europe and Russia. Jefferson was the beneficiary of these happy circumstances. Although the price tag for this real estate acquisition was steep at the time, the fee was far less expensive than a war against Napoleon for control over the vast tract of land.

As Napoleon set forth on his ill-fated mission to conquer all of Europe and Russia, the United States again found itself caught up in the eddies of foreign conflict, hopes to the contrary notwithstanding. Angered by America's burgeoning trade with France, British ships engaged in the impressment of U.S. merchant sailors: naval recruitment by force—kidnapping—to man British warships against the French fleet. When the British fired on the American frigate the USS *Chesapeake* in 1807, killing three crew members, President Jefferson responded by persuading Congress to enact an embargo against the sale of American goods to Britain. The embargo proved widely unpopular among New Englanders, who were largely pro-British and depended on foreign trade with Britain for their livelihood. Members of Congress from that region managed to have the law overturned in 1809. The New Englanders argued that the French had been as despicable as anyone toward the new republic, marauding American vessels at sea at least as often as the British. While the French did refrain from impressment, it is true that they frequently captured U.S. ships and sold them to the highest bidder, imprisoning the crews.

Elsewhere in the country, though, the British were considered far more objectionable than the French, especially among the ultranationalist war hawks, who supported the administration of James Madison (America's fourth president) and longed for another war against Great Britain. The time had come, they insisted, to put an end to England's insulting attempts to dominate shipping across the Atlantic Ocean. "Embargoes, nonintercourse, and negotiations are but illy [badly] calculated to secure our rights," war hawks proclaimed at a Fourth of July celebration in Kentucky in 1811. "Let us now try old Roman policy, and maintain them with the sword."[6]

Aggravating as well to the war hawks was the British presence in Canada, which fairly bristled with the presence of His Majesty's gunboats and row after row of redcoats. More to the point, the British were interfering with America's march of destiny toward the west. As pioneers began to move across the Allegheny Mountains, they encountered the understandable resistance of Native Americans who resented this intrusion into their homelands. Instead of bows and arrows, however, many of the indigenous peoples turned out to be well-armed by the British with muskets, and had been encouraged to dispatch as many of the encroaching Americans as possible. War hawks wanted America's infantrymen to drive the British out of Canada—the only military option, since the U.S. navy remained an outgunned deterrent to King George's daunting flotilla of warships. They believed that since Napoleon had so easily surrendered his Louisiana stakes in the New World maybe the British would also tuck tail and flee from Canadian soil.

Thus was America riven with debate over who most warranted an attack from the United States: the British (a policy supported by the Francophiles, who were mostly rural Jeffersonian Republicans) or the French (a policy supported by the Anglophiles, mostly New England Federalists). The United States did not have the resources to take on both challenges at the same time. Soon Americans tilted toward taking up arms once more against the British, with impressment the first article to justify the decision. The ensuing War of 1812 against the British proved to be a disaster, however—indeed, "the greatest disgrace ever dealt to American arms."[7]

As historian Thomas A. Bailey notes, the war "was a rash departure from the judicious policy of Washington, Adams, and Jefferson—of playing for time and letting America's booming birthrate and Europe's recurrent distresses fight the nation's battles."[8] The nation, still in its infancy, was unable this time to repel the British military. The Congress refused to appropriate funds to combat the redcoat siege against Washington. Admiral Sir George Cockburn of the Royal Navy torched the Capitol and the White House, while President Madison fled on horseback into the Virginia countryside. Cabinet members hid in their home states; federal lawmakers adjourned; Anglophiles in New England denounced "Mr. Madison's war"; and Connecticut, Massachusetts, and Rhode Island went so far as to seek a separate peace with the British Crown. American infantrymen sought to rout British and Canadian forces, and a rout is what they got—but in the wrong direction. Only General Andrew Jackson's spirited victory at New Orleans, Admiral Oliver Hazard Perry's triumph in the Battle of Lake Erie, and Brigadier General Winfield Scott's great courage displayed at the battles of Chippewa and Lundy's Lane in Canada provided occasions for national pride.

At last, on Christmas Eve of 1814, both the British and the Americans—war-weary, tax-burdened, and bloodied—decided they were fed up with the war. Fortunately for the United States, at the time, Napoleon attracted greater attention in London than the unruly former colonialists. The British needed to marshal their resources for a final push against the French emperor, who more directly threatened the British way of life than the faraway, obstreperous republic in the New World. American and British diplomats signed the Treaty of Ghent in 1814, an initiative acclaimed throughout the United States, even though the peace treaty delicately sidestepped any mention of freedom on the high seas or curbing the evils of impressment—the original cause of war.

In the Rush-Bagot Agreement of 1817 (America's first significant arms control pact), the British and the Americans further agreed to remove their naval ships from the Great Lakes, defusing an ongoing explosive situation. Though humiliated in the War of 1812, the United States had demonstrated some skill at diplomacy—although, again, thanks in large part to Britain's greater interest in maintaining its military strength on the high seas and in defense of the British Isles against the French and other European rivals.

Its efforts to annex Canada quickly rebuffed by the independent-minded Canadians, the United States turned toward Florida where Spanish armies and their indigenous allies often disrupted the flow of commerce from farmers in Georgia and Alabama into eastern seaboard ports for shipment to Europe. President James Monroe sent the indomitable "Hero of New Orleans," Andrew Jackson, into the Florida Territory in 1817 to protect America's interests. With questionable authority but unquestioned brio, Jackson swiftly deposed the Spanish governor, executed suspected British spies who got in his way, and announced that henceforth America held legal jurisdiction over the entire Florida Territory. Apparently this bullfighter's swagger impressed the Spanish, who left the military arena and entered into protracted diplomatic negotiations with the Monroe administration that ended in a tradeoff with the signing of the Adams-Onís Treaty of 1821. Americans took over the Florida Territory in exchange for assurances that the Spanish would enjoy unfettered rule over Texas and the southwest. Some questioned the wisdom of this bargain, but most were happy to have Spain permanently out of the new nation's southeast corner.

Monroe Delivers a Lecture

America's central foreign policy interests—securing its territorial integrity and protecting its commercial activities—were underscored in a celebrated lecture to the Europeans delivered by President Monroe in 1823 as part of his State of the Union address. It was a case of the pupil sternly wagging his finger at the headmasters. In this most heralded of all American foreign policy pronouncements, subsequently labeled the Monroe Doctrine, the president warned the capitals of the Old World that the nations of the Western Hemisphere were "henceforth not to be considered as subjects for future colonization by any European power."

Speaking brashly on behalf of a weak nation that not long before had lost the War of 1812, Monroe further advised:

> In the wars of the European powers in matters relating to themselves we have never taken any part, nor does it comport with our policy so to do. It is only when our rights are invaded or seriously menaced that we resent injuries or make preparations for our defense. With the movements in this hemisphere we are, of necessity, more immediately connected. . . . We owe it, therefore, to candor, and to the amicable relations existing between the United States and those powers, to declare that we should consider any attempt on their part to extend their system to any portion of this hemisphere as dangerous to our peace and safety . . . It is equally impossible, therefore, that we should behold such interposition, in any form, with indifference.[9]

These words had a strong effect on many who read them, including retired president Thomas Jefferson. "This sets our compass and points the course which we are to steer through the ocean of time opening on us," he wrote.[10] In an ironic twist of history,

President Monroe enjoyed the support of a strong-armed ally who backed the president's desire to preserve the Americas for the Americans: none other than the nation's recent foe, Great Britain. The British sought to block the rumored French and Spanish economic designs on the Americas (more figments of the overheated imagination of London strategists than real) and, at least for the moment, they found it convenient to stand with the United States. His Majesty's government even offered to issue a joint U.S.-British declaration of warning to the Europeans. Monroe's secretary of state, John Quincy Adams, sagely suggested to the president, however, that the United States take a stance on its own and avoid leaving the impression to other nations that the young republic was merely a "cockboat in the wake of the British man-of-war."[11] The president's address had little influence at the time in world capitals; still, the prestige of Monroe's famous name and the "aura of antiquity"[12] associated with the statement would allow future presidents to invoke the Doctrine's principles as if they were a hallowed American tradition.

Westward Ho!

When Senator Frank Church spoke of the United States during the Cold War as a beacon of hope for the world, he was reiterating a view that has long been a part of the nation's culture: a feeling of American exceptionalism, a moral and religious belief that this land has a special mission in history. As Thomas Jefferson put it, the United States was "the last best hope of mankind." Presidents from Abraham Lincoln to Ronald Reagan would refer to the nation as a "light on a hill"; and the poet Walt Whitman went so far as to suggest that the whole world gazed upon America with a sense that

> Humanity with all its fears,
> With all the hopes of future years
> Is hanging breathless on thy fate![13]

Initially, the self-perceived mission of the United States was to tame the western frontier in the name of democracy and commerce. The nation turned to the task with an admirable gusto during the Monroe administration (1817–25), as captured by the slogan "manifest destiny" that sprang from the pages of newspaper editor John L. O'Sullivan in 1845.[14] A rising number of ambitious farmers and trappers ventured into the continental heartland, followed by merchants with dreams of harbors on the Pacific coast and sea-lanes to the markets of Asia. The march into the territories was underway, as Americans envisioned unlimited possibilities for themselves and their progeny in the vast reaches of the west.

The westward movement was costly, though, not just in terms of depleting the federal treasury (as with the Louisiana purchase) but in the blood spilled in wars with American Indians. The tragedies visited upon the Cherokees, driven from their ancestral lands along the Trail of Tears, and upon other Native Americans are—along with slavery—wretched episodes in the nation's history.

In the name of further expansion, Americans seemed prepared in 1846 to fight the British in yet a third war, this time for land in the Pacific northwest. "54°40' or Fight" became the rallying cry for presidential candidate James K. Polk and his supporters, who insisted the United States dissolve an agreement signed with the British in 1818 that established joint control over the region. The

Polk faction sought to take over the Northwest Territory all the way to 54°40' north latitude. Once elected president, cooler heads prevailed and Polk managed to avoid war by negotiating a compromise that divided the territory between the United States and Great Britain at the 49th parallel.

Next on the real estate acquisitions list was the prospect of more land in the southwest and along the Pacific coast. Of particular appeal to Polk was the prospect of ports in California, opening up the Asian "frontier." In 1846, the American president intentionally provoked Mexico into war by placing the bait of U.S. cavalry troops along the Rio Grande. When Mexico attacked the troops, Polk had the pretext he needed to seek a declaration of war from Congress. The lawmakers obliged and war with Mexico was underway. The struggle would last for two years, ending in a U.S. victory and the signing of a peace accord known as the Treaty of Guadalupe Hidalgo. Polk got his California ports and much more, as the treaty ceded to the United States all of New Mexico, Arizona, California, and an extension of the Texas boundary to the Rio Grande. The United States conveniently forgot the earlier promises in the Adams-Onís Treaty that this part of the New World would fall within Spain's sphere of influence.

Once they arrived at the west coast, gateway to the Pacific, Asia beckoned to the restless spirit of southern cotton growers and western fur trappers, along with business entrepreneurs, adventurers, and missionaries from across the United States. Two years before the Mexican War, the administration of James K. Polk had dispatched an emissary to China for the purpose of negotiating access to markets for American goods. Then, in 1854, Commodore Matthew C. Perry steamed into the Bay of Yedo (now Tokyo) with an armada of

U.S. naval ships worthy of a major power. He carried a letter of friendship from President Franklin Pierce addressed to the Emperor of Japan. While in the region, Perry visited China as well, nudging this market of a half-billion consumers further toward a trading relationship with the United States. America was hardly the only nation to dream of commercial profits in Asia; European rivals had their own merchant and warships plying the waters along the Chinese and Japanese seaboards. The long history of isolationism practiced by the two Asian powers was beginning to erode.

On the missionary front, American Christians sought to convert untold millions of people living in the Far East to their faith. Defending U.S. interests in the Philippines, a senator from Minnesota maintained that "we come as ministerial angels, not as despots."[15] President William McKinley agreed wholeheartedly. It was the duty of Americans in the Philippines, he would declare at the end of the nineteenth century, to "uplift and civilize and Christianize."[16] The goal of American church leaders to save the world from the devil had introduced a distinctive and enduring moral dimension into the evolution of American foreign policy.

Thus, at mid-nineteenth century, the United States had established two quite different stances toward the world: keeping Europe at a distance, while at the same time reaching out to Asia— isolationism, on the one hand, and involvement on the other hand. This ambivalence would remain a hallmark of American foreign policy through the decades. "Americans did not feel that a vigorous and far-reaching policy in the Pacific contradicted their basic isolationist premise," observes Charles O. Lerche, Jr., "even though great-power intrigue complicated their every move."[17] America would try to isolate itself from the political wrangling of

Europe, but its evangelizing religious spirit would encourage a reaching out to the unsaved souls of Asia.

Civil War

Missionary work, coupled with trade for cotton and furs in exchange for Asian tea and spices, were hardly the sole preoccupations of the United States at this time. For, in fact, the "United" States stood on the brink of disintegration. Nothing since the War of Independence so turned the nation inward as the "War Between the States" (or, for southerners, the "War of Northern Aggression") that ignited in 1861. The nation now had dual foreign policies, as both the north and the south turned toward Europeans for help in their separate causes. Great Britain flirted with the idea of a formal alliance with the south, the source of 80 percent of the cotton used in British textile mills. "We do not like slavery," said British Prime Minister Lord Palmerston, "but we want cotton."[18] After the north's military victory at Antietam in 1862 (however unimpressive, in light of the failure of the federal troops to pursue the retreating Army of Northern Virginia), London had second thoughts and chose the more prudent course of neutrality.

In the midst of President Abraham Lincoln's internecine woes, France spotted an opportunity: the Americans were now too distracted to worry much about defending the principles of the Monroe Doctrine. French troops invaded Mexico and placed an Austrian archduke, Ferdinand Maximilian, on its throne. The calculations of the government in Paris, a monarchy led by Napoleon III, were correct. Officials in Washington wrung their hands and protested the invasion but, preoccupied by the Civil War, they could manage nothing more.

When the Civil War ended in 1865, however, the United States sent a stern warning to Paris: cease and desist from the Mexican venture—or face the consequences. The French withdrew, perhaps in part because America's military might (as demonstrated in the Civil War) impressed Napoleon III, but probably more so because of the unpopularity of the expensive Mexican initiative among the people of France. Further considerations included the fear in Paris of rising German militarism, along with a concern about a mounting guerrilla war fought by the Mexicans against the French interlopers. Left in the lurch was poor, handsome Maximilian (the "Archdupe"), who for all his troubles soon found himself standing before a Mexican firing squad.

The period of the American Civil War represented a low ebb in the nation's foreign policy, as the country turned sharply inward. Paradoxically, though, the war had a significant influence on U.S. relations with the world. The firepower and battlefield skill displayed by the north and the south sent a signal around the globe that the United States was now a potent military force. Moreover, America's apparent determination to push the French out of Mexico, by the point of a bayonet if necessary, revealed a tenacious adherence to Monroe's principles of 1823. No foreign power would seriously challenge the Monroe Doctrine again until the Cuban missile crisis of 1962.

A Bolder Nation

Civil war behind them, Americans returned once more to the task of nation-building. In 1867, Secretary of State W. H. Seward, a zealous expansionist, purchased the Alaskan Territory ("Seward's Icebox") from the Russians for $7.2 million—about two cents an acre. Not every American shared his enthusiasm for expansion, referring to the Alaskan purchase as "Seward's Folly." Opponents objected not only to the immediate costs but to the longer-term burdens of added territory. Lawmakers voted against efforts to buy the Virgin Islands and to establish a protectorate over Haiti. Like earlier generations, Americans remained of two minds about the involvement of the country in affairs beyond these shores. "The nation lunged into the future at breakneck speed," writes Lerche, "but with constant nostalgic glances to the simpler past it was leaving behind."[19]

Emboldened by its growing military and economic strength, the United States flatly told the British in 1895 that officials in Washington would be the ones to arbitrate a diplomatic dispute between the United Kingdom and Venezuela. Magisterially, Secretary of State Richard Olney informed his British counterpart that "the United States is practically sovereign on this continent, and its fiat is law upon the subjects to which it confines its interposition." As historian Gaddis Smith notes, "this blustering affirmation quickly became known as 'the Olney corollary'—the first of many expansions and interpretations of the original [Monroe] Doctrine."[20]

Olney's puffery aside, the United States resumed its long-standing policy of noninvolvement with the powers of Europe. After all, there was work enough to be done at home: a bountiful continent to lace together with roads, rails, and canals; factories to build; farmlands to seed. In blissful oblivion of a world that would soon violently intrude upon the naive and ill-prepared nation, Americans savored their state of provincialism as the sands of isolation ran quickly through the hourglass. The events of 1898 would snatch from the United States this luxury of detached introspection.

AMERICA'S EMERGENCE AS A WORLD POWER

"There can be little question that the year 1898 is a landmark in the development of American foreign policy," writes historian Dexter Perkins, ". . . roughly, it can be said that up to 1898 the United States looked inward; after 1898 she looked outward."[21] America's plunge into world affairs was a result of the Spanish-American War, which marked the beginning of the nation's concern for questions of human rights in the world. Spanish troops had dealt harshly with insurrections in Cuba and the Philippines, to the extent of herding men, women, and children into concentration camps in Cuba, where tens of thousands perished. Even in the face of these stark human rights abuses, President William McKinley hoped to keep the United States out of war and he pursued diplomatic negotiations to end the Spanish barbarism. As is often the case in foreign policy, though, events overwhelmed intentions.

The Spanish-American War

On February 15, 1898, a mysterious explosion sank the U.S. battleship *Maine*, moored in Havana harbor, killing more than 250 sailors on board. Sunk, too, were McKinley's hopes for a diplomatic settlement. Inflamed by the war-mongering, sensationalist ("yellow") journalism of newspaper titans Joseph Pulitzer and William Randolph Hearst, the American public demanded revenge. "Remember the *Maine*! To hell with Spain!" became the battle cry. Diplomacy now began to look more attractive to officials in Madrid, but it was too late. Congress declared war in April and, within days, Admiral Thomas E. Dewey destroyed the Spanish navy at Manila Bay in the

Philippines. Spurred on by this stunning victory, U.S. troops and cavalry liberated Cuba and, for good measure, Puerto Rico as well. Then, as icing on the cake, America added Hawaii, the Philippines, Wake Island, and part of Samoa to its list of territorial acquisitions. Annexation of the Philippines alone cost the United States the lives of seven thousand soldiers, and led to the death as well of some two hundred thousand Philippine civilians.

Examining this period of global emergence for the United States, Amos Perlmutter maintains that America sought no domination over other peoples. "The United States had the opportunity to conquer and occupy Mexico, Cuba, and islands in the Caribbean," he writes, "but doing so was always rejected and unacceptable to the American people."[22] For some critics, however, this is a fine line to draw. After all, several presidents from McKinley and Woodrow Wilson to George W. Bush seemed so intent on forcing America's form of democracy on others—by armed intervention in Iraq, in the case of the Bush administration: "Wilsonianism in boots"[23]—that the nation's avowed benevolence toward other nations could be questioned by those on the receiving end.

Spreading Democracy and Opening Markets

One point was clear: at the opening of the twentieth century, most of the world saw the United States as a new colonial—for some, imperial—power. Once consisting of thirteen tremulous colonies clinging to the eastern seaboard of an untamed continent, the maturing republic now had far-flung interests that stretched across the Pacific Ocean—and, at last, a world-class military prepared to defend them. Further, the United States had an inspiring new mission that would begin to figure prominently in its foreign policy, namely, "the repeated presidential calls to promote the creation of democratic government abroad."[24] Most recently, in 2005, President George W. Bush advocated this theme in his second inaugural address. "So it is the policy of the United States to seek and support the growth of democratic movements and institutions in every nation and culture," he said, "with the ultimate goal of ending tyranny in our world."

Yet the expansion overseas that began to unfold in the watershed year of 1898 "did not constitute so sharp a departure from the isolationist tradition as has often been assumed," emphasizes historian Foster Rhea Dulles. "For the United States made no commitments to foreign nations as it emerged upon the international scene." In harmony with its founding principles and over a century of experience as a nation, "it entered upon no entangling alliances with other powers."[25] Nonetheless, something had changed profoundly. The world realized that the United States was a player in international affairs, with a global presence and a willingness to back up diplomacy with military muscle. To believe that a nation could be a world power but at the same time remain free of "entangling alliances" was naive; nevertheless, so remained the hopes at the time of strategists in Washington. As the United States gained more experience in dealing with well-armed rivals in the Far East, this approach to foreign policy would prove inadequate.

The United States looked upon the Philippines and Guam as attractive "stepping stones" to China[26]—locations where Americans could establish a base of operations to foster commercial inroads into the populous marketplaces that beckoned on the Asian mainland.

Inconveniently, though, Europe and Japan seemed intent on creating their own spheres of influence in China, regardless of what the Chinese themselves may have wished, and these rivals were quite prepared to jostle aside any efforts by the United States to find a place in the Chinese market. With entrepreneurs at home stiffening his backbone, President McKinley vowed to compete aggressively for the alluring economic opportunities on the Asian mainland. In 1899, McKinley's secretary of state, Jay Hay, proposed an "open-door policy" in China, whereby each major power (the United States included) would have a sphere of trading influence honored by other nations. The leaders of Europe and Japan nodded in America's direction with expressions of agreement with the concept; but then they went about their business as usual, essentially ignoring Hay's unilateral proclamation.

A faction of overzealous Chinese xenophobes were less than impressed by the plans of foreigners to divide up their nation for an economic banquet. Known as the "Boxers" (or *Yehequan* in China), they instigated the Boxer Rebellion of 1900: an armed resistance to the infidels from Japan and the West. Their modus operandi was simple enough: kill every foreigner in sight. In America's first significant stab at global diplomatic leadership, Hay proposed that the major trading powers work together to defuse the rebellion by assuring the Chinese of their territorial integrity, and by emphasizing the commercial benefits that would accrue to the Chinese. This time, the secretary of state's call for an "open door" was taken more seriously by the Europeans and the Japanese, and even the Boxers calmed down—no doubt in part because European and American soldiers inside China displayed greater strength than the Boxers had anticipated.

The negotiations were largely a success, but the Japanese felt affronted by America's interference in what they viewed as their own exclusive sphere of influence, that is, all of China. Hay's bold practice of diplomacy in China stirred resentment in Japan that would simmer for four decades, before boiling over in the attack against Pearl Harbor in 1941. Other grievances, especially America's unwillingness to stand by and allow Japanese expansion throughout Asia, added to Tokyo's growing distaste for the United States.

America's interest in the Far East was not driven by commercial ambitions or the hope of missionary conversions alone. The issue of human rights that had found legs during the Spanish-American War continued forward. The foreign policy of the United States took on an idealistic strain that would carry the homegrown concepts of freedom and civil liberty to other parts of the world. Despite this concern for human rights, power politics (realism, or realpolitik in the language of Europeans) remained preeminent in the calculations of America's leaders, as was true in every other major capital of the world. According to the precepts of realism, a nation's external relations should rest on a foundation of military and economic strength, since international affairs is a struggle for power in a global setting "unmediated by any referee."[27]

The preeminence of realism in the calculations of American foreign policy was well illustrated by the activities of McKinley's successor, the irrepressible Theodore Roosevelt, a hero in the spirited fight against the Spanish in Cuba during the Spanish-American War. Teddy Roosevelt sided early in his presidency with insurgents in a Colombian civil war. Successful in their rebellion, the insurgents established a new land—Panama—where they allowed their powerful patron, Roosevelt, to carry out his vision of a canal connecting the Atlantic and Pacific oceans. The waterway was a triumph for American commercial shipping interests, as well as a bold manifestation of Roosevelt's interest in the expansion of U.S. power in the region and beyond. Now the president and his successors could move U.S. warships more quickly from one great ocean to another.

Roosevelt also took steps to ensure that Europeans got the message that the Monroe Doctrine was still alive and well. In 1904, he issued an eponymous amendment to the famous pronouncement. Henceforth, according to the "Roosevelt Corollary":

> Chronic wrongdoing, or an impotence which results from a general loosening of the ties of civilized society, may in America, as elsewhere, ultimately require intervention by some civilized nation, and in the Western Hemisphere the adherence of the United States to the Monroe Doctrine may force the United States, however reluctantly, in flagrant cases of such wrongdoing or impotence, to the exercise of an international police power.[28]

The United States was not (yet) a policeman for the world; nevertheless, Roosevelt had claimed this role with respect to Latin America. One of the president's favorite expressions was the West African proverb, "Speak softly and carry a big stick." The Roosevelt Corollary was a classic expression of this "big-stick diplomacy," which provided a rationale for some thirty U.S. military interventions into Latin America over the next few decades. Often the big-stick approach to foreign affairs went hand in hand with another form of diplomacy that gained prominence during this era: "dollar diplomacy." Favored particularly by Roosevelt's successor, William Howard Taft, here was the exercise of unbridled government support for U.S. corporate interests in Latin American and elsewhere. The U.S. government's military might, coupled with corporate money and an occasional expression of interest in the question of human rights abroad, were the driving forces behind America's foreign policy at the dawn of the twentieth century.

Wilsonian Idealism

With the advent of the Wilson administration (1913–21), the nation worked hard to keep its traditional distance from European affairs. Isolationism, the dream of turning back the clock to a more pleasant and peaceful time when America could concentrate on its internal development, became the order of the day. Wilson, though, did not allow this renewed introspection to weaken the hold of the United States over its self-proclaimed sphere of influence in Latin America. He was particularly concerned about a civil war in Mexico that had erupted in 1910. When President Huerta of Mexico rejected Wilson's efforts to settle the war, the American president ordered military expeditions into Mexico in 1914 to subdue the rebels. When the Mexican Pancho Villa crossed into the United States in 1916 and fought with Americans, killing eighteen in the town of Columbus, New Mexico, Wilson order General John J. Pershing to hunt down the bandit-turned-general south of the border. Not until 1917 did Pershing return home with his seven thousand U.S. soldiers, without capturing Villa but managing to sow resentment toward the United States throughout Mexico.

Just as the sinking of the *Maine* in 1898 had drawn Americans into war, in 1915 the sinking of the British liner *Lusitania* by a German submarine (with 128 U.S. citizens perishing along with 1,070 other passengers) stirred impassioned anti-German sentiments from New York to California. Resisting these public passions, the idealistic Wilson struggled to keep the United States out of a war with Germany. He received thunderous applause from Democratic Convention delegates in 1916 for his pledge to keep the peace. Reelected to the White House, Wilson advocated "peace without victory" and a new "league of nations." The German response: unrestricted submarine warfare against any ship entering the Atlantic Ocean, including those flying an American flag.

Adding to the insult, in 1917 the German Foreign Secretary Arthur Zimmermann sent a secret telegram to his envoy in Mexico (intercepted by British naval intelligence and passed along to Washington) that ordered him to seek a pact of aggression with Mexico against the United States, should the Americans enter the war against Germany. The "quid" for the "quo," according to this scenario, would be a return of Texas, New Mexico, and Arizona to Mexico, once the Germans had defeated the United States. Disclosure of the Zimmermann telegram by the American press threw more fuel on the fire of anti-German sentiment.[29]

The degree of bellicosity from the Germans was too much even for Wilson. "We shall fight . . . for the rights and liberties of small nations," he proclaimed before Congress in April of 1917. Following a congressional declaration of war against the Germans, the president sent two million American soldiers overseas to help tip the scales against the kaiser. In Wilson's words, the war would be fought to make the world "safe for democracy." It would be a "final war for human liberty." Wilson's famous "triad" became the quest for peace, liberal democracy, and free markets.[30]

After eight million soldiers—including 116,516 in American uniform—had perished, the war finally came to an end on November 11, 1918. President Wilson turned to the task of preventing all future wars through the establishment of a League of Nations—the last of "Fourteen Points" he had presented to Congress on January 8, 1918 (among them, independence for Poland, Austria, Hungary, and the Balkans).

The major powers of Europe and, indeed, senators in Wilson's own government viewed the prospects for lasting peace in the world through a more jaded lens. "God gave us his Ten Commandments and we broke them," observed Clemenceau, the hard-boiled French premier. "Wilson gave us his Fourteen Points—we shall see."[31] Brushing aside such cynicism, Wilson sailed for France in 1918 (the first American president to set foot in Europe) to negotiate the terms for the end of the war through the Treaty of Versailles. In elegant, if damning, words, the brilliant British economist John Maynard Keynes sketched a profile of the key negotiators:

> These were the personalities of Paris—I forbear to mention other nations or lesser men: Clemenceau, aesthetically the noblest; the President [Wilson], morally the most admirable; Lloyd George [the British prime minister], intellectually the subtlest. Out of their disparities and weaknesses the Treaty was born, child of the least worthy attributes of each of its parents, without nobility, without morality, without intellect.[32]

During the course of the negotiations, Wilson bartered away thirteen of his Fourteen Points in exchange for support of his cherished

League of Nations. Upon returning to the United States, the president discovered that his toughest trial was still before him, as the Senate expressed disapproval of the League concept. The Republican leader and chairman of the august Foreign Relations Committee, Senator Henry Cabot Lodge (R-MA), disliked the president on a personal level and would probably have sought to block the League proposal on these grounds alone.[33] Lodge also opposed the notion of involving the United States in an international organization of any kind, preferring a unilateral American foreign policy with Washington, DC, calling its own shots in world affairs—an approach popular with the second Bush administration today.

Joined by the mesmerizing orator William E. Borah (R-ID) and other "irreconcilables," Lodge stalled the League proposal in committee. In 1919, President Wilson decided to take his case to the American people. In an exhausting series of speeches across the nation that would break his health and lead to a severe stroke, the president spelled out to the public the merits of having a League of Nations. Lodge and his colleagues remained unimpressed and proceeded to amend the proposal beyond recognition. Exhausted and embittered, Wilson withdrew his support from the transfigured document and the Senate put the kibosh on the treaty.

The United States would not become a member of the League of Nations, even though its own president had authored the initiative. Underscoring the widespread public opposition to the League proposal, in 1920 the voters threw out the Democrats (who continued to cling to the idea of a League) and elected Republican Warren G. Harding, a nicely profiled, vacuous candidate who promised a return to "normalcy" and attention to issues at home. Nor was his successor, Calvin Coolidge, much interested in foreign affairs. With the exceptions of notable efforts by the United States to negotiate European debt relief and seek agreements of naval arms control, with Harding and Coolidge, the time had come to concentrate on the domestic political agenda. The public and leading politicians had rejected Wilson's internationalism in favor of an isolationist resurgence—a return to the halcyon days of aloofness from world politics in the manner of presidents Washington, Jefferson, and Monroe.

Reluctant Leader

The rest of the world, though, was becoming increasingly difficult to ignore. Moreover, as a result of Woodrow Wilson's proselytizing, many Americans now had a greater interest in global affairs. Even if they had not bought into the idea of a League of Nations, they did share Wilson's longing for peaceful relations among nations. So despite the preference of Harding and Coolidge for domestic affairs, the public supported America's involvement from 1922–28 in international disarmament talks. This diplomacy led to the Kellogg-Briand Treaty, negotiated by Secretary of State Frank Kellogg and French Foreign Minister Aristide Briand. The treaty grandly renounced war "as an instrument of national policy." Nevertheless, officials in Washington refused to enter into any kind of permanent international organization that might have had the authority to enforce this objective. As a result, the pact (ratified by President Coolidge in 1929) became little more than a rhetorical dash of Wilsonian internationalism in America's isolationist stew.

Just as the Civil War had done, the Great Depression of 1929 turned the United States inward as the nation tried to cope with a period of severe unemployment and financial dislocation. Only Latin America received much attention from Washington officials. Republican President Herbert Hoover swept aside the Roosevelt Corollary, viewed by some neighbors to the south as a haughty expression of Yankee imperialism, and declared in 1930 that nothing in the Monroe Doctrine justified U.S. intervention in the internal affairs of Latin American nations. His successor, Democrat Franklin D. Roosevelt (Teddy's cousin), carried this benevolent philosophy a step further. He removed all U.S. troops south of the Rio Grande (with the exception of those stationed in the Panama Canal Zone) and, in 1933, proclaimed a new "good neighbor policy" toward Latin America. Mostly, though, Franklin Roosevelt focused his energies on restoring the U.S. economy, while keeping a wary eye on the totalitarian regimes in Germany, Italy, and Japan as they began to amass troubling military arsenals, as if their signatures on the Kellogg-Briand peace pact had been written in disappearing ink.

The United States was about to be yanked out of isolationism by the greatest challenges the nation had faced from overseas since the early wars with Great Britain: the rise of fascism and communism, twin threats that would dominate American foreign policy for the next half-century. Japan was the first of the fascists to exhibit an alarming militancy, invading Manchuria in 1931 and Shanghai the following year. The League of Nations proved too feeble to halt the aggression. Critics quickly blamed the absence of the United States from its membership as the chief cause of the League's failure. No nation did anything to reverse the Japanese advance and, through their passivity, set a match to the papers on which the League and the Kellogg-Briand Treaty had been written. An opportunistic witness to the ease with which Japan carried out the plunder of Manchuria and Shanghai, the Italian dictator Mussolini subsequently invaded Ethiopia in 1936 and entered into a military alliance with Germany. Japan joined these "Axis" powers in the same year and turned toward its main objective, overrunning China with troops in 1937.

The United States and the rest of the world did nothing, looking away as the Japanese slaughtered the Chinese people. Americans did not like what was happening, but they disliked even more the idea of sending their own flesh and blood into the fray. Disillusioned by the carnage of the First World War, which many saw as an unfortunate entry by the United States into Europe's petty bickering, isolationists moved to avoid another costly foreign intervention.

Hitler ordered German troops into Austria in 1938—again, with barely a murmur from other nations. Then, with seven divisions massed along the borders of Czechoslovakia, he sent threats to the Prague government, demanding the return to Germany of the Sudetenland, a western and northern section of the Czech Republic where a majority of the populace was of German descent. British Prime Minister Neville Chamberlain led a diplomatic rescue attempt, meeting in Munich with Hitler, Mussolini, and the French Premier Daladier. Chamberlain held out to Hitler a policy of appeasement: Germany could have the Sudetenland in exchange for a promise not to invade the rest of Czechoslovakia, as though the British and the French somehow had the right to dismember the Czech nation, which at the time had a larger and better equipped army than Germany.

Following this fateful meeting in Munich, the irenic British prime minister flew back to London. Smiling in triumph, he descended the airplane stairs with the signed four-party agreement held aloft in his hand, assuring the crowd gathered to cheer his arrival home that Europe would have "peace in our time." The document, signed by Hitler and Chamberlain on September 30, 1938, proclaimed "the desire of our two peoples never to go to war with one another again." Six months later, Nazi tanks rumbled across the borders to devour the rest of Czechoslovakia, a proud nation weakened by the loss of the Sudetenland and demoralized by the readiness of the British and the French to turn their backs on its sovereignty. In Bailey's felicitous phrase, the pact with Hitler and Mussolini proved to be "merely surrender on the installment plan."[34] The site of the surrender, Munich, became a word forever synonymous with "appeasement" and the futility of attempting to satiate fanatics by yielding to their demands. It came to mean "a lack of backbone in foreign affairs."[35]

Hitler next signed a nonaggression pact with Russia, opening the way for a German invasion of Poland by promising Moscow the eastern half of his latest territorial spoils. On September 1, 1939, Panzer tanks crushed the brave but feckless Polish resistance, whose defenders rode into battle on horseback. Two days later, the British and the French honored a defense alliance with Poland and declared war against the Nazis. (In a reckless error, the amateurish German Foreign Minister, Joachim von Ribbentrop, had advised the delusional Führer that the British—ever spineless—would remain on the sidelines.[36]) The Second World War had erupted.

Despite these chilling events in Europe, isolationist opinion remained strong inside the United States. President Franklin Roosevelt reassured the public that the United States would remain neutral. Even when rumors of a pogrom against Germany's Jews filtered out to the West, the Roosevelt administration issued expressions of concern and protest, but took no action. This was an internal German problem, reasoned the Department of State; America's hands were tied. Besides, two major European powers—Britain and France—were already responding to the Nazi threat; American intervention was unnecessary. This illusion quickly shattered, however, as France fell before a German blitzkrieg in early 1940. A few months later, the British barely escaped a tightening Nazi noose in a desperate evacuation from the continent at Dunkirk.

These unsettling developments gave Roosevelt a new perspective on the danger facing the United States. Although the American people were still unwilling to enter into the war, the president began to take steps toward aiding the British. He failed in his attempt to persuade Congress to repeal the Neutrality Acts; but, undeterred, he proposed a Lend-Lease Act to assist the struggle against the fascists. The United States would lend or lease supplies to the British and others fighting Germany, sidestepping the inability of the Allied powers at the time to pay cash for arms. As the president put it, America would lend a garden hose to a neighbor whose house was on fire. Isolationists in Congress opposed the measure, fearing both a slide toward war and too much power in the hands of a liberal president. The proposal passed in March 1941, despite their opposition.

The Lend-Lease Act, along with Roosevelt's use of an executive agreement to further aid the United Kingdom (authorizing the exchange of fifty U.S. warships for American naval base rights at British bases in the Western Hemisphere), along with the president's introduction of conscription in 1940, signaled an end to neutrality. These initiatives greatly agitated the isolationists. "We have torn up 150 years of traditional foreign policy," complained their leader in

Congress, Senator Arthur H. Vandenberg (R-MI). "We have tossed
Washington's Farewell Address into the discard. We have thrown
ourselves squarely into the power politics and power wars of
Europe, Asia and Africa. We have taken the first step upon a course
from which we can never hereafter retreat."[37]

Then came December 7, 1941, and the Japanese surprise bom-
bardment of Pearl Harbor—a day that would "live in infamy," in
Roosevelt's imperishable phrase. America's insistence that Japan
withdraw from China, coupled with a U.S. ban on the sale of avia-
tion fuel and scrap metal to the Japanese, had produced a deep
sense of humiliation in Japan. With growing paranoia, leaders in
Tokyo managed to convince themselves that it was only a matter
of time before the American "imperialists" attacked their homeland. All of these feelings pointed the way to Pearl Harbor. After
the sneak attack, even the staunchest isolationists were ready to
fight. "The only thing now to do is lick hell out of them," declared
a prominent isolationist, Senator Burton K. Wheeler (R-MT).[38]

Embracing Internationalism—Gingerly

Four years of global warfare that sent sixty million people to pre-
mature graves and left Europe, Russia, and Japan in smoldering
ruins finally ended in 1945 with twin victories for the United
States and its allies in both Europe and the Pacific. The war ush-
ered in the nuclear age when the United States dropped a uranium,
and then a plutonium, bomb on Japan in August 1945. The blast
effects revealed how atomic weapons could destroy whole cities in
an instant flash of light and heat, with ground-zero temperatures
of fifty million degrees centigrade.

The end of the war also generated a new era of international cooperation in which the United States was the acknowledged leader. In a revival of Wilsonianism spurred by the horrors of the war, most of the world's nations gathered in San Francisco in July 1945 to establish a United Nations—"the boldest experiment in international organization yet adopted by man."[39] From the beginning, the United Nations exhibited a fatal flaw. Like the League of Nations, it had no workable international police force to halt military aggression by rogue nations. Still, hopes remained high among internationalists that this would be an important step toward Wilson's dream of a lasting world peace.

Containment and the Cold War

In the decades that followed the Second World War, the United States moved dramatically away from its lifelong isolationist instincts toward a new posture of global engagement. On the economic side of foreign policy, for example, by century's end "you could buy a Coke in deepest Africa or stay at a Holiday Inn in Urumqi in northwestern China."[40]

Yet no sooner had the United States demobilized its troops after the victory against fascism than another new conflict emerged: a "Cold War" between the Western democracies and the Soviet-dominated communist nations of the world (who never demobilized). "Within six months after war's end all pretense at friendship was being dropped," writes David S. McLellan. "Henceforth each side would interpret all moves as basically hostile and therefore would act accordingly. The Cold War had begun."[41] The Soviet leader, Joseph Stalin, seemed increasingly truculent toward the

United States, not to mention extraordinarily cruel to his own people and domineering over contiguous nations. As former British Prime Minister Winston Churchill declared in a speech at Westminster College in Fulton, Missouri, in 1946:

> From Stettin in the Baltic to Trieste in the Adriatic, an iron curtain has descended across the continent. Behind that line lie all the capitals of the ancient states of Central and Eastern Europe. Warsaw, Berlin, Prague, Vienna, Budapest, Belgrade, Bucharest and Sofia, all these former cities and the populations around them lie in the Soviet sphere and all are subject in one form or another, not only to Soviet influence, but a very high and increasing measure of control from Moscow.[42]

Every president from Harry S. Truman to George H. W. Bush would place the Soviet Union at the top of their list of national security threats to the United States, and rightly so because the Soviets had the capacity to strike North America with atomic bombs by airplane and, later, by intercontinental ballistic missiles. In the sobering and all-too-accurate acronym of the era, each of the two "superpowers" had the capacity to retaliate against an attack from the other with mutual assured destruction (MAD)—a deadly rain of atomic (and later, even more destructive hydrogen) bombs that could leave each civilization in rubble.

The Cold War lasted until 1991, when the Soviet Union finally crumbled from the inefficiencies of its overly centralized economic system. For Americans and Russians, and indeed much of the world, the intervening years felt like a roller-coaster ride, with many a dangerous turn. During the Kennedy years, tank-to-tank confrontations in Berlin and a missile crisis in Cuba took the superpowers perilously close to a Third World War, this time with city-busting nuclear warheads. Throughout the Cold War, America's leaders felt compelled to maintain a costly defense establishment. In addition, the United States and the Soviet Union constructed vast intelligence organizations to spy on one another and to engage in covert operations designed to advance their cause.

The overriding approach to foreign policy followed by the United States during the Cold War was the doctrine of containment. Soviet power "is a fluid stream which moves constantly, wherever it is permitted to move, toward a given goal," wrote the American diplomat George F. Kennan in an article in *Foreign Affairs* published in 1946. "Its main concern is to make sure that it has filled every nook and cranny available to it in the basins of world power." He recommended "a long-term, patient but firm and vigilant containment of Russian expansive tendencies."[43] Forty years later, experts looked back on Kennan's influential article as a manifestation of "the final collapse of nostalgia for prewar isolationism."[44]

Certainly the Truman administration eschewed isolationism. In March 1947, President Truman told Congress that it would be the policy of the United States "to support free people who are resisting attempted subjugation by armed minorities or by outside pressures"—a philosophy of American foreign policy soon known as the Truman Doctrine.[45] When Britain withdrew its military and economic support for Greece and Turkey, Truman rushed to fill the power vacuum before the Soviets had a chance to step in. As historian John Lewis Gaddis has observed, the president's initiative implied "a world-wide commitment to resist Soviet expansionism wherever it appeared."[46] Also in 1947, the United States turned to an even more ambitious project: providing billions of dollars in economic aid to European countries through a European Recovery Program, labeled the Marshall Plan in honor of George Catlett Marshall, the secretary of state who proposed it. The United States proposed the economic assistance in order to make the limping economies of Europe more sturdy and resistant to communist influence. A further incentive existed: the establishment of viable markets in Europe for U.S. exports—an obvious boon to the American business community.

Truman's initiatives notwithstanding, many Americans continued to feel ambivalent about the far-reaching involvement of the United States in the world. Isolationists, led by Senator Robert A. Taft (R-OH) during this period, complained about the large, spendthrift government that was throwing away U.S. dollars on foreign policy instead of domestic needs. "Don't be Santa Claus!" they cried. Nonetheless, other political factions inside the United States believed that President Truman was insufficiently involved in world affairs, and was being far too tough on the Russians—a posture guaranteed to ruin the chances for peaceful coexistence. In its salesmanship of the Marshall Plan to lawmakers, the Truman administration portrayed the Soviets as an implacable foe. Gaddis recalls the unfortunate consequences: "Trapped in their own rhetoric, leaders of the United States found it difficult to respond to the conciliatory gestures which emanated from the Kremlin following Stalin's death and, through their inflexibility, may well have contributed to the perpetuation of the Cold War."[47]

Setting the stage for the Korean and Vietnam wars, in 1950 the Truman administration drafted a top secret document to guide its foreign policy planning: National Security Council Paper No. 68

(NSC 68, for short). The document stated that "the assault on free institutions is worldwide now, and in the context of the present polarization of power a defeat of free institutions *anywhere* is a defeat everywhere."[48] The Eisenhower administration preached the same gospel, only with more fire and brimstone. "As there is no weapon too small, no arena too remote, to be ignored, there is no free nation too humble to be forgotten," declared President Dwight D. Eisenhower, who also made rash promises to the "captive nations" behind the Iron Curtain that America would secure their freedom.[49]

The United States had now become a world policeman. The goal was to subdue the villains of the communist world and spread democracy—or at least shore up anti-communist dictators—to help ensure America's own security. In 2001, the second Bush administration would adopt a similar goal of propagating worldwide democracy. President George W. Bush pointed to a new set of villains: the despots who ruled along an "axis of evil" in Iraq, Iran, and North Korea. According to a foreign policy expert, within the second Bush administration, "revival Wilsonians believe that traditional American values are so compelling, so demonstrably superior, and so widely popular that they can sweep and reshape the world."[50]

During the period from the Truman to the Nixon administration, the United States fought major wars in Korea and Vietnam in defense of democratic values and in opposition to the spread of communism. America would lose over ninety thousand troops in regional wars on the Korean peninsula and in the jungles of Vietnam—the latter "the most disastrous foreign adventure in American history"[51] and the nation's only military defeat abroad. In between the two wars, the superpowers came close to a nuclear war over the crisis of Soviet missile emplacements in Cuba.

Though geographically distant from the United States, the outbreak of war on the Korean peninsula in 1950 represented a test of Western resolve against communist expansion. McLellan sums up why the United States decided to enter into a faraway war when North Korean troops moved into South Korea:

> The Korean aggression was immediately interpreted in light of Britain's experience at Munich. Dictators' appetites grow with eating and if allowed to get away with one aggression, they will be encouraged to perpetrate another. The integrity of America's pledge to defend its European allies would be judged by the resolution with which it acted to stem aggression in Korea. And it was felt that the strategical balance already shaken by the loss of China would be irretrievably upset should the United States fail to respond.[52]

The Korean War ended in a stalemate in 1953. Strategist Thomas C. Schelling concluded: "We lost 30,000 dead . . . to save face . . . and it was undoubtedly worth it."[53]

During the High Noon superpower confrontation in Cuba in 1962, top members of the Kennedy administration wondered if the nation would survive. Many Washington, DC, bureaucrats sent their families out of town; some tried to build makeshift bomb shelters in their backyards. At the height of the crisis, the Soviet leader, Nikita Khrushchev, chose to call back freighters carrying more missiles to Cuba, and agreed as well to dismantle the missiles already under construction on the island. "We are eyeball to eyeball, and the other fellow just blinked," commented Secretary of State Dean Rusk when he heard the good news.[54]

A far more costly confrontation with communists would soon follow in Vietnam.[55] The war went badly for the United States. Here was combat where the innocent-looking seventy-year-old grandmother in a rice paddy might have a hand grenade tucked in her basket, where every turn on the jungle trail might hold a booby trap, where the North Vietnamese enemy would appear and disappear like deadly phantoms in the thick underbrush. For ten years the fighting went on. Over fifty-eight thousand Americans lost their lives; over three hundred thousand more required hospitalization from wounds. Many returned home badly maimed, physically and mentally; some seventy-four thousand survived as quadriplegics or multiple amputees.

As in Korea, the United States attempted to contain communism in Vietnam, yet steer clear of an escalation of the conflict to a global level, with Chinese and Soviet forces entering the fray. The end result was a wearing battle of attrition. Never before had the nation witnessed on a daily basis televised reporting of warfare's agony and carnage. Gruesome pictures of death and destruction entered America's living rooms: villages engulfed in napalm; wounded GIs evacuated by helicopter, their faces twisted in pain; rag-doll figures of men, women, and children lying dead in rice paddies; Buddhist monks aflame in suicidal protests. The American public began to turn against a continuation of the war during the Johnson administration.

The cost of the war, in blood and money, was enormous, and the long struggle had torn the nation asunder like nothing in its history since the Civil War. Massive street demonstrations took place against the war. As President Lyndon B. Johnson's domestic programs faltered, black Americans rioted and torched cities.

Students burned American flags, their draft cards, and even banks supposedly implicated in the financing of the war. Young men fled to Canada to avoid the draft for a war they believed was immoral and illegitimate. Some individuals joined radical antiwar groups like the "Weathermen," resorting to terrorism against their own government. Campuses closed across the land; and, at the height of the protests, the Nixon administration circled the White House with city buses for protection against youthful dissenters. The White House, the Central Intelligence Agency (CIA), the Federal Bureau of Investigation (FBI), and military units carried out Orwellian and illegal espionage operations against antiwar protesters.[56] Throughout most of the war, the United States seemed in a state of siege. Finally, in 1973, the Nixon administration withdrew U.S. forces from Indochina and two years later the last Americans fled from South Vietnam as the North Vietnamese army tightened the noose around Saigon.

In the midst of the turmoil, President Richard M. Nixon and his secretary of state, Henry Kissinger, pursued a policy of détente toward the Soviets, until the Watergate scandal drove the president from office in 1974. The Ford and Carter administrations tried again to achieve warmer relations with Moscow, but a Soviet invasion of Afghanistan in 1979 disillusioned President Jimmy Carter and brought back feelings of distrust between the two nations. Under President Ronald Reagan, the Cold War revved up like a neglected engine given a fresh quart of oil. The president labeled the Soviet Union an "evil empire" and his administration dramatically increased U.S. military spending.[57] Quite distinct in many ways, Wilson the idealist and Reagan the realist nonetheless shared a common interest in the promotion of global democracy.

Reagan is remembered as "the first Republican president emphatically to embrace the essential tenets of liberal democratic internationalism, or what might be called Wilsonianism."[58]

In what became known in the media as the Reagan Doctrine, the White House ordered the CIA to engage in widespread covert actions to assist nations in their resistance to Soviet influence, especially in Nicaragua and Afghanistan. The prior history of covert action during the Cold War had been uneven, with short-term successes in Iran (1953) and Guatemala (1954), but followed by ugly failures at the Bay of Pigs in Cuba (1961) and—though less spectacular—in many other places around the globe.[59] The Reagan administration's operations in Nicaragua not only failed to oust the pro-Marxist Sandinista regime, but led to the Iran-contra affair involving the violation of laws meant to maintain accountability over the CIA. The administration's reputation suffered great damage from the scandal, including the president's 21 percent plunge in the public opinion polls. During the 1980s, the CIA experienced a short-term covert action success in Afghanistan, helping to drive the Soviets out of the country; however, the repressive Taliban regime rose up to dominate the nation and, in turn, provided safe haven for the Al Qaeda terrorist group that attacked the United States in 2001.

Despite President Reagan's initial hostility toward the Soviet Union, he and Soviet leader Mikhail S. Gorbachev began to seek an accommodation with one another in 1985, meeting in Geneva for a spirited exchange on prospects for the reduction of nuclear weapons and then again in Iceland in 1986, the United States in 1987, and the Soviet Union in 1988, for formal negotiations on arms-control agreements and a final withdrawal of Soviet troops from Afghanistan. The unlikely duo of Reagan and Gorbachev had embraced a new round of détente. Within a year, during the first Bush administration, the Cold War started to unravel, beginning in November 1989 with the fall of the Berlin Wall that separated East from West Berlin.

A Fragmenting World

The collapse of the Soviet Union as a global power dramatically altered world politics. Abruptly, the focus of American foreign policy shifted and broadened. "Our mission is to understand the world," said Director of Central Intelligence (DCI) William H. Webster in 1991.[60] The CIA resources directed toward Russia declined from some 60 percent of the total to about 17 percent.[61] As another DCI put it, "America had slain the dragon [the Soviet Union]. Now it faced a world filled with poisonous snakes."[62] Anyone who had hoped the United States could safely retreat from world affairs was in for disappointment. The nation had now become the only superpower—or, as the *Economist* put it (borrowing a phrase coined by the French foreign minister), the only "hyperpower."

During the tenure of President Bill Clinton, who led the first post-Cold War administration, the world refused to go away, as much as the president would have preferred to focus on the economy and other domestic issues. America's enemies had become more ghost-like: insurgents and terrorists who vanished into the winding alleys of Mogadishu or hid in the caves of mountainous Afghanistan. The first Bush administration had already had a taste of the new threats that were emerging in the world as the Cold War wound down, with military conflicts in Panama (1989) and Iraq

(1991). The Clinton administration faced ongoing disputes with Iraq over its suspected development of WMDs and, in 1993, found itself embroiled in street warfare in Somalia, with disastrous results leading to the death of eighteen U.S. soldiers and a hasty American retreat. The terrorist attacks against the United States in 2001, though, provided the cruelest wake-up call about the dangers that still existed in the world following the end of the Cold War.

Wars Against Terrorism and Rogue States

Stunned by the 9/11 attacks, the second Bush administration immediately went to war against Al Qaeda and other terrorists who might further threaten the nation, focusing on the overthrow of the Taliban regime in Afghanistan and routing Al Qaeda members hiding in the rugged terrain of South Asia. After the Taliban regime was defeated in 2001–03, Iraq became the object of the administration's wrath—the same regime, led by Saddam Hussein, that had preoccupied the president's father when he had been the nation's chief executive and had tried to assassinate him on a visit to Kuwait after he left the presidency.

The second Bush administration's rationale for an Iraqi invasion in 2003 rested on a fear that Hussein could be developing WMDs that he might pass on to terrorists or use directly against the United States or perhaps Israel. Rebuffed by the UN after President George W. Bush sought backing for war against Iraq, the administration gathered together its own "coalition of the willing" (in the president's phrase) of thirty-three mostly small nations, and launched an invasion against the Hussein regime. In the 2002 National Security Strategy document, the Bush administration argued that a "preemptive war" was necessary to protect the United States against the possibility of a future use of force against America by the Iraqi, or some other, regime. The president's national security adviser, Condoleezza Rice, spoke darkly of a "mushroom cloud" that could appear over an American city, the result of a terrorist nuclear attack against the United States that would be far more catastrophic than the September 11th attacks.

The evocation of this doctrine of preemption raised questions among critics, at home and abroad, about whether the Bush administration had become too shrill and aggressive in seeking quick military solutions to tangled problems in the Middle East.[63] Historian Gaddis, though, reasoned that it would be "irresponsible to have such great power, and not to try to use it in this way," that is, preempt evildoers from striking first at the United States with potentially devastating modern weapons.[64]

The U.S.-led coalition organized by the Bush administration rapidly defeated the Iraqi military and, at the end of 2003, captured Hussein himself. The hard part of the war, however, turned out to be its aftermath: trying to establish security and democracy in a country without a tradition of representative government. In the meantime, remnants of the old Iraqi regime continued to kill American troops, abetted by terrorists from various countries who traveled to Iraq to advance the global jihad against the United States proclaimed by Osama bin Laden, the Al Qaeda leader, on behalf of Muslim extremists.

The failure to find WMDs in Iraq raised further questions about whether the administration's argument for the war had been justified in the first place. Had the American people been misled by a president with an agenda that went far beyond fighting Al Qaeda and other terrorists, one that involved a continuation of Reagan's embrace of Wilsonian democracy-building—only this time by imposing by force America's form of government in the Middle East? Had the Iraqi invasion distracted the United States from its war against Al Qaeda, which was, after all, the enemy that struck New York City and the Pentagon in 2001? While such questions filled the political talk shows and the presidential primaries in 2004, Bin Laden and his top aid, Ayman al-Zawahiri, remained at large.

As several Washington commissions carried out inquiries into the 9/11 and WMD intelligence failures, one thing was certain: much of the world, including key U.S. allies in Europe, had started to doubt America's global leadership. The good will toward the United States evident in the immediate aftermath of the 9/11 catastrophe had dissipated, replaced with harsh denunciations. "Why does the world hate America?" became a favorite topic of rumination for media pundits and op-ed essayists. Those who took the time to delve below the surface of this question soon realized the extent to which the world's displeasure with the United States had long historical roots. From another vantage point, it was also clear Americans themselves continued to feel ambivalent toward the world, drawn by the profits of global commerce and with hopes for the spread of free markets, Christianity, and democratic governments, yet repelled by the prospect of costly wars and the quicksand of foreign political intrigues.

Despite a lingering admiration in many places around the world for all the good things Americans had achieved over the years—from the establishment of an admirable form of government in 1789 and an evolving embrace of civil liberties and civil rights over the years, to the nation's victories in Europe and the Pacific in 1945, its generosity through the Marshall Plan, and its steadfast resistance to global communism—many people overseas had come to doubt the wisdom of the United States and its capacity for responsible world leadership. Some even feared America's motives, an armed colossus with armies and navies spread across the latitudes in the style of a would-be hegemonic power. Americans, too, were divided on the question of how far around the globe the nation's military, political, and economic ties should extend: the persistent ambivalence toward the world that has been an integral part of the nation's heritage.

The next seven chapters explore the roots of this anguish, here and overseas, about the capabilities and intentions of the United States. Each chapter takes up a specific limitation or "sin" of American foreign policy that has contributed to the nation's divisions at home and loss of goodwill abroad.

NOTES

1. Frank Church, "Covert Action: Swampland of American Foreign Policy," *Bulletin of the Atomic Scientists* 32 (February 1976), p. 11.
2. See Nancy L. Hoepli, *A Cartoon History of United States Foreign Policy* (New York: Morrow, 1975), p. 1.
3. Ibid.
4. Ralph K. Andrist, ed., *George Washington: A Biography in His Own Words* (New York: Harper & Row, 1972), pp. 373–374.
5. Robert Wallace, "The Barbary Wars," *Smithsonian* (January 1975), p. 91.
6. Thomas A. Bailey, *A Diplomatic History of the American People*, 9th ed. (Englewood Cliffs, NJ: Prentice-Hall, 1974), p. 137.
7. James Sterling Young, *The Washington Community: 1800–1828* (New York: Columbia University Press, 1966), p. 184.
8. Bailey, *A Diplomatic History*, p. 145.
9. See Ernest R. May, *The Making of the Monroe Doctrine* (Cambridge, MA: Harvard University Press, 1975).
10. Letter from Thomas Jefferson to President James Monroe (October 24, 1823), in Merrill D. Peterson, ed., *Jefferson* (New York: Library of America, 1984), p. 1481.

11. Hollis W. Barber, *Foreign Policies of the United States* (New York: Dryden Press, 1953), p. 232. See also Dexter Perkins, *Hands Off: A History of the Monroe Doctrine* (New York: Little, Brown, 1941), p. 43. These sources draw upon John Quincy Adams, in C. F. Adams, ed., *Memoirs of John Quincy Adams*, vol. VI (Philadelphia: 1974–77), p. 179.

12. The "aura of antiquity" quote is from Bailey, *A Diplomatic History*, p. 180. Not every foreign head of state was impressed by presidential evocation of the Doctrine's principles over the years. Hollis notes, for example, that the German chancellor (1877–90) Otto von Bismark dismissed the edict as little more than an "international impertinence" (*Foreign Policies*, p. 232).

13. These quotes are from Daniel S. Papp, Loch K. Johnson, and John E. Endicott, *American Foreign Policy: History, Politics, and Policy* (New York: Pearson Longman, 2005), p. 40.

14. Cited by Richard N. Current, Alexander DeConde, and Harris L. Dante, *United States History* (New York: Scott, Foresman, 1967), p. 234.

15. Cited in Gary A. Donaldson, *American Foreign Policy: The Twentieth Century in Documents* (New York: Longman, 2003), p. 3.

16. Quoted by Frances FitzGerald, "Reflections: Foreign Policy," *The New Yorker* (November 11, 1985), p. 112.

17. Charles O. Lerche, Jr., *America in World Affairs* (New York: McGraw-Hill, 1963), p. 36.

18. Quoted in Hoepli, *A Cartoon History*, p. 27.

19. Lerche, *America in World Affairs*, p. 38.

20. Gaddis Smith, "The Legacy of Monroe's Doctrine," *New York Times Magazine* (September 9, 1984), p. 46.

21. Dexter Perkins, *The Evolution of American Foreign Policy* (New York: Oxford University Press, 1948), p. 58.

22. Amos Perlmutter, *Making the World Safe for Democracy: A Century of Wilsonianism and Its Totalitarian Challengers* (Chapel Hill: University of North Carolina Press, 1997), p. xi.

23. David C. Henrickson, "The Lion and the Lamb: Realism and Liberalism Reconsidered," *World Policy Journal* 20 (Spring 2003), p. 97.

24. Tony Smith, *America's Mission: The United States and the Worldwide Struggle for Democracy in the Twentieth Century* (Princeton: Princeton University Press, 1994), p. xiii.

25. Foster Rhea Dulles, *America's Rise to World Power: 1898–1954* (New York: Harper & Row, 1954), p. 58.

26. Norman Stone, ed., *The Times Atlas of World History*, 3rd ed. (Maplewood, NJ: Hammond, 1989), p. 246.

27. J. Martin Rochester, *Between Two Epochs: What's Ahead for America, the World and Global Politics in the Twenty-First Century* (Upper Saddle River, NJ: Prentice Hall, 2002), p. 61.

28. Richard H. Collin, "Roosevelt Corollary," in Bruce W. Jentleson and Thomas G. Paterson, ed., *Encyclopedia of U.S. Foreign Relations*, vol. 4 (New York: Oxford University Press, 1997), p. 32.

29. Barbara W. Tuchman, *The Zimmermann Telegram* (New York: Dell, 1958).

30. See Michael Mandelbaum, *The Ideas That Conquered the World: Peace, Democracy and Free Markets in the Twenty-First Century* (New York: Public Affairs, 2002).

31. W. A. White, *Woodrow Wilson* (Boston: Houghton Mifflin, 1929), p. 384, cited by Bailey, *A Diplomatic History*, p. 608. See also August Heckscher, *Woodrow Wilson* (Newtown, CT: American Biography Press, 1991).

32. John Maynard Keynes, *Essays and Sketches in Biography* (New York: Meridian, 1956), p. 180.

33. Alexander L. George and Juliette L. George, *Woodrow Wilson and Colonel House: A Personality Study* (New York: Dover, 1956).

34. Bailey, *A Diplomatic History*, p. 708.

35. Peter McGrath, "The Lessons of Munich," *Newsweek* (October 3, 1988), p. 37. In 1991, President George H. W. Bush would justify a U.S.-led invasion of Iraq with the phrase: "No more Munichs."

36. Michael Bloch, *Ribbentrop* (London: Time Warner Books, 2003).

37. Arthur H. Vandenberg, Jr., and J. A. Morris, eds., *The Private Papers of Senator Vandenberg* (Boston: Houghton Mifflin, 1952), p. 10, cited in Dulles, *America's Rise to World Power*, p. 198.

38. Bailey, *A Diplomatic History*, p. 740.

39. Ibid., p. 771.

40. Donaldson, *American Foreign Policy*, p. xii.

41. David S. McLellan, *The Cold War in Transition* (New York: Macmillan, 1966), p. 6.

42. Winston Churchill, "The Sinews of Peace" (March 5, 1946), in *Vital Speeches of the Day*, vol. 12 (March 15, 1946), p. 332.

43. George F. Kennan (who signed his article anonymously as X), "The Sources of Soviet Conduct," *Foreign Affairs 25* (July 1947), pp. 566–582.

44. "Containment Forty Years Later," *Foreign Affairs 65* (Spring 1987), p. 829.

45. Harry S. Truman, speech before a Joint Session of Congress, March 12, 1947.

46. John Lewis Gaddis, *Strategies of Containment: A Critical Appraisal of Postwar American National Security Policy* (New York: Oxford University Press, 1982), p. 22.

47. Ibid., p. 352.

48. Quoted in Gaddis, *Strategies of Containment*, p. 91, emphasis added.

49. Ibid., p. 130. See also Townsend Hooper, *The Devil and John Foster Dulles: The Diplomacy of the Eisenhower Era* (Boston: Little, Brown, 1973).

50. Walter Russell Mead, *Power, Terror, Peace, and War: America's Strategy in a World at Risk* (New York: Knopf, 2004), pp. 88–89.

51. Frank Rich, "Oldest Living Whiz Kid Tells All," *New York Times* (January 25, 2004), sec. 2, p. 1.
52. David S. McLellan, *The Cold War in Transition* (New York: Macmillan, 1966), p. 23.
53. Thomas C. Schelling, *Arms and Influence* (New Haven: Yale University Press, 1966), p. 124.
54. Dean Rusk, with Richard Rusk, *As I Saw It* (New York: Norton, 1989), p. 237.
55. Stanley Karnow, *Vietnam: A History* (New York: Viking, 1983).
56. Loch K. Johnson, *America's Secret Power: The CIA in a Democratic Society* (New York: Oxford University Press, 1989).
57. Daniel Wirls, *Buildup: The Politics of Defense in the Reagan Era* (Ithaca, NY: Cornell University Press, 1992).
58. Smith, *America's Mission*, p. xv.
59. Loch K. Johnson, *Secret Agencies: U.S. Intelligence in a Hostile World* (New Haven: Yale University Press, 1996).
60. Loch K. Johnson, *America as a World Power* (New York: McGraw-Hill, 1995), p. 113.
61. Author's interview with DCI Robert M. Gates, Washington, DC (March 27, 1994).
62. R. James Woolsey, testimony, *Hearings*, U.S. Senate Select Committee on Intelligence, 103d Cong., 2d. Sess. (March 6, 1993).
63. See, for example, Norman A. Graebner, "Adamsian Unilateralism vs. The Bushian Imitation," *American Diplomacy* (December 4, 2004), at www.unc.edu/depts/diplomat/archives_roll/2004_10–12/book/book_graebner_adam.
64. John Lewis Gaddis, "The Past and Future of American Grand Strategy," Charles S. Grant Lecture, Middlebury College (April 21, 2005).

CHAPTER I

Ignorance

ALL ABOARD FOR TIMBUKTU

One could be forgiven for failing to know the precise spot of the remote location referred to in the old expression "From here to Timbuktu." More accurately spelled "Tombouctou," this town of some twenty thousand lies near the Niger River in the West African nation of Mali. In the late thirteenth century Tombouctou served as a thriving trading center for trans-Saharan commerce. Tipperary may be a challenge to pinpoint on a map as well, even if you're familiar with the once-popular song that begins, "It's a long ways to Tipperary . . . " Whether or not it is a long way would depend upon how close one is to southern Ireland, where Tipperary is a county.

More distressing is the average American's lack of knowledge about this planet's far less obscure geography, and about key events that occur around the world. Poll after poll indicates that most Americans live in blissful ignorance about the rest of the world. In light of the long shadow cast by the United States across the globe as the only superpower, one might reasonably expect its citizens to know something about international affairs, if only to judge more wisely whether policy officials have persuasive reasons for spending taxpayer monies beyond these shores and sending soldiers overseas to die.

Consider results from surveys on U.S. citizen awareness of world geography, one indicator of a person's interest in and understanding of America's involvement abroad:

- 30 percent of the students at the University of Miami in Florida could not locate the Pacific Ocean on a world map
- 25 percent of the high school students in Dallas could not name the country that lies immediately to the south of the United States
- 50 percent of the students in Hartford, Connecticut, could not name three countries in Africa
- 45 percent of the high school students in the state of Washington could not name the large nation that borders the United States on the north
- Nearly 50 percent of college students in a California poll could not locate Japan on a map
- 95 percent of the first-year students at a college in Indiana could not place Vietnam on a map[1]

In a 1988 Gallup survey of individuals between the ages of 18 and 24 living in nine Western nations, the United States finished last in geographic literacy.[2] Three-fourths of the Americans in this poll failed to identify the Persian Gulf on a world map, even though at the time the U.S. Navy had gathered a sizable flotilla of warships in this waterway to protect commercial shipping (especially oil bound for the West). Moreover, a report from the American Council of Trustees and Alumni indicated that students at 55 of the nation's top colleges are able to graduate without taking a single course in world history. They are not even required to take a course on American history, which presumably would give them a better sense of U.S. relations with the world since this nation's birth.[3] As a Gallup youth survey concluded in 2000, teenagers in the United States have an "appalling low awareness of facts related to world events and leaders."[4]

A few months before the United States led a multinational invasion force into Iraq in 2003, a National Geographic Society international survey found that only about one in seven—13 percent—of Americans between the ages of 18 and 24 could find Iraq, Iran, or Israel on a world map.[5] Only 17 percent could locate Afghanistan, where the United States was already at war; and a mere 24 percent could point to Saudi Arabia, a prime source of gasoline for America's automobiles. Americans could find only seven of sixteen prominent nations on the map; 30 percent could not locate the Pacific Ocean, the world's largest body of water; and 56 percent did not know where India was, home to 17 percent of the world's population. Only 19 percent could name four countries that officially acknowledge having nuclear weapons. Overall, Americans came in next to last in the quiz (after Mexico), with a "D" grade. The youth of Sweden came out on top, followed by Germany and Italy. In reporting on the survey, the president of the National Geographic Society, John Fahey, observed that "more students can tell you where an island is located that the *Survivor* TV series came from [the Marquesas Islands in the eastern South Pacific] than can identify

Afghanistan or Iraq. Ironically, a TV show seems more real or at least more meaningful and interesting or relevant than reality."

Ignorance of world affairs is hardly the special preserve of America's youth. Gallup pollsters discovered in the 1980s that barely half of a broad sample of U.S. citizens realized the Marxist-led Sandinistas and the American-backed contras were at war in Nicaragua, or that Arabs and Jews were at odds in Israel. Only a third could name a single member of the North Atlantic Treaty Organization; and 18 percent thought the Soviet Union was a member of the NATO defense pact, even though it had been established in 1949 precisely to thwart Soviet expansion.[6]

Of course, one could argue that whether or not citizens know the location of the Persian Gulf does not really have much to do with actual foreign policymaking, such as the decisions to invade Iraq in 1990 and again in 2003 made by the National Security Council, whose members presumably have a good sense of world geography. While this is true, a widespread lack of knowledge about the world among U.S. citizens can pose significant repercussions for American foreign policy. For instance, public ignorance of international affairs suggests that government officials are held to a lower level of accountability with respect to the nation's external relations, since poorly informed citizens will be deficient in their ability to evaluate foreign policy decisions and act accordingly, whether in the voting booth or through pressure-group politics and other expressions of public opinion. Presumably, if citizens were better informed about the world, their leaders in Washington would have to take public opinion more into account and, further, would be expected to explain in a more timely and fulsome manner their rationales for foreign-policy initiatives.

Americans have shown a capacity to respond eventually, and with a reasonable degree of rationality, to international objectives pursued by Washington officials, if the public is unhappy with the course of a foreign-policy decision.[7] If citizens were more consistently aware of world affairs in the first place, however, they could weigh in earlier and possibly help to avoid missteps. The average American has neither the time nor the interest to become a bona fide expert on the intricacies of global affairs but a higher level of knowledge and concern than presently exists would lead to a more robust form of public accountability for foreign policy, and that is the essence of democracy.

Moreover, public ignorance of the world signals to those in other countries that Americans do not really care about them or what happens beyond the borders of the United States. Such an impression does little to win allies for this nation in key votes taken at the United Nations and other important international forums. Nor does it help in the securing of commercial opportunities abroad, or attracting foreign students and tourists to study, visit, and spend money in this country. Some of the students and tourists who might have otherwise visited these shores will go on to become leaders of their nations; it would behoove the United States to be more welcoming to them. Above all, the perception of a limited interest in the rest of the world (fewer than one in five Americans have a passport) raises doubts about the worthiness of the United States as a global leader—an honor and a potential advantage that is imprudent to squander away.

Another dimension of this nation's engagement with the rest of the world is the foreign-language proficiency of Americans. Their foreign-speaking abilities lag behind the citizens of many other countries. My travels in Europe suggest that many people (at least in the cities) speak English, along with one or two European tongues beyond their own. Yet most Americans have never formally studied a language other than their own, despite the fact that about 95 percent of the people in the world speak a language other than English (though many study English as a second language). Figures from 1970 to 2000 indicate that only 43.8 percent of all public high school students in the United States enrolled in a foreign-language class.[8] Moreover, the United States is the only nation in the world where scholars can earn a doctorate without demonstrating competence in any foreign language.

At least America remains a melting pot of different heritages, which means that a fair number in its population know some foreign language as a result of family legacy. This could be a great advantage for the United States in world affairs. "The circumstances of our origin, as a nation, mixed up the nationalities . . . thoroughly in the crucible of our life," the well-known U.S. statesman George F. Kennan has observed. "This has given us, potentially, a flexibility and cosmopolitanism of understanding which probably surpasses that of any other people."[9]

This blending of ethnic backgrounds in the United States contributes significantly to the degree of language facility among Americans: about twenty-eight million speak Spanish, ten million speak another Indo-European language, and seven million speak an Asian or Pacific Island language. Other than English and Spanish, the ten languages most frequently used at home in the United States as of 2000 were: Chinese (2.0 million people); French (1.6 million); German (1.4 million); Tagalog, the language of the Philippines and nearby nations (1.2 million); Vietnamese (1.0 million); Italian

(1.0 million); Korean (0.9 million); Russian (0.7 million); Polish (0.7 million), and Arabic (0.6 million).[10] Among the ten most-studied foreign languages by Americans are Spanish, French, German, and Italian at the top of the list (in descending order); yet the languages of the Middle East and South Asia, places where the United States has its greatest foreign policy challenges at the moment, are nowhere to be found among the top ten.[11]

The K–12 educational system in the United States is notoriously weak in the teaching of world history, geography, and foreign languages. Few precollege curriculums offer instruction in Chinese and Japanese, let alone Arabic; and K–12 textbooks on Arabic are "practically non-existent."[12] Nor for that matter are many institutions of higher learning in the United States properly equipped and staffed to teach Arabic, Pashto, or Farsi. Efforts to improve student awareness of different world faiths and cultures are limited, too. Sometimes these efforts can lead to controversy and opposition among citizens. In 2002, for example, the University of North Carolina at Chapel Hill asked first-year students to read an assigned text about the Koran. Carolinians in large numbers reacted in protest across the state, writing scurrilous letters to the University's president, blasting the homework assignment on talk shows, and filling the newspapers with letters and op-eds in opposition. In this case, the University may have brought much of the grief on itself by choosing a text with a strong bias in favor of the Koran, without balancing the students' intellectual experience with other religious points of view from around the world (including readings from the Bible).

University programs focused on area studies have been in decline, even at the nation's premier academies. For example, the

New York Times reported in 2002: "Try finding a full-time political scientist who specializes in the Middle East or South Asia at the nation's top universities and you'd almost be out of luck. Stanford and Princeton don't have a single political scientist who specializes in the Middle East; Yale has no political scientist on South Asia."[13] Universities are no doubt improving in this regard, but still have a long way to go.

The decline in media coverage of international events has added to America's ignorance about the rest of the world. Joseph S. Nye, Jr., reports that "between 1989 and 2000, the television networks closed foreign bureaus and cut their foreign news content by two-thirds."[14] An analysis of the leading topics on the television network morning shows throughout 2004 reveals that the Olympics, a murder trial (the Laci Peterson case), criminal charges against pop star Michael Jackson, and the jail sentencing of homemaking celebrity Martha Stewart all received more coverage than the 9/11 Commission Report or the Iraq prisoner abuse scandal at Abu Ghraib. International events and the 9/11 Commission fared better on the nightly news programs, although the issue of same-sex marriage outdistanced reportage on the Israel-Palestinian conflict. So did Ms. Stewart's lockup.[15]

On the brighter side, the statistics on those studying foreign language in the United States are trending upward (even if the study of German and French is in decline), a result stimulated significantly by the terrorist attacks of September 11, 2001. Urgent calls from the nation's intelligence agencies and from the Department of Defense for translators of Arabic, Pashto, and Farsi have brought about a surge in the study of "exotic" languages. Classes on Middle Eastern and South Asian languages, cultures, and religions have filled at some universities, as student demand surges beyond the supply of competent instructors. Still, fifty students enrolled in Arabic—out of, say, thirty-five thousand undergraduates at a state university—remains a small number. A recent memo from the dean at one major state university announced to faculty that, in the name of efficiency, all classes with less than a twenty-student enrollment would be cancelled, evidently including one in which only a few undergraduates had signed up for Arabic. After strong objections from the faculty, the dean rescinded the order.

University bureaucracy aside, students themselves often demonstrate little interest in understanding foreign cultures. Many continue to equate foreign-language study with the pain of root-canal work. Moreover, typically less than 20 percent of undergraduates at state universities study abroad for a semester, although at some institutions this figure has shot up from 3 percent to nearly 20 percent just in the past five years, and the national growth rate is a heartening 9 percent.[16] According to my telephone surveys with their administrative offices in 2005, colleges and universities in the state of Georgia alone have over two hundred fifty study-abroad programs that place thousands of students all over the world, from Innsbruck and Oxford to Kyoto and Verona. All too often, though, study-abroad programs sponsored by American universities are of short duration—a semester at best—and place U.S. students in dormitories together overseas, rather than living with indigenous families. A full year abroad, integrated into a local community, is likely to be the most enriching experience, as well as the best way to learn a foreign language and culture.

These few promising post-9/11 trends to the contrary, the fact remains that the overwhelming majority of Americans are without fluency in a non-English language. Obviously this creates a communications barrier between U.S. citizens and people of other societies. In a phrase from a recent Census Bureau report, the United States is a nation "linguistically isolated" from the rest of the world. This affects the ability of Americans traveling abroad to develop rapport with local citizens, or to relate well to those foreigners who visit our nation. It places the United States at a disadvantage in global commerce as well. According to a report published in the 1980s, ten thousand Japanese fluent in English conducted business in the United States, while only about nine hundred American businesspeople—few of whom who could speak Japanese—plied the boardrooms in Tokyo.[17] That skewed ratio is unlikely to have improved much since then. In several American universities, it is possible to earn a degree in international business without taking a single foreign-language course. Little wonder the United States has fallen behind in world commerce, currently suffering record trade imbalances with much of the world.[18]

Scholars, too, have seen their opportunities to study foreign languages and cultures erode. J. William Fulbright (D-AR), who served an unprecedented thirteen years as chair of the Senate Foreign Relations Committee, fathered the Fulbright International Educational Exchange Program. Established in 1946, the Fulbright Fellowships have allowed thousands of American professors and artisans to travel and study overseas, where they meet and befriend local citizens. As Senator Fulbright lamented near the end of his distinguished career:

> There are fewer fellowships now than there were 25 years
> ago. It is evident that some important political leaders in

Washington have failed to recognize that the exchange program is more than just a laudable experiment, that it is also an important instrument of foreign policy, designed to mobilize human resources of intellect and judgment, just as military and economic programs mobilize physical resources.[19]

Harmful, too, has been the sudden downturn in the number of international students studying in the United States—a 2.4 percent overall decline in 2003 and even higher drop-offs in the nation's major research universities.[20] In part, this reflects the growing difficulty foreigners face in acquiring visas to come to America in the aftermath of the terrorist attacks of 2001. As Nye notes, "Ever since the terrorist attacks of Sept. 11, getting an American visa has been a nightmare of red tape, and the hassle has deterred many foreign student applicants."[21] The figures are probably a manifestation, also, of a concern among students from the Middle East and South Asia that, since the attacks, they may face prejudice if they come to the United States. According to a survey of the Council of Graduate Schools, the number of Indian students who applied to attend U.S. graduate schools in the fall of 2004 dropped 28 percent compared to the previous fall. Applications from the Far East have dropped, too, with a 45 percent decline in applications by students from China.[22] Many of the foreign students who might have come to study in the United States may have gone home after their studies with an abiding affection for America and its values—"the best way of building friends," argues Thomas L. Friedman.[23]

Eminent scholars from abroad who wish to visit the United States face similar problems. In 2004, J. M. Coetzee, the South

African winner of the 2003 Nobel Prize for Literature, declined an invitation from the University of Texas, citing the headache of acquiring a visa. Reacting to the American visa bureaucracy, scholarly international conferences have begun changing their meeting venues from U.S. sites to other locations, as when the International Astronomical Union recently switched from Hawaii to Brazil for its 2009 annual meeting.[24]

Until larger numbers of Americans commit themselves to learning more about the world, including travel overseas with the intent of making friends and gaining a better appreciation of foreign cultures, other nations are apt to look upon citizens of the United States as unworthy of global leadership. Continued ignorance of foreign languages, geography, customs, economic practices, and politics seems a sure prescription for a decline in this nation's international standing. Professor Robert H. Swansbrough, a political scientist and administrator at the University of Tennessee, Chattanooga, has suggested the establishment of special educational scholarships and loans (something equivalent to the National Defense Education Act of the Cold War years) for students willing to prepare themselves for careers related to area studies and language arts. The loans could be forgiven for those who graduate from college and devote five years to public-service pursuits.[25]

Along these lines, Senator Pat Roberts (R-KS), chair of the Senate Select Committee on Intelligence, instituted a special scholarship for U.S. students who enroll in foreign languages and area studies at American universities. Under a law passed in 2004 that created an "Intelligence Scholars Program," the successful applicant will receive payments from the government for one year of study in return for a promise of eighteen months of service as an analyst in one of the nation's intelligence agencies.[26]

GLOBAL KNOWLEDGE DEFICITS WITHIN THE GOVERNMENT

Even more disturbing than gaps in the public's knowledge about world affairs is ignorance inside the government itself, where day-to-day decisions are made that affect the future of the United States. Spotty knowledge of the world's languages extends into the very agencies expected to gather information about foreign events and advise top policymakers. For example, the U.S. Foreign Service is the only diplomatic corps in a major industrialized nation that does not insist that its officers be fluent in another language.

Inside the nation's intelligence agencies, speakers of Middle Eastern and African languages (such as Farsi, Arabic, and Amharic) are in short supply. So are analysts with a deep under-standing of the history, politics, and culture of places like Afghanistan, Iraq, Iran, Syria, and North Korea. When the CIA set up a Center for Counterterrorism in 1986, it had only two Arabic speakers.[27] The Defense Intelligence Agency (DIA) had only two Iraqi analysts at the time of the first Persian Gulf War in 1990.[28] During the buildup to the NATO bombing of Serbia during the Clinton administration, Serbo-Croatian translators were hard to find in the U.S. government. Prior to September 11, 2001, the FBI had only one strategic analyst with the skills needed to track the Al Qaeda terrorist organization.[29]

America's intelligence agencies have an abundance of documents and transcripts of telephone intercepts from around the world but much of this information—upward of 90 percent—lies dust-covered in vaults, untouched because the agencies lack enough skilled translators.[30] On September 10th, the day before the terrorist attacks against the United States in 2001, the National Security Agency (NSA) intercepted an Al Qaeda message that proclaimed: "Tomorrow is zero hour." These fateful words were not translated until September 12th.[31] Whether or not knowledge of this warning would have tightened U.S. airport security and prevented the 9/11 tragedy is, of course, unknown but it might have. Regardless, the point is clear: fast translations could be vital in the future. By 2004, FBI linguists had still failed to translate over one hundred twenty thousand hours of potentially valuable recordings related to terrorist activities at the time of the 9/11 attacks.[32] Some of these Al Qaeda recordings were accidentally erased as a result of the Bureau's antiquated computer systems.

The influx of new communications interceptions—telephone calls, e-mail messages, audio from electronic listening devices, documents stolen from terrorist cells or provided by defectors—continue to outpace the FBI's capacity to provide quick and accurate translations. The inspector general in the Justice Department, home of the FBI, concluded in 2005 that the Bureau "cannot translate all the foreign-language counterterrorism and counterintelligence material it collects."[33]

Throughout the government, a crash program is underway to remedy these translation deficiencies. The government also faces the challenge of recruiting U.S. intelligence officers with the language skills and cultural acumen to travel abroad and, in turn, recruit foreign agents to infiltrate important targets in the Middle

East, South Asia, and wherever else Al Qaeda and other terrorist cells are located. Director of Central Intelligence (DCI) George J. Tenet estimated in 2004 that reliable U.S.-directed spy rings with the capacity to infiltrate Al Qaeda could take upward of five years to develop. His successor, Representative Porter J. Goss (R-FL), thought the task would take even longer, perhaps as long as ten years. It will take time, as well, to train a new generation of analysts with insights into the nations of the Middle East and South Asia—regions largely overlooked during America's focus on the Soviet empire and other Communist-dominated regions of the world during the Cold War.

Of course, an improved facility with foreign languages will hardly solve all of America's intelligence problems. For instance, the WMD fiasco leading up to the war in Iraq in 2003 was mostly a product of the CIA having no reliable human agents in Iraq, coupled with faulty intelligence analysis throughout most of the U.S. intelligence community (and the world, for that matter) that presumed the Iraqi dictator, Saddam Hussein, would continue to develop powerful weapons, just because that had been his behavior in the previous ten years. Nor are the most accurate and rapidly translated communications intercepts from abroad of any use if they are ignored by officials who engage in the selective use ("cherry picking")—or outright rejection—of information that fails to meet their policy preconceptions or political needs. As Pushkin observed in the poem "The Hero" (1830), "Uplifting illusion is dearer to us than a host of truths." Nonetheless, improvements in translation will solve some intelligence problems and, quite possibly, could alert the United States to developments in the world that otherwise might never come to the attention of decision-makers in Washington.

INTELLIGENCE FAILURES IN IRAQ AND AFGHANISTAN

The costs to the American people that arise from faulty intelligence at the highest levels of government became painfully obvious in the recent cases of the 9/11 attacks and the belief that there were WMDs in Iraq. It would be an impossible standard to think the nation's intelligence agencies should be able to foresee and thwart all threats to the nation; the world is simply too vast and adversaries too cunning for that level of success. Still, Americans were shocked to discover that the CIA and its companion agencies had little understanding about the Islamic world before Afghanistan and Iraq became dangers to the United States.

The CIA had a brief flirtation with Afghanistan during the Reagan administration, providing local anti-Soviet mujahedeen fighters with Stinger missiles and other arms to counter the intervention of the Red Army in the poor, mountainous nation in 1979. When the Soviet military finally retreated a decade later, all but a few CIA personnel departed from Afghanistan as well. After the exit of the Soviet Union, the United States adopted an attitude of indifference to the fate of Afghani people.[34]

Iraq, too, attracted little American attention during the Cold War years, other than as a foil against the possible expansion of Iran in the region. The United States provided arms and intelligence to Saddam Hussein in Iraq's war against Iran during the 1980s. Beyond these peripheral concerns, foreign policy officials in Washington largely discounted this part of the world and concentrated their attention on the machinations of the Communist states.

When the Taliban regime took hold of Afghanistan in the 1990s and provided a safe haven for any and all fellow radical Islamists (including the incipient terrorist group Al Qaeda), and when Iraq invaded its neighbor Kuwait in 1990, the United States suddenly had to play catch-up and try to understand the dynamics of these events. Devoid of well-placed human intelligence or "humint" agents on the ground, and only belatedly shifting satellite surveillance platforms into new orbits over these nations, the U.S. intelligence community had little information about the inner workings of the governments in Kabul and Baghdad, or about their troop movements. The involvement of the United States in warfare in the Persian Gulf in 1990–91, to drive its erstwhile ally Iraq out of oil-rich Kuwait, further distracted the CIA from focusing on Afghanistan, the Taliban, and Al Qaeda.

Even after this brief war, in which the Iraqi troops were quickly routed, America's intelligence agencies had little success in, and minimal motivation for, the development of spy rings in Iraq or Afghanistan. Both Saddam Hussein and the Taliban dictators had extensive security and counterintelligence forces that largely succeeded in keeping the CIA at bay. Moreover, the CIA found itself in the post-Cold War years with a full plate of other global intelligence requirements, most notably a responsibility for tracking and curbing the proliferation of WMDs. This bailiwick included everything from guarding against the disappearance of "loose nukes" in Russia and investigating sarin gas attacks in Japan, to finding out about possible atomic bomb construction in Pakistan, North Korea, and Iran—not to mention tracking black market sales of uranium to a variety of rogue nations and terrorist organizations. Iraq and Afghanistan were just two items, and not even the most important, on the long list of threats to the United States, known inside the White House and the National Security Council (NSC) as the "threat assessment" and sorted according to priorities from Tier 1A to Tier 4. After the 9/11 attacks, Al Qaeda leapt to Tier 1A, with Iraq lower down on the ladder of perceived dangers.

When Al Qaeda terrorists struck the United States on September 11, 2001, and when the Bush administration feared the added possibility that Saddam Hussein might use WMDs against the United States directly or through allied terrorists, the CIA and the other American intelligence agencies had only scanty information about Afghanistan and Iraq to offer strategists in the White House. A high-level penetration of Al Qaeda with a U.S. intelligence agent, a mole, had proved virtually impossible. Some wondered why a penetration was so difficult. After all, when the United States and its local ally, the Northern Alliance, moved against Al Qaeda and the Taliban regime in Afghanistan, captured in the fighting was a twenty-year-old U.S. citizen by the name of John Walker Lindh. He had received Al Qaeda training, had met the leader of the terrorist organization (Osama bin Laden), and, at the time of his apprehension in Kunduz, Afghanistan, was under arms with the Taliban military. Moreover, within America itself, Al Qaeda sympathizers were known to frequent Islamic mosques in Brooklyn and elsewhere. Why couldn't the FBI recruit some of them as double agents?

Simply because Al Qaeda had trained Lindh did not mean that he or any other American might be able to infiltrate the terrorist organization at a high echelon, with access to important information about Bin Laden's future schemes against the United States.

Al Qaeda is a clan-based, tightly knit ethnic and religious entity that carefully guards access to its inner sanctum, especially proximity to its leader Bin Laden. Nor was Baghdad an easy place to infiltrate with CIA agents, since Saddam had constructed a security system almost as hermetically sealed from outsiders as the locked-down regime of North Korea, with layers upon layers of guards and Saddam himself constantly on the move to avoid assassination by internal dissidents or an external intelligence hit squad.

With respect to Iraq, the CIA was left to speculate and extrapolate about conditions inside the country based on the knowledge base it did have when Americans were on the ground there during the U.S./UN invasion of 1991. At that time, the CIA's analysts were startled to discover that Saddam's WMD programs—including the Iraqi quest for a nuclear bomb—had moved much further along than the CIA and other American intelligence agencies had anticipated. This revelation probably added to the CIA's inclination later in the 1990s and early 2000s to overestimate the likelihood that Saddam had returned with zeal to the development of WMDs.

In Afghanistan, when Americans hit back after 9/11 with a combination of CIA paramilitary operations; military special forces; and unmanned aerial vehicles (UAVs, armed with surveillance cameras and Hellfire missiles), B-52 bombs, and cruise missiles, the Taliban and Al Qaeda forces melted into the rugged terrain of the Texas-sized nation. Some sought refuge in remote caves; others vanished across Afghanistan's porous boundaries into Pakistan and other neighboring countries before the U.S. Army, the Marines, and the CIA were able to seal the borders.

In Iraq, the United States settled on the assumption that Iraq had WMDs; in Afghanistan, U.S. troops and intelligence officers turned to the hard task of hunting down Al Qaeda members one by one in inhospitable terrain. The Bush administration reported that the CIA and the military had been successful in capturing or killing three-quarters of the senior Al Qaeda leadership; but Bin Laden and his top aide remained on the loose and, by all accounts, Al Qaeda was recruiting new members as quickly as the old ones were captured or killed.

The mistakes of the American intelligence agencies related to Iraq began with their prediction—a best guess—in October of 2002, reported to top policy officers in a National Intelligence Estimate (NIE), that WMDs were likely to be present there. This hunch, based on extrapolations from the state of the Iraqi weapons program in 1991, gained further credibility after a German intelligence asset (codenamed "Curveball") and a captured Al Qaeda operative (Ibn al-Shaykh al-Libi) reported that the WMDs did exist. Only after the war had started were these reports discredited. Further support for the WMD hypothesis came from Ahmad Chalabi and his Iraqi National Congress faction—Iraqi exiles in opposition to Saddam Hussein who had much to gain by a U.S. invasion that would overthrow the Iraqi regime and perhaps elevate Chalabi as the new ruler.

The clinching moment in support of the WMDs argument came from an oral briefing presented to President George W. Bush by DCI Tenet in early 2003, during which the intelligence chief went so far as to suggest that the existence of WMDs in Iraq was a "slam dunk."[35] Using this frightening possibility as the main pretext for going to war in Mesopotamia for a second time, the White House warned the American people that if the United States failed to act quickly, Americans might suffer disastrous consequences, perhaps even the appearance of a "mushroom cloud" from a nuclear detonation in its own backyard. Los Angeles, Chicago, New York City. Who could tell where? The threat had to be nipped in the bud through the use of armed force against Saddam's regime.

But as the U.S. military poured into Iraq, no one could find the anticipated cache of weapons. Charles A. Duelfer, a former CIA analyst chosen by the Bush administration itself to investigate Iraq's development of WMDs, reported in 2004 that—contrary to the prewar assertions of the administration—there was no evidence of "concerted efforts to restart the program." The United States was "almost all wrong" on the subject of Iraqi WMDs, concluded Duelfer's formal report.[36]

Mistaken WMD predictions were not the only source of American ignorance surrounding Iraq. The CIA and the other American intelligence agencies anticipated that U.S. soldiers would be greeted enthusiastically by Iraqis when they arrived in 2003 to "liberate" the nation from its murderous dictator. One CIA officer came up with a plan to smuggle in hundreds of small American flags to distribute, so that Iraqis could gratefully salute the U.S. Marines and the Army as they marched victoriously along the roads into Baghdad. A propaganda coup, the spectacle could be filmed and disseminated throughout the Arab world. Instead, the reality was quite different. American soldiers were "welcomed" by rocket-propelled grenades (RPGs) and improvised explosive devices (IEDs) triggered by a much stronger anti-U.S. insurgency force than the CIA and military intelligence had anticipated—yet another intelligence failure. Nasiriya, one of the towns the CIA predicted would cheer the arrival of the liberators, turned out to be a place where the Marines faced some of the fiercest resistance from insurgents.[37]

Other intelligence mistakes became obvious. The Kean Commission, headed by Republican former governor of New Jersey Thomas H. Kean, reiterated in 2004 a key finding of an earlier Congressional Joint Committee that looked into the 9/11 tragedy: the CIA and the FBI had been unable or unwilling to share what little information they did have about suspected Al Qaeda operatives. The CIA realized in early 2001 that two of the terrorists had entered the United States, but failed to raise a red flag in its communications with the FBI about these suspects. Plagued by its own mistakes, the Bureau rebuffed warnings from its field agents about suspicious men of Middle Eastern descent who were enrolled in flight schools in the United States. Moreover, Bureau headquarters failed to check the names of these student pilots against CIA and State Department terrorist watchlists. The CIA and FBI databases on foreign terrorists proved electronically incompatible and unable to exchange this kind of information; and a face-to-face culture of sharing information in interagency meetings was almost nonexistent, characterized by petty bureaucratic rivalries and deep-seated differences in professional training—as if the FBI and the CIA were adversaries rather than partners against the likes of Al Qaeda.

An even larger problem arose from the lack of good information from CIA stations overseas and FBI field offices at home about Al Qaeda and related terrorist threats. "What we missed was the fine granularity that you get from a physical presence on the ground, by interacting with the Iraqi people over the years," recalled Maj. Gen. James M. (Spider) Marks, who led the military intelligence effort for the land war command in Iraq during the 2003 war. "Since 1991, we lost our finger on the pulse of the Iraqi people and built intelligence assessments from a distance."[38] A former senior

CIA official, Richard J. Kerr, whom DCI Tenet asked to review the causes of the Agency's inadequate Iraq intelligence findings, concluded that ". . . there was too little research on important social, political, and cultural issues."[39] The CIA also bit too soon on the notion, floated its way by British intelligence (which, in turn, apparently got the idea from an Italian intelligence source), that Saddam had sought to acquire yellow cake uranium from the African nation of Niger. Even though the CIA eventually concluded that this intelligence was based on forged documents and warned the Bush administration to that effect, the yellow cake "evidence" ended up in the president's State of the Union address in 2003 anyway, as one of the notes in the trumpet of war against Iraq.

Fooled, too, on a related matter was Secretary of State Colin L. Powell. In 2003, on the eve of the Iraqi invasion, he stood before delegates to the United Nations in a special session, DCI Tenet at his side. Powell argued that the U.S. intelligence agencies had incontrovertible evidence linking Saddam to the purchase of aluminum tubes whose purpose could only be the construction of a nuclear bomb. In fact, as reliable U.S. scientists subsequently pointed out, these tubes were more likely meant to be used to launch conventional battlefield rockets.[40] Equally skeptical before the UN presentation were analysts in Powell's own State Department intelligence unit, the Bureau of Intelligence and Research (INR). So were analysts in the home of America's most experienced nuclear weapons experts, the intelligence unit within the Department of Energy. The reservations of these two small agencies were shouldered aside, however, by more muscular intelligence organizations, like the CIA and the DIA, which had concluded (not without some internal dissent) that the aluminum tubes were highly suspicious.

During the tumultuous years from 2001–04, the CIA and the other intelligence agencies sometimes got things right. Analysts accurately predicted that the people of Iraq would quickly weary of a U.S. military presence in their country. The agencies also provided the military with first-rate information on Iraq's oil infrastructure and defense perimeters. The National Geospatial-Intelligence Agency (NGA) supplied street-by-street maps of downtown Baghdad, indispensable as U.S. troops moved into the Iraqi capital. Further, the CIA consistently refuted the administration's obsession with the belief that Saddam and Bin Laden were coconspirators in the 9/11 attacks and other nefarious terrorist activities. The Agency also rejected the view that Iraq itself was a bastion of terrorism—an hypothesis popular with Vice President Dick Cheney, who visited the CIA an unprecedented eight times to discuss intelligence with analysts. Instead, the CIA maintained that it would only become so if the United States invaded Iraq; then "Afghan Arabs" from around the world who had fought with the mujahedeen against the Soviets would materialize in Iraq to fight against another superpower intent on occupying a Muslim nation. So it came to be.

When intelligence agencies provide policy officials with information that runs contrary to their preconceptions, a common response—regardless of which party occupies the White House—is the phenomenon of politicization, that is, the twisting or outright dismissal of intelligence that fails to fit into the procrustean bed of an administration's foreign policy strategies. One might excuse President George W. Bush to some degree for having confidence about the widespread supposition that Iraq possessed WMDs on the eve of America's invasion of Iraq in March of 2003. After all, a majority of his intelligence agencies thought so, and his trusted DCI emphasized that the weapons were a "slam dunk" certainty. Still, a more prudent commander in chief—one who was truly open-minded about the wisdom of attacking the Hussein regime—would have insisted on harder evidence before taking the nation to war. The president might have sought out the nation's top intelligence experts on Iraq for a personal briefing, especially those in INR and the Energy Department who dissented from the conventional wisdom about WMDs. If he had, he might have discovered how soft the WMD estimate was, based primarily on just a single, questionable German intelligence source in Iraq (aptly named "Curveball") and extrapolations from what the CIA knew about Iraq's weapons programs more than a decade earlier, in 1991.[41]

Critics have claimed, however, that the Bush administration was never interested in the facts, but was hell-bent on going to war with Iraq, whether to see democracy bloom in a Muslim state in the Middle East, gain access to Iraqi oil reserves, acquire land for U.S. military bases in the region, rid Israel of an Iraq threat, or to avenge Saddam's attempt to assassinate the president's father (former President George H. W. Bush) in 1993. Perhaps all of the above.[42] In the same manner, one must wonder, too, about the firmness of the intelligence and strategic rationales for President Bill Clinton's air attacks on Iraq (Operation Desert Fox), which seem more of an excuse to look tough at home than to respond to any genuine threat to the interests of the United States.

During the second Bush administration, one Pentagon response to intelligence that did not fit into the policy aspirations of its leaders was their creation of a Policy Counterterrorism Evaluation Group. (The Pentagon also established an Office of Special Plans, often confused with the intelligence-oriented Evaluation Group, to plan for the stabilization of a post-war Iraq.) Aides to the secretary of defense used the Evaluation Group to analyze intelligence on their own terms, since the CIA could not seem to find data in support of the administration's views, especially information to confirm the vice president's unyielding belief that Saddam had a connection to Al Qaeda. There is nothing intrinsically wrong about the secretary of defense, or any other Cabinet official, seeking additional analysis focused on their specific departmental planning. This is often known as "alternative analysis" and can play a constructive role.

The use of alternative analysis becomes bankrupt, however, if it involves the dissemination of dubious information to policymakers, or discards altogether (or bends) analysis from throughout the intelligence community just because the findings fail to resonate with the Department's policy plans. The Policy Counterterrorism Evaluation Group sent to the White House a conclusion—rejected by the rest of the intelligence community and others who had looked into the case, including the 9/11 Commission—that the leader of the 9/11 hijackers, Mohammed Atta (an Egyptian), had met with an Iraqi intelligence agent in Prague on the eve of the attacks against the United States. According to Senator Carl Levin (D-MI), a member of the Select Committee on Intelligence, the director of the Evaluation Group "was giving the Administration analysis that they wanted to hear. It was misleading, it was deceptive, it was based on feeble intelligence." The director of the Evaluation Group lamely retorted that he was merely engaged in alternative analysis.[43]

The appropriate lesson to be drawn from the Iraqi WMD case is that it is not enough to have good information about a dangerous regime like Saddam Hussein's. (Even this first test was failed by the U.S. intelligence community.) One must also have government officials who resist twisting the meaning of the reliable intelligence that does exist, whether selectively choosing only those items of information that support their preconceptions ("cherry picking") or reaching conclusions that have no merit in the judgment of seasoned analytic experts from throughout the intelligence community.

In Great Britain, the politicization of intelligence regarding WMDs in Iraq was particularly stark. The British intelligence agency responsible for foreign intelligence, the Strategic Intelligence Service (SIS or MI6), reported to Prime Minister Tony Blair that quite possibly Saddam Hussein could bring tactical WMDs of a chemical or biological nature to the battlefield front lines in Iraq within forty-five minutes if American and British troops invaded in 2003. Based on this top-secret report, the prime minister's public spokesman left the British media (and therefore the British public) with the impression that MI6 had concluded that the United Kingdom itself was vulnerable to an Iraqi WMD assault—including perhaps weapons that could strike London forty-five minutes after war began. This was a rather different and far more frightening scenario than what MI6 had actually imparted to the Blair government.

Subsequently, critics charged that this rhetorical escalation in the original meaning of MI6's report might have been a ploy by the government to play on the fears of British citizens as a means to gain their support for the war effort, much as the Bush administration had spooked the American public with talk of "mushroom clouds."[44] Once the war was well underway, an investigative panel in England exonerated the prime minister of this charge, but the fact remained that his media aide had exaggerated the Iraqi threat in a press conference and Great Britain soon went to war. In the 2005 British national elections, the voters bloodied Blair's nose with a low percentage vote for his party, though—like George W. Bush in 2004—Blair managed to gain reelection despite the controversies over the possible "cooking" of intelligence to advance public support for the war in Iraq.

In both the U.S. and the U.K. examples, missing were intelligence chiefs willing to stand up in a public arena and clarify the intelligence record, before citizens on both sides of the Atlantic were misled. In the United States, DCI Tenet could have insisted that the yellow cake allegations be excised from the State of the Union address, or at least could have publicly corrected the record after the speech. More significantly, he could have made it clear to the president and, if necessary, to the public, that the CIA and its companion agencies actually knew little about contemporary Iraq and were basing their estimates on a dubious agent (Curveball), a fabricating Al Qaeda detainee (al-Libi), a politically ambitious Iraqi exile (Chalabi), and a hunch from what they had learned on the ground in Iraq—a dozen years before the 2003 invasion. Although Tenet did object strongly to many of the Bush administration's exaggerations about Iraq,[45] he could have been more circumspect, too, about having Secretary of State Colin L. Powell place his good reputation on the line at the UN with intelligence on aluminum tubes that remained a subject of contention among the intelligence agencies. The secretary himself could have conceded publicly that much of the intelligence was debatable and had been rejected by his own intelligence unit, as well as the nuclear weapons analysts in the Department of Energy (and Air Force Intelligence). Instead, the rush to war was on.

Another secretary of state, Dean Rusk of the Kennedy and Johnson administrations, once said that all intelligence reports should begin with the caveat: "We don't really know for sure, but this is our best guess."[46] Instead, DCI Tenet—and even more so the president and his government—left the public with the impression that WMDs in Iraq and the risk that they might be used on American soil demanded a policy of preemption against Saddam's regime—even if several of America's leading allies (among them, Canada, France, and Germany) and many prominent Americans (such as General Wesley Clark) believed that more time should be taken to allow UN inspectors an opportunity to confirm the existence of the alleged weapons.

IGNORANCE AND AMERICAN
FOREIGN POLICY

Ignorance of international affairs can take many forms that are harmful to the pursuit of America's proper place among nations. At the level of the general public, it can prevent citizens—voters—from properly evaluating the choices made by their elected surrogates in Washington, DC. In a democracy, decisions of war and peace, trade and aid, diplomacy and covert action all rest upon the foundation of an informed and consenting public. Yet polls and studies of how poorly informed the public is on matters of global affairs lead to an obvious conclusion: the United States can do better in the education of its citizens about the role of this nation in the world, both in its schools and universities and through better explanations from public officials about the true facts of America's activities abroad.

Presently, citizens of the United States are nowhere near as well informed about international affairs as they should be, or as are the citizens of other industrialized nations. American students in high school and college know little about China, for example, although Chinese students understand much about America and Americans: from the basics of how many states there are and how presidents are elected to the details of U.S. policies that affect China—not to mention all the latest U.S. movies, popular music, and best-selling books.

The United States is making headway, though, especially since the 9/11 attacks shocked Americans to the reality that we may not be as admired and respected throughout the world as we might wish to be. The Kean Commission report on the terrorist attacks became a best-seller, which presumably means that many Americans now know a fair amount about terrorism and their own government's missteps in trying to cope with this danger. Arabic studies are on the rise, and college students are filling classes on international affairs and expressing the strongest interest in public-service careers since President John Kennedy called upon the youth of America to serve their country. According to my conversations with CIA officials in 2005 and 2006, intelligence job applications are at an all-time high, as are the qualifications of young aspirants.

Ignorance can be especially dangerous at the government level, because this is where decisions are made on behalf of the people of the United States. This nation can no longer tolerate the slipshod approach to intelligence collection around the world that too often characterized espionage operations in the Middle East and South Asia during the Cold War and after. If the 9/11 attacks have taught us nothing else, they have made it clear that the United States will only be able to protect itself against surprise attacks if it has accurate, timely, and detailed ("actionable") information about the plans of its enemies. There will never be a perfect intelligence system that can provide the nation's leaders with unerring transparency of the entire globe. Nevertheless, much can be done to chase away the clouds of ignorance that settled over the government in the years leading up to 9/11 and the second Iraqi invasion.

The remedy begins with better humint, along with improvements in all the other intelligence "ints": sigint (signals intelligence to intercept the phone calls and e-mails of Al Qaeda operatives); imint (image intelligence to provide clearer pictures of battlefields and other areas of interest, through more innovative use of UAVs, U2s, smaller but more plentiful satellites, and inexpensive camera-laden blimps stationed at 80,000 feet); and osint (open source intelligence, a more skillful and quicker mining of the public literature to place the secretly acquired nuggets of information into context). Success with humint will require men and women with language skills and knowledge of the world that will enable them to live overseas and work secretly with locals who can tap into the information America needs for its protection. Locals will respond best—usually only—to Americans whom they trust, which in turn requires that U.S. intelligence officers and diplomats speak their language reasonably well, know their customs, and understand their politics and history.

The same is true for the next ingredient for success: well-trained analysts who can provide insight to the stream of "raw" information that is brought home by human agents and spying machines. Analysts, too, must have advanced training in language, satellite-photo interpretation, international politics, area studies, cultures, and world history. The intelligence reports that go to the president and other policy officials are only as good as the wisdom analysts can bring to them—and the courage to say "we're not really sure" or "we think the president has misstated the facts," when that is the case. Speaking truth to power is not a job for the meek. An old Turkish proverb advises that he who tells the truth should have one foot in the stirrup. Nonetheless, intelligence officers must tell the truth to policy officials for the sake of rational, fact-based decisions. A former U.S. intelligence director properly warns that "there is no greater threat to world peace than poorly informed or misinformed leaders and governments."[47]

When he served as chairman of the Joint Chiefs of Staff, General Colin Powell offered sage advice for policymakers who interact with intelligence analysts. Intelligence consumers should say to those briefing them on world developments: "Tell me what you know, tell me what you don't know, tell me what you think, [and] always distinguish which is which."[48] Unfortunately, Powell failed to insist on adherence to his own advice when he became secretary of state and had to brief the UN on the issue of WMDs in Iraq.

The nation will also need policymakers who have the wisdom and integrity not to bend the facts that are presented to them by analysts, however unwelcome and contrary to an administration's political objectives they may be. Not that those with policy responsibilities should never question the conclusions reached by analysts or engage in alternative analysis. There is nothing sacrosanct about the sixteen intelligence agencies; they, too, are comprised of humans and are therefore fallible, as this chapter illustrates. Yet a king's ransom is spent each year for the purpose of having intelligence agencies gather and assess information from around the world; their judgments should be taken seriously and rejected only in the presence of strong evidence to the contrary. Vice President Cheney was much criticized for visiting the CIA often during 2003 to probe the estimates of intelligence analysts. Some thought this was an example of politicization and efforts by the Bush administration to intimidate the CIA into changing its estimates to support the war in Iraq and the suspected ties between Saddam Hussein and Al Qaeda. Yet, most of the analysts did not feel intimidated and, in fact, appreciated the willingness of the vice president (and his aide, I. Lewis Libby, Jr.) to take their work seriously and ask about it.[49] They did not feel intimidated by the vice president ("despite his perpetually curled lip," as one said to me).

The Pentagon's second-in-command during the 2003 Iraqi war, Paul Wolfowitz—often accused of dismissing CIA reports out-of-hand during the lead-up to the war—once himself employed a medical analogy to explain the ultimate reason why one should not politicize intelligence. "Policymakers are like surgeons," he said before joining the Bush administration as undersecretary of defense in 2001. "They don't last long if they ignore what they see when they cut an issue open."[50]

The ignorance about foreign affairs that has plagued the United States can be dispelled. The government must search more energetically for facts from around the world, bring the best insights to these facts that well-trained minds can provide, and speak the truth to those in office and to the public. In turn, decision-makers must carefully weigh the information as they make choices, resisting the temptations of bias, preconception, groupthink, or other barriers to the honest and careful weighing of America's best interests abroad. None of this is easy, but it can be achieved by men and women of talent and integrity who are open-minded. Surely the most unforgivable act of ignorance is for government officials—across party lines and administrations—to spend some $44 billion a year on intelligence,[51] only to dismiss, spin, or selectively embrace the results.

NOTES

1. Lee Schwartz, "We're Failing Geography 100," *Washington Post* (December 29, 1987), p. 29.
2. Connie Leslie, "Lost on the Planet Earth," *Newsweek* (August 8, 1988), p. 3.
3. Valerie Strauss, "History Students Going Beyond the Book," *Washington Post* (June 6, 2000), p. A13.
4. Gallup Organization, *Gallup Youth Survey* (May 5, 2000), p. 1.
5. Cited by "Global Goofs: U.S. Youth Can't Find Iraq," CNN.com/education (November 22, 2002).
6. Leslie, "Lost on the Planet Earth," p. 3.
7. See Ole R. Holsti, *Public Opinion and American Foreign Policy* (Ann Arbor: University of Michigan Press, 2004); Bruce W. Jentleson, "The Pretty Prudent Public: Post-Vietnam American Opinion on the Use of Military Force," *International Studies Quarterly* 36 (1992), pp. 49–73; and John Mueller, *War, Presidents and Public Opinion* (New York: Wiley, 1973).
8. U.S. Census Bureau, *Statistical Abstract of the United States* (2003), p. 176, citing the American Council on the Teaching of Foreign Languages, *Foreign Language Enrollments in Public Secondary Schools* (Yonkers, NY: 2000).
9. George F. Kennan Papers, Firestone Library, Princeton University, File 1–13, p. 1 (December 2, 1960), brought to the author's attention by Yale University historian John Lewis Gaddis.
10. U.S. Census Bureau, Census 2000 *Summary File 3*.
11. Association of Departments of Foreign Languages, Modern Language Association, *Foreign Language Enrollments in the United States Institutions of Higher Education* (Fall 2002).
12. Sally Morrison, "Arabic Language Teaching in the United States," *Language Link*, Center for Applied Linguistics (June 2003), p. 4.
13. Stephen Kotkin, "A World War Among Professors," *New York Times* (September 7, 2002), p. A15.
14. Joseph S. Nye, Jr., *The Paradox of American Power: Why the World's Only Superpower Can't Go It Alone* (New York: Oxford University Press, 2002), p. ix.

15. "What Just Happened?" *New York Times* (December 26, 2004), p. E10, based on the Sloan Digital Sky Survey and the Tyndall Report.

16. Survey, Institute of International Education, cited in Andrea Jones, "Far-Flung Classrooms Lure Students," *Atlanta Journal-Constitution* (November 16, 2004), p. E1.

17. Reported in Jane O. Hansen, "U.S. Students are 'Internationally Ignorant,'" *Atlanta Journal Constitution* (November 22, 1986), p. A6.

18. "Foreign Trade Statistics," U.S. Census Bureau (February 10, 2006), p. 1. The goods and services deficit in 2005 was $725.8 billion, the highest on record.

19. J. William Fulbright, "Fulbright Exchanges Enhance Our National Security," *Chronicle of Higher Education* (December 10, 1987), p. 104.

20. Max Bixler, "Foreign Student Ranks Decline," *Atlanta Journal Constitution* (November 10, 2004), p. F1, citing a report from the Association of International Educators.

21. Joseph S. Nye, Jr., "You Can't Get Here from There," *New York Times* (November 29, 2004), p. A25.

22. Sam Dillon, "Foreign Enrollment Declines at Universities, Surveys Say," *New York Times* (November 10, 2004), p. A15.

23. Thomas L. Friedman, "The Calm Before the Storm?" *New York Times* (April 13, 2005), p. A29.

24. Ibid.

25. Personal correspondence with Robert H. Swansbrough (December 18, 2002).

26. See David Glenn, "Cloak and Classroom," *Chronicle of Higher Education* LI (March 25, 2005), pp. A14–A17.

27. Steve Coll, *Ghost Wars* (New York: Penguin, 2004), p. 141.

28. William E. Burrows and Robert Windrem, *Critical Mass: The Dangerous Race for Superweapons in a Fragmenting World* (New York: Simon & Schuster, 1994), p. 26.

29. Author's interview with senior FBI official, Washington, DC (June 16, 2005).

30. John Mills, staff director of the U.S. House Permanent Select Committee on Intelligence, author's interview, Washington, DC (September 28, 1996).

31. Bob Woodward, *Plan of Attack* (New York: Simon & Schuster, 2004), p. 215.

32. Eric Lichblau, "F.B.I. Said to Lag on Translations of Terror Tapes," *New York Times* (September 28, 2004), p. A1.

33. Quoted by Frank Davies, "In Fight vs. Terrorism, Linguists Gain Clout," *Miami Herald* (May 2, 2005), p. A1.

34. See Coll, *Ghost Wars*.

35. Bob Woodward, *Plan of Attack* (New York: Simon & Schuster, 2004), p. 249.

36. Dana Priest and Walter Pincus, "U.S. 'Almost All Wrong' on Weapons," *Washington Post* (October 7, 2004), p. A1. Another American arms expert, David A. Kay, had led a UN inspection team into Iraq and similarly could

find no weapons of mass destruction [see David Kay, statement, "Interim Progress Report on the Activities of the Iraq Survey Group," House Permanent Select Committee on Intelligence, U.S. House of Representatives (October 2, 2003)].

37. Michael R. Gordon, "Faulty Intelligence Misled Troops at War's Start," *New York Times* (October 20, 2004), p. A1.

38. Cited in ibid., p. A12.

39. Ibid.

40. David Barstow, William J. Broad, and Jeff Gerth, "How the White House Used Disputed Arms Intelligence," *New York Times* (October 3, 2004), p. A1.

41. See Loch K. Johnson, "A Framework for Strengthening U.S. Intelligence," *Yale Journal of International Affairs* 1 (winter/spring 2006), pp. 116–131.

42. See, for example, Woodward, *Plan of Attack*; and Richard A. Clarke, *Against All Enemies* (New York: Free Press, 2004).

43. See Jeffrey Goldberg, "A Little Learning," *The New Yorker* (May 9, 2005), p. 40.

44. Author's conversations with members of a British Parliamentary delegation, Washington, DC (October 4, 2004).

45. See Douglas Jehl, "Through an Indictment, a Glimpse into a Secretive and Influential White House Office," *New York Times* (October 30, 2005), p. A28.

46. Comment to the author, Athens, Georgia (July 4, 1984).

47. Richard Helms, with William Hood, *A Look Over My Shoulder: A Life in the Central Intelligence Agency* (New York: Random House, 2003), p. 164.

48. "Fundamentals of Naval Intelligence," *Naval Doctrine Publication 2: Naval Intelligence, Chapter 2* (U.S. Department of the Navy, Office of the Chief of Naval Operations and Headquarters, U.S. Marine Corps, 1994).

49. Author's interviews at the CIA, Langley, Virginia (October 1, 2004).

50. Jack Davis, "The Challenge of Managing 'Uncertainty': Paul Wolfowitz on Intelligence-Policy Relations," interview with Paul Wolfowitz (March 1995), unpublished, p. 8.

51. Scott Shane, "Official Reveals Budget for U.S. Intelligence," *New York Times* (November 8, 2005), p. A18.

CHAPTER 2

Executive Branch Dominance

THE PRESIDENT AS SUPERHERO

Despite the disturbing lessons of Watergate, Vietnam, CIA domestic spying, and the Iran-contra affair—all instances in which the executive branch broke faith with the American people—there remains in the United States a strong predilection to rally around the White House and the rest of the executive branch when it comes to matters of foreign affairs. One of the oldest adages in America's political folklore is "politics stops at the water's edge." The idea is that we should all stand united behind the same flag and president when confronting the rest of the world, rather than have the president and lawmakers at odds. This may seem a sensible notion at first glance; after all, this planet is a hostile place bristling with weapons and terrorist cells, and, to paraphrase Benjamin Franklin, if we are unable to hang together, we might end up hanging separately. Understandably, we would like to avoid exhibiting weakness to our adversaries by seeming to be in a state of disarray. Further, at times the United States may need to act with secrecy and dispatch, attributes associated with the executive branch, not Congress with its fragmented structure and hurly-burly procedures.

In the case of domestic policy, the nation can afford the luxury of muddling through, moving incrementally while making slight changes to existing policy when necessary—widely considered the hallmark of how the United States transacts its political business at home.[1] With foreign policy, however, the dangers from abroad may be too dire for politics as usual. Protection against everything from weapons of mass destruction to terrorist attacks and the infiltration of foreign spies may require bold and quick initiatives. During the Cold War, the ten-minute flight time for a nuclear-tipped missile to trace the arc from a Soviet submarine in the Atlantic Ocean to ground zero in the heart of Washington, DC, stood as a chilling reminder of how vulnerable the United States had become to a swift and devastating attack. Such perils then, and surprise attacks by terrorists today, have led proponents of bold presidential leadership to advocate an approach to America's foreign policy that is dramatically different from what they would tolerate for domestic policy. For the nation's external affairs, proponents of presidential power embrace hierarchy, secrecy, and deliberation by only a few in the White House inner circle. They believe that the hallowed traditions of democracy—openness, debate, the careful consideration of a wide range of options, a role for public opinion—have to be sacrificed from time to time on the altar of national security.

Upon closer inspection, however, one can see deep flaws in the "water's edge" argument. It implies that it would be unpatriotic, perhaps even treasonous, for a citizen to point out that something might be wrong with a particular foreign policy stance taken by the president on behalf of the United States. Perhaps a citizen or a member of Congress believes that war in Country A is unnecessary; that foreign aid to Country B is likely to end up in a dictator's Swiss bank account; that to cozy up to Country C—with its history of human rights abuses—is wrong, even if the United States might thereby gain access to airbase landing rights for possible missions against suspected terrorist havens in nearby Country D. Should citizens and lawmakers be silenced if they have reservations about decisions made by foreign policy bureaucrats or even the president? Clearly not, unless one wishes to annul the Constitution's first amendment right to free expression.

The debate and the openness characteristic of domestic policy-making can and must be permitted for foreign policy, too, with the obvious exception of a few necessary secrets, such as the names of America's undercover intelligence officers and foreign agents, the blueprints of U.S. weapons systems, and the Pentagon's battlefield plans. To surrender foreign policy to a small group of officials in the executive branch is to risk the making of decisions contrary to the will of citizens across the land, as if the United States had adopted an elected monarchy as a form of government. In the name of national security, the very essence of American democracy—the opportunity for debate—would be abandoned.

Bob Woodward has observed that "the real threat to America is not so much terrorists, Iraqi insurgents, or Asian bird flu, but secret government." He recalls with a sense of disquiet President George W. Bush's comment to him during an interview about planning for the Iraqi war. "I consult my War Cabinet and no one outside," the president said. "I live in a bubble."[2]

The United States is the world's oldest democracy, with public institutions that are well regarded and emulated in many countries around the globe. The National Security Council (NSC), for example, has been widely adopted as a useful means of governance in many other nations, as have America's intelligence oversight procedures.[3] At its best—the Marshall Plan, the creation of NATO, arms-control accords, the advancement of human rights—the nation has made open decisions after extensive debate within Congress, embracing a working partnership between lawmakers and the president. At its worst—the Bay of Pigs, assassination plots, the Vietnam War, the Cambodian incursion, the Iran-contra scandal—the United States has bypassed debate and ignored the need for comity between the branches of government. When the government is functioning contrary to constitutional design, the White House proceeds as it wishes, in secrecy, free of "outside interference" from Congress—an approach championed by National Security Adviser Vice Admiral John M. Poindexter during the Iran-contra affair.[4] Poindexter seemed to view Congress as an alien body, rather than an important instrument of popular control over the government and a vital forum for debate and compromise.

All too often Americans and their elected representatives in Washington fail to exercise their right of expression. They lose their courage, even though the emperor parading before them in the guise of president may wear no clothes. They tamely fall in line behind the president's leadership in foreign affairs, even if he is marching the nation over a cliff.

The roots of this presidential veneration run deep. For school children, the president is one of the first public figures they can identify, along with police officers and firefighters.[5] In textbooks, the chief executive is often portrayed as a hero: George Washington on horseback rallying the nation against the repressive British, or Abraham Lincoln in top hat—the Great Emancipator—saving the Union and championing the end of slavery. Political scientist Thomas E. Cronin examined high school and colleges textbooks on government and discovered that the president is portrayed as someone who can do no wrong, who has all the information and skilled advisers needed to make wise decisions.[6] One text went so far as to refer to Lincoln as "the martyred Christ of democracy's passion play."[7] This same volume, widely used in college courses on the presidency in the 1960s, suggested further that "there is virtually no limit to what the President can do if he does it for democratic ends and by democratic means."[8] Even the savvy journalist Theodore H. White lapsed into unfettered adulation of the presidency in his best-selling book, *The Making of the President 1960.* "So many and so able are the President's advisors of the permanent services of Defense, State, Treasury, Agriculture," wrote White, "that when a crisis happens all necessary information is instantly available, all alternative courses already plotted."[9] Rest at ease. Father president will save the day.

Yet consider the reality about presidential power. Chief executives and their aides, mere mortals all, are as fallible and flawed as anyone else. For example, during the Iran-contra affair, President Ronald Reagan failed to rein in the National Security Council staff before it bypassed the constitutionally based appropriations process on Capitol Hill. The NSC staff created an organization known as The Enterprise. This supersecret "off-the-shelf, stand-alone, self-sustaining" organization was designed, according to one of the staffers, Lt. Col. Oliver L. North, to operate outside the framework of government for the purpose of conducting covert action against the rulers of Nicaragua during the 1980s—even though such activities had been banned by the Boland Amendments (sponsored by the chair of the Permanent Select Committee on Intelligence in the House of Representatives, Edward P. Boland, D-MA). Some presidents have committed crimes more directly, as when Richard M. Nixon attempted to cover up the Watergate break-in during 1973. Further, the moral lapses of some presidents have become well known, none so well in the modern era as Bill Clinton's impeachment by the House (the Senate failed to convict) for circumstances related to a sex scandal with a White House intern.

Not that the Congress has been above reproach. House Speaker Newt Gingrich (R-GA) is reported to have consorted with his own staff aide while publically attacking Clinton for similar behavior. Senator Joseph McCarthy (R-WI), the leader of a witch-hunt for communists in the 1950s, was a notorious drunk. Prominent Democrat Daniel Rostenkowski (Illinois) went to jail for stealing money from a House account. Moreover, with respect to policymaking, Nye has pointed to serious congressional shortcomings in recent years. "Not only did Congress refuse to ratify more than a dozen treaties and conventions over the last decade," he writes, "but it reduced foreign aid, withheld our dues to the United Nations and other international agencies, slashed spending at the State Department, and abolished the U.S. Information Agency."[10]

These institutional flaws in both branches of government underscore the central point: neither Congress nor the presidency is a paragon of virtue—no human organization is—and that is why the constitutional framers espoused checks and balances, the involvement of both the executive and legislative departments of government in the making of policy to help ensure (although there are no guarantees) that, in Madison's famous words from *Federalist Paper No. 51*, "ambition may be made to counter ambition."

The fact remains that the power of every president is far more limited than one would ever realize from the textbook glorification they often enjoy. Regardless of how skilled a chief executive may be, the events the White House faces can be simply unmanageable. Looking back on the problems confronted by the Carter administration, the president's national security adviser, Zbigniew Brzezinski, expressed dismay at the inability of the White House and the executive branch to control events abroad. Particularly vexing was the fate of American hostages held in Tehran by Iranian insurgents from November 1979 until the end of President Carter's term, a total of fourteen months. Neither diplomacy nor military intervention succeeded in freeing the hostages during the Carter years.

"History is much more the product of chaos than of conspiracy," Brzezinski concluded. "The external world's vision of internal decision-making in the Government assumes too much cohesion and expects too much systematic planning. The fact of the matter is that, increasingly, policymakers are overwhelmed by events and information."[11] The ill-fated rescue mission attempted by the Carter administration to free the hostages is replete with examples of events that revealed mistakes by the executive branch, including a crash of rescue helicopters in the Iranian desert and a series of military communications snafus.

Fortunately, in reality the president does not enjoy the exaggerated powers suggested in some of the textbooks. Nonetheless, when it comes to international affairs, Congress and the people have been willing to place excessive and unwarranted trust in presidents, vice presidents, and their aides in the executive branch. All too often the wisdom of the framers, who advocated limited presidential authority and a robust role for lawmakers in the making of foreign policy, has been cast aside. In Article I of the Constitution—the first for a reason—the framers laid out the powers of Congress related to America's relations with the rest of the world, including the authority to declare war and approve or disapprove treaties. These powers are considerable, and considerably ignored in the modern era by lawmakers and the public alike, who have apparently forgotten the dangers of power concentrated in the executive branch—the animating fear that guided those who drafted the Constitution in 1789.

UP AGAINST THE BUREAUCRACY

One reason for avoiding a reliance on the president alone to make foreign policy is that, often, the White House is unable to control its own executive branch. President Harry S. Truman's classic prediction about the experience that his successor, General Dwight D. Eisenhower, would have in the Oval Office serves as a poignant reminder of the difficulties faced by chief executives in commanding the vast executive domain. "He'll sit here," Truman foresaw, "and he'll say, 'Do this! Do that!' And nothing will happen. Poor Ike—it won't be a bit like the Army. He'll find it very frustrating."[12] President Lyndon B. Johnson also expressed frustration over a president's lack of power. "Power?" he once said. "The only power I've got is nuclear—and I can't use that."[13] The real power had slipped beyond his grasp, into the crevices of the Pentagon and other behemoth organizations within the executive branch.

During the Cuban missile crisis in 1962, President John F. Kennedy decided it would be prudent to move a U.S. Navy blockade ("quarantine," in more polite diplomatic language) closer to Cuba. This would give the leaders in the Kremlin more time to evaluate the danger of an impending war with the United States as Soviet warships steamed across the Atlantic toward the Caribbean island. The Kennedy administration hoped Moscow would order those vessels nearing the blockade to return home. The U.S. Navy, however, had its own ideas about how to conduct the operation, as the secretary of defense, Robert S. McNamara, soon found out. After consultations with the president, McNamara and his deputy drove from the White House to the Pentagon to inquire about the Navy's progress on the blockade plan. The defense secretary presented Navy officials with incisive questions about their management of the operation. Finally, the chief of naval operations (CNO), upset over this civilian interference, waved the Manual of Navy Regulations in the secretary's face and shouted: "It's all in there!"

"I don't give a damn what John Paul Jones would have done," McNamara responded. "I want to know what you are going to do, now."

At the end of the angry exchange, the CNO concluded brusquely, "Now, Mr. Secretary, if you and your Deputy will go back to your office the Navy will run the blockade."[14]

Even mundane matters can bog down in bureaucratic resistance. The Kennedy administration ordered the Central Intelligence Agency to remove its "CIA Headquarters" sign from alongside the George Washington Parkway in Virginia. The president pointed out to the director of central intelligence that it was indiscreet to advertise the location of America's foremost spy agency. After several weeks of telephone calls from the president's aides to the Agency, the sign finally came down. (It is now back up.)

The president's bureaucrats, in short, often have their own agenda, and it can be quite distinct from the objectives of the White House. No wonder Roger Hilsman, a former high official in the Kennedy administration, concluded: "In action after action, responsibility for decision [within the executive branch] is as fluid and restless as quicksilver and there seems to be neither a person nor an organization on whom, it can be fixed. At times the point of decision seems to have escaped into the labyrinth of governmental machinery, beyond layers and layers of bureaucracy."[15] A former secretary of the navy during the Reagan administration also expressed chagrin over the Pentagon's lack of responsiveness: "No matter who is Secretary of Defense, it is not a rational decision-making organization. It is too big. It is big, big, big . . . It makes any management person laugh out loud."[16]

An expert on the national security bureaucracy, Morton Halperin, notes further that "career officials, including those who will come to head organizations such as the Joint Chiefs of Staff, often develop their position largely by calculating the national interest in terms of the organizational interests of the career service to which they belong."[17] The U.S. Air Force, for example, steadfastly resisted efforts to develop intercontinental ballistic missiles (ICBMs), as favored by the Kennedy administration. The leaders of the U.S. Air Force favored, instead, the use of manned bombers, which they considered the heart and soul of their mission. "Sitting in [missile] silos just cannot compare to flying bombers," Halperin continues, summing up the Air Force point of view. Presidents be damned; Air Force generals wanted to *fly*! For the same reason today, the Air Force has resisted the development of unmanned aerial vehicles (UAVs). Drones, like the "Predator," have proven highly useful in Afghanistan during the war against the Taliban regime and Al Qaeda but, for the Air Force, UAVs point to a disconcerting future: airplanes without pilots.

The history of American intelligence is filled with illustrations about slippage in the executive branch chain of command. Senator Frank Church (D-ID) accused the CIA in 1975 of acting like a "rogue elephant" on a rampage, out of control. This outburst was prompted by the senator's discovery of documents on CIA assassination plots against Fidel Castro of Cuba, Patrice Lumumba of Congo, and other foreign leaders. Church was appalled at the notion of the United States serving as a "Godfather" of the world, bumping off heads of state who happened to disagree with the United States. The CIA countered that Senator Church overstated the case; the Agency was just following presidential orders from Eisenhower (in the case of Lumumba) and Kennedy (in the other cases). No documentation could be found, however, in support of presidential authority for the murder plots. High officials, including secretaries of state and defense (Dean Rusk and Robert McNamara, respectively), testified under oath that they found it unlikely the president had ordered assassination. Yes, it was true that President Kennedy had complained, "Won't someone do something about Castro!" Did that mean assassination? Not according to Rusk and McNamara. Yet that was clearly the interpretation adopted by Richard Helms, the CIA's deputy director for operations at the time. He in turn told his underlings to plan Castro's murder. Subsequently, and without authority from the White House, they recruited the Mafia to assist in the murder plot.

Such a sequence of events is probably what Kennedy's national security adviser, McGeorge Bundy, had in mind when he presented testimony on the subject before Senator Church's investigative committee. "It can happen and I think it has happened," Bundy said, "that an operation is presented in one way to a committee [of the NSC] and executed in a way that is different from what the committee thought it had authorized."[18] Similarly, presidential adviser Clark Clifford (who served several Democratic presidents, beginning with Truman) told the Church Committee:

> I believe, on a number of occasions, a plan for covert action has been presented to the NSC and authority is requested for the CIA to proceed from Point A to Point B. The authority will be given and the action will be launched. When Point B is reached, the persons in charge feel it is necessary to go to Point C, and they assume that the original authorization gives them such a right. From Point C, they go to D and possibly E, and even further. This has led to some bizarre results, and, when an investigation is started, the excuse is blandly presented that authority was obtained from the NSC before the project was launched.[19]

It is true that most CIA operations have been approved by the White House; and, since the Church Committee investigation in 1975–76, covert actions must be formally approved by the president and reported to the two congressional intelligence oversight committees. Yet the Agency has continued to be haunted by the "rogue elephant" label. During the Iran-contra scandal, Representative Boland concluded that the CIA was "almost like a rogue elephant, doing what it wanted to."[20] Again, the Agency blanched at the criticism, arguing that only a few members of the CIA had been involved in the scandal. Those members, however, included the Agency's own director, William J. Casey! One could perhaps appreciate Representative Boland's concern. More recently, in 2004, a leading conservative member of Congress, John McCain (R-AZ), lamented that the CIA is still "in some ways a rogue agency."[21]

The problems of accountability are magnified in the nation's foreign policy and security agencies, where most officials are virtually invisible to the public. Commenting on this problem during the Carter administration, a senior official in the CIA's Operations Directorate said, with anguish about how to handle his officers and agents trained in paramilitary (warlike) activities: "What do you do with the fire horses when there's no fire?"[22] Ruthless former Nicaraguan national guardsmen in the contra army, underworld figures, ideologically fervent Cuban exiles, Afghan Arabs armed with Stinger missiles once aimed at Red Army gunships and now taken up in a jihad against the United States—all have numbered among the CIA's agents who proved difficult, and sometimes impossible for the Agency (not to mention more distant White House officials), to control.

Before entering into alliances with such unpredictable elements, presidents would be well served—just like patients facing difficult surgery—to get a second opinion. As the government has grown larger, the widely cited conclusion of the Brownlow Commission is even more valid today than when its commissioners concluded in 1936 that "the President needs help." By turning to other elected officials in Congress, the president may have a better chance to tame the bureaucracy and tether it to the will of the people in the conduct of the nation's foreign affairs.

THE WHITE HOUSE VERSUS
CAPITOL HILL

A central issue in any appraisal of American foreign policy, then, is the degree to which it ought to be an executive function—indeed, narrowly defined to encompass only the top officials in the executive branch—or whether, as in domestic policy, the United States can afford the luxury of a wider range of participants, to include representatives of the American people on Capitol Hill. The nation's founders had strong views on the subject. In *Federalist Papers No. 51*, James Madison advised in 1788:

> . . . If angels were to govern men, neither external nor internal controls on government would be necessary. In framing a government to be administered by men over men, the great difficulty lies in this: you must first enable the government to control the governed; and in the next place oblige it to control itself. A dependence on the people is, no doubt, the primary control on the government; but experience has taught mankind the necessity of auxiliary precautions.

The primary control would be elections; but Madison foresaw the need for a separation of powers, checks and balances, and the vigorous exercise of accountability in all its forms, from congressional hearings to budget reviews—the "auxiliary precautions" referred to in his celebrated essay.

Thomas Jefferson agreed, in his own memorable language. "Confidence is everywhere the parent of despotism," he cautioned. "Free government is founded in jealousy . . . It is jealousy and not confidence which prescribes limited constitutions to bind down those we are obliged to trust with power." His prescription: "In questions of power, then, let no more be heard of confidence in man, but bind him down from mischief by the chains of the Constitution."[23] Neither the nation's second president (Madison) nor its third (Jefferson) governed as a freewheeling chief executive. The greatest insight of the founders was their appreciation of power's corrupting influence; their greatest gift to the nation was the safeguards they built into the Constitution to protect against this human condition, most notably the strong authority they lodged in the Congress over spending, and the war and treaty powers. Congress would hold the purse strings; Congress would declare war; and the Senate would approve treaties, but by way of a difficult two-thirds majority.

A government might be more efficient with a single strong person at the helm, but that was not the point; more important was the protection of liberties, stripped away from the colonists in the New World by the autocratic decrees of King George III. As Supreme Court Judge Louis Brandeis would state more than one hundred years later:

The doctrine of the separation of powers was adopted by the [Constitutional] Convention of 1787, not to promote efficiency but to preclude the exercise of arbitrary power. The purpose was not to avoid friction, but, by means of the inevitable friction incident to the distribution of the governmental powers among three departments, to save the people from autocracy.[24]

Even on the efficiency side of the equation, constitutional scholar Louis Fisher has noted that "for all its slowness and fractiousness, the deliberative process in Congress is generally far more effective and efficient in formulating national policy than unilateral decisions by the President."[25]

A FOREIGN POLICY COMPACT

Consider two extreme approaches to the making of foreign policy: relying on the president and his or her top aides exclusively or relying on members of Congress exclusively. (The judicial branch has a role in foreign policy and pronouncements by the Supreme Court can be far-reaching, but it is not involved in the formulation of policy.) The first approach enjoys widespread support for the reasons of urgency and secrecy mentioned earlier, and because the far-flung intelligence apparatus within the executive branch presumably provides the White House with better information about world affairs than the Congress has at its disposal. Moreover, many continue to believe that the nation must speak with one voice in its relations with other nations—the water's-edge argument—and, therefore, dissent should be muffled. In addition, some lawmakers have been more than happy to pass on to the White House responsibility for knotty and controversial foreign problems that might spell trouble for them in their next election. Let the president take responsibility for covert actions like the disastrous Bay of Pigs invasion, or overt wars that turn sour.

Others, though, balk at the notion of foreign policy by executive fiat. Even before Vietnam and Watergate raised serious doubts about relying on presidential power, a pro-Congress viewpoint could be heard, especially from the conservative side of the political spectrum. Economic conservatives lamented the centralism that Franklin Roosevelt had brought to the marketplace. States-rightists fretted over international agreements signed by presidents that might lead indirectly to a further strengthening of presidential authority. Some lawmakers from the South even feared that the federal government might establish new civil rights regulations by way of executive agreements with African nations.[26] Isolationists looked on the presidency as the agent of interventionism abroad, which so often had led (in their view) to a drain on American resources—or to a complete sellout of American interests, which conservatives charged Roosevelt with in 1945 when he used executive agreements to negotiate with Stalin at Yalta.

In more recent years, many conservative Republicans—with three of their own in the White House: Reagan and the two Bushes—have changed their tune, now favoring broad authority for the president in foreign policy. During the Reagan years, conservative Republicans maintained that the president should be given leeway to carry out whatever policies were necessary to halt communist aggression in Central America—even if that meant rising above laws such as the Boland Amendments, which between 1982 and 1986 placed limits on covert military assistance to the CIA-backed anticommunist contras in Nicaragua. The Boland legislation was "unconstitutional," declared Senator Barry Goldwater (R-AZ), adding: "It's another example of Congress trying to take away the constitutional power of the President to be Commander in

Chief and formulate foreign policy."[27] A majority of lawmakers in both chambers disagreed with Goldwater, however, and steadily tightened the Boland legislative restrictions on covert action in Nicaragua. In response, the Reagan administration moved underground with its establishment of The Enterprise to conduct secret operations in Nicaragua.

Regardless of political leanings—Republican, Democrat, or Independent—some students of democratic theory have felt that lawmakers are closer to the grass roots than presidents, especially members of the House of Representatives with their perpetual reelection pressures. As a result, those serving in Congress better comprehend what kind of foreign policy the people in Pocatello and Tuscaloosa really want. Are citizens back home willing to send their sons and daughters to war in Afghanistan and Iraq? Are they prepared to run up a huge national debt to pay for the rebuilding of these querulous nations after war? How about U.S. military intervention in Iran or North Korea? Do they favor spending additional billions on research for an antiballistic missile defense shield? The nation's lawmakers, according to this perspective, are like raw nerve endings reaching into each of the fifty states and 435 congressional districts across America, sensing the likely response of the people to vital foreign policy and national security issues. The president cannot possibly visit each district even once, let alone on a regular basis; members of Congress do so usually every week—some every day, if their districts are close to the nation's capital. This makes Congress a unique, continuous forum filled with elected officials who have a fine-tuned sense of public opinion in their constituencies.

During his second term, President Reagan blocked the shipment of U.S. wheat to the Soviet Union—the "evil empire," in the president's characterization. Lawmakers complained vociferously, however, that he ought to spend more time listening to the plight of American farmers and less time playing Cold War politics. Reacting to this political unrest in the nation's heartland, and to pressure from Capitol Hill led by Senate majority leader Robert Dole (R-KS), the president reversed course and allowed the wheat exports to move forward.

Between the extremes of foreign policymaking by the White House, on the one hand, or by the Congress, on the other hand, lies a third approach: a constitutional balance between the branches. Here the emphasis is on a healthy cooperation between coequal departments of government—an engine with all its cylinders at work. At times the first Bush administration displayed an appreciation for this approach. During his first months in office, President George H. W. Bush patiently and quietly negotiated an interbranch agreement with Congress that allowed nonlethal aid for the contras in Nicaragua, successfully defusing what had become the most controversial foreign policy issue of the 1980s. In June 1989, when Chinese troops attacked pro-reform students in Beijing, President Bush immediately called top members of the legislature in both parties to the White House and together they worked out a strategy of criticism and sanctions against the People's Republic of China in punishment for the regime's brutal repression of peaceful demonstrators.

President Carter's undersecretary of state, Warren M.Christopher, who later served as secretary of state in the Clinton administration, presented the case for interbranch cooperation in foreign policy in terms of an executive-legislative compact. "As a fundamental precept," he wrote, "the compact would call for restraint on the part of the Congress—for Congress to recognize and accept the responsibility of the Executive to conduct and manage foreign policy on a daily basis." In return, the executive branch must be prepared to provide lawmakers "full information and consultation." Moreover, "broad policy should be jointly designed." For its part, Congress should only rarely, in extreme circumstances, attempt "to dictate or overturn Executive decisions and actions."[28]

Employing another image, when he served as chair of the Foreign Relations Committee, Senator J. William Fulbright (D-AR) suggested that the Congress and the president should jointly chart the desired global routes for the American ship of state. Then it would be up to the president to take command as an able captain and steer the vessel safely to port, making periodic adjustments as necessary, in consultation with experienced hands in the Congress.[29]

FOREIGN POLICYMAKING BY THE PRESIDENT AND THE CONGRESS

The American people want neither an imperial president free of legislative restraints nor an imperiled president dominated by an overbearing Congress. The disastrous Smoot-Hawley protectionist legislation of the 1930s and the investigative shenanigans of Senator Joseph McCarthy serve as lessons on how lawmakers can misuse their power. The excesses of modern presidents, of which the Watergate cover-up and the mendacity associated with the war in Vietnam and the paramilitary operations of the Iran-contra affair are only the most well known, should also have taught us anew the danger of an executive branch that operates in secrecy, without legislative consultation or accountability. This cautionary principle of governance stands at the center of the American Constitution.

In the modern era, the aggrandizement of power by Presidents Lyndon Johnson and Richard Nixon shocked the nation, as did the Iran-contra affair during the Reagan years. But the institutional wisdom that should be extracted from these cases of malfeasance in the White House is, as political scientist Aaron Wildavsky explains, "not that the presidency should be diminished, but that other institutions should grow in stature. The people need the vigor of all their institutions."[30] Whether planning improvements in health policy or a war against an outlaw nation, reliance on the judgment of the president and vice president alone is a foolish and risky course, no matter which party is in control of the White House.

This principle has been poorly appreciated by recent presidents. Only at the eleventh hour did President George H. W. Bush turn to the Congress for authorization to use military force against Iraq in 1990. He claimed—before the clamor on Capitol Hill became too loud to ignore—that he already had sufficient "inherent" authority to make war based on the implicit meaning of the war powers in the Constitution (an argument first advanced by President Truman). The first President Bush maintained as well that he enjoyed added authority granted by the United Nations, as if that international organization had the right to decide when the United States could go to war. The first President Bush left the impression that, even if Congress formally decided to oppose his military plans against Iraq, he would proceed anyway. A potential constitutional crisis was narrowly averted when the Senate approved military action by a four-vote margin (and in the House by a solid majority).

President Clinton offered an even weaker argument on behalf of his intention to invade Haiti in 1994, with or without congressional approval. He said simply: "It is the right thing to do."³¹ Yet, as Louis Fisher has pointed out, "This is a strikingly superficial foundation for national policy, domestic or foreign. More important than doing the right thing is doing things the right way—following constitutional procedures, developing a national consensus and pubic support, and working with the legislative branch instead of circumventing it."³²

In 2002, President George W. Bush, echoing his father's arguments from 1990, stated that he, too, had sufficient constitutional authority as president to use the war power as he saw fit in a second, preventive ("preemptive") war against Iraq—or, presumably, any other country. In the president's opinion, it was unnecessary for lawmakers to express their opinion through a formal declaration of war, or even by way of a less formal authorization to use force abroad (as stipulated by the War Powers Resolution passed in 1973). Yet, as Jack Rakove pointed out at the time: "If an invasion of Iraq on the scale contemplated does not represent a decision for war within the meaning of the Constitution, it is hard to imagine any other military action that would ever again be subject to congressional approval or restraint."³³

Following in his father's footsteps, President George W. Bush eventually sought legislative and UN backing for a war against Iraq, but only after public anxiety and congressional reaction to his theory of war by executive fiat became intense. When UN members urged delay on military intervention, Bush turned to Congress for its endorsement to use armed intervention against the Hussein regime. Unlike 1991, this time—with concern about WMDs in Iraq—Congress quickly and overwhelmingly provided open-ended support for the war. Debate was minimal and lawmakers displayed virtually no interest in holding hearings or a serious floor debate to examine implications of a war, even though the WMD "crisis" was thought by many at the time (and still is today) to have been manufactured by the White House and the Pentagon in support of the administration's desires to topple the regime for other reasons.

Whether the president would have honored a congressional resolution that prohibited a preemptive invasion of Iraq in 2003, or proceeded anyway, will never be known. Neither of the two Bush presidents—like several Democratic and Republican presidents before them—seemed to care much about a bedrock tenet of American government, well expressed in the modern era by Professor Eugene Rostow of Yale University (himself well-known as a strong proponent of presidential power). "If the President and the executive branch cannot persuade Congress and the public that a policy is wise," he wrote, "it should not be pursued."[34] Adds Fisher: "There are no shortcuts to that end, nor should there be."[35]

Vice President Dick Cheney, though, has expressed quite a different outlook. Looking back at the first Persian Gulf War in 1990–91, he concludes: "I firmly believe to this day even if the Congress had voted no, we had no option but to proceed." Little wonder former President and Nobel Laureate Jimmy Carter worries about the "tendency to isolate the president, to exalt the president, to make it almost unpatriotic to criticize the president."[36]

Sometimes a U.S. president—even though hemmed in by all the constraints presented earlier—can be too strong, as when Johnson took the nation into Vietnam without a national debate in Congress. Sometimes the executive branch bureaucracy can be too strong for the president to control and guide. In both instances, the nation would benefit from a more active participation by lawmakers in the making of policy—535 elected surrogates of the people in Washington, DC, who have a constitutional duty to check power in the White House and the executive branch and to weigh in with their own, often highly experienced views on the proper conduct of international relations. Why is executive branch dominance in foreign policy a bad thing? The answer lies in the Constitution and the *Federalist Papers*, because concentrated government power presents a danger to liberty at home. "Power, lodged as it must be in human hands, is ever liable to abuse," warned James Madison.[37] Moreover, a course of action in foreign affairs that seeks enduring public support will succeed only as a result of openness and public debate, not by means of secret schemes hatched behind the walls of hidden bureaucracies.

NOTES

1. Charles E. Lindblom, *Intelligence of Democracy* (New York: Free Press, 1965).
2. Bob Woodward, remarks, Yale University (October 25, 2005).
3. See Karl F. Inderfurth and Loch K. Johnson, *Fateful Decisions: Inside the National Security Council* (New York: Oxford University Press, 2004); and Hans Born, Loch K. Johnson, and Ian Leigh, eds., *Who's Watching the Spies? Establishing Intelligence Service Accountability* (Washington, DC: Potomac Books, 2005).
4. Testimony, John M. Poindexter, *Hearings*, Joint Select Committee to Investigate Covert Arms Transactions with Iran, the Inouye-Hamilton Committee 8 (July 1978), p.159.
5. Fred I. Greenstein, *Children and Politics* (Princeton: Princeton University Press, 1968).
6. Thomas E. Cronin, "Superman, Our Textbook President," *Washington Monthly* 2 (October 1970), pp. 47–54.
7. Clinton Rossiter, *The American Presidency*, rev. ed. (New York: New American Library, 1960), p. 108.
8. Ibid., p. 69.
9. Theodore H. White, *The Making of the President 1960* (New York: Atheneum, 1961), p. 441.

10. Joseph S. Nye, Jr., *The Paradox of American Power: Why the World's Only Superpower Can't Go It Alone* (New York: Oxford University Press, 2002), p. xii.

11. Quoted in Hedrick Smith, "Brzezinski Says Critics Are Irked by His Accuracy," *New York Times* (January 18, 1981), p. A3.

12. Quoted by Richard E. Neustadt, *Presidential Power: The Politics of Leadership from FDR to Carter* (New York: Wiley, 1980), p. 9.

13. Remark by Senator Hubert H. Humphrey (D-MN), Congressional Fellows Program, American Political Science Association, author's notes, Washington, DC (February 7, 1977).

14. Elie Abel, *The Missile Crisis* (Philadelphia: Lippincott, 1966), pp. 154–155.

15. Roger Hilsman, *To Move a Nation* (New York: Delta, 1967), p. 7.

16. John F. Lehman, Jr., quoted by John H. Cusman, Jr., "Ex-Insider Who Elects to Remain on Outside," *New York Times* (January 6, 1989), p. 11.

17. Morton H. Halperin, "Organizational Interests," in Daniel J. Kaufman, Jeffrey S. McKitrick, and Thomas J. Leney, eds., *U.S. National Security: A Framework for Analysis* (Lexington, MA: D. C. Heath, 1985), pp. 201–232.

18. Archives, Senate Select Committee to Investigate Intelligence Activities (the Church Committee), U.S. Senate (1975). On the Church Committee inquiry, see Loch K. Johnson, *A Season of Inquiry* (Lexington: University of Kentucky Press, 1985).

19. Ibid.

20. Quoted by Don Oberdofer, *Washington Post* (August 6, 1983), p. A13.

21. Interview, *This Week with George Stephanopoulos*, ABC Television Network (November 14, 2004).

22. Remarks to the author, CIA headquarters, Langley, Virginia (February 24, 1978).

23. Thomas Jefferson, "Draft of the Kentucky Resolutions" (October 1798), in Merrill D. Peterson, ed., *Thomas Jefferson: Writings* (New York: Library of America, 1984), p. 455.

24. *Myers v. United States*, 272 U.S. 52.293 (1926).

25. Louis Fisher, "A Constitutional Structure for Foreign Affairs," *Georgia State University Law Review* 19 (Summer 2003), p. 1067.

26. Loch K. Johnson, *The Making of International Agreements: Congress Confronts the Executive* (New York: New York University Press, 1984).

27. Quoted in *U.S. News & World Report* (May 2, 1983), p. 29.

28. Warren Christopher, "Ceasefire between the Branches: A Compact in Foreign Affairs," *Foreign Affairs* 60 (Summer 1982), p. 999.

29. Remarks by Senator Fulbright, heard by the author while serving as a staff aide on the Foreign Relations Committee, U.S. Senate, 1970, Washington, DC.

30. Aaron Wildavsky, "The Past and Future Presidency," *The Public Interest* 21 (Fall 1975), p. 75.

31. Press conference, September 15, 1994.
32. Fisher, "A Constitutional Structure," p. 1103.
33. Jack Rakove, "Who Declares War?" *New York Times* (August 2, 2002), p. A13.
34. Eugene Rostow, "Searching for Kennan's Grand Design," *Yale Law Journal* 87 (1978), p. 1536. For a starkly different view in favor of unbridled presidential power in foreign policy, see John Yoo, *The Powers of War and Peace: The Constitution and Foreign Affairs after 9/11* (Chicago, IL: University of Chicago Press, 2005).
35. Fisher, "A Constitutional Structure," p. 1105.
36. The Cheney and Carter quotes are from Bob Woodward, "Cheney Upholds Power of the Presidency," *Washington Post* (January 20, 2005), p. A7.
37. James Madison, "Speech before the Virginia State Constitutional Convention," December 1, 1829, at www.jmu.edu/madison/center/main_pages/madison_archives/life/retirement/speech. My thanks to Professor Eugene Miller for locating this source for me, after I came across the quote etched in marble in the lobby of the Madison Building, Library of Congress, Washington, DC.

CHAPTER 3

Excessive Emphasis on the Military

THE INSTRUMENTS OF AMERICAN FOREIGN POLICY

"We're the ones who respond when the world dials 911," a U.S. official in the second Bush administration told a reporter.[1] In a BBC interview, National Security Adviser Condoleezza Rice (who would become secretary of state in the second term of the George W. Bush presidency) suggested that grave consequences could result if the United States failed to respond to the Al Qaeda attacks. "Historically," she asked, ". . . how many dictators who ended up being a tremendous global threat and killing thousands, and indeed, millions of people, should we have stopped in their tracks?"[2]

Diplomacy

When the world dials 911, America's means for response are considerable. Among the nation's instruments of foreign policy is diplomacy (from the Greek *diplomata*, meaning "folded documents"). In the words of the renowned American statesman George Kennan, diplomacy is the "business of communicating between governments."[3] Jaw-jaw, not war-war, as Winston Churchill often put it. The aspiration is to settle disputes with others through the signing of international agreements, rather than the use of force. The successful diplomat's skills include the arts of persuasion and negotiation, along with an ability to observe and report on events and personalities overseas. As another exemplary American diplomat, David D. Newsom, once observed:

> The politics the United States pursues . . . must, to be acceptable, be expressed and explained and defended to skeptical, distracted, and occasionally unfriendly governments and peoples abroad. This becomes the task of the American diplomat who, in a mediating role, must also explain the realities that confront America to those in Washington who may be unready to accept the anomalies of an outside world.[4]

The practice of diplomacy lacks the drama of sending in the Marines or infiltrating CIA agents. The victories of the diplomat "are made up of a series of microscopic advantages," wrote British statesman Lord Salisbury (1830–1903), "of a judicious suggestion here, of an opportune civility there, of a wise concession at one moment and a farsighted persistence at another; of sleepless tact, immovable calmness and patience that no folly, no provocation, no blunders can shake."[5] In the hands of great diplomats like France's Richelieu, Great Britain's Canning, Germany's Bismarck, and America's John Quincy Adams, such small and intricate moves can spell the difference between war and peace. In the annals of recent American diplomacy, U.S. negotiators have demonstrated the value of this approach to foreign policy by eliminating a whole category of nuclear weapons held by the superpowers during the Reagan years (the Intermediate Range Nuclear Forces [INF] Treaty of 1987) and, more recently, with breakthroughs in 2005 that promise a dismantling of the North Korean nuclear weapons program.[6]

Economic Statecraft

In the nation's quiver, too, are the arrows of trade and aid, which can be used to advance America's interests abroad. David A. Baldwin has exhaustively examined the broad range of sanctions and inducements available to governments in this domain, from the offering of favorable tariffs (including most-favored-nation rights) and investment guarantees, on the positive side, to such negative sanctions as embargoes, boycotts, blacklisting, freezing assets, and suspension of foreign aid.[7]

Intelligence

Intelligence is a vital arrow as well. The nation's sixteen secret agencies gather and analyze information from around the world; seek to penetrate other governments with moles (in large part to learn if other nations have burrowed their agents inside America's government); and, from time to time, carry out aggressive covert actions—propaganda, political and economic operations, paramilitary activities—in hopes of manipulating world affairs in a direction favorable to the United States.[8]

Public Diplomacy

Information in a broader sense than intelligence is important, too: public diplomacy, in which the Department of State tells the American story to the world—ideally, with warts and all to make the portrayal honest, and therefore credible. It is a good story and can stand the harsh light of full truth. After over a decade of neglect following the end of the Cold War, in 2005 the second Bush administration created an office of undersecretary of state for public diplomacy in the Department of State. This official, Karen P. Hughes, would tell the American story worldwide, with a special focus on the Middle East and South Asia. The undersecretary's first trip to these regions in the fall of 2005 was an eye-opener for her; many local people informed the undersecretary that they were entirely content with their way of life and did not wish to become "Americanized." For example, Muslim women said they did not want to drive automobiles or wear Western clothing.

"Soft power" is part of this information stream to the world. Joseph S. Nye, Jr., has popularized this concept, which in his words is the ability to "entice and attract" people abroad to the U.S. point of view through film, television, popular music, literature, and popular sports figures.[9] "Cultural power" may be a more descriptive term for this approach to foreign policy. Although Nye does not, one can separate out from this cultural mix the appeal of America's political ideals (the support of human rights, for instance) and its widely copied constitutional and legal procedures—the power of moral suasion. America is admired abroad, noted Supreme Court Justice William O. Douglas, not "so much for our B-52 bombers and for our atomic stockpile, but . . . for the First Amendment and the freedom of people to speak and believe and to write, have fair trails." Here was "the great magnet" that made the United States a respected and worthy world power.[10]

The results of America's cultural power and moral suasion are particularly difficult to measure. In recent years, though, they seem to have done little to curb the rising unpopularity of the United States in other countries.

The Military

Despite Justice Douglas's eloquent argument that moral suasion has been America's long suit, rather than B-52s, bombers, cruise missiles, and combat soldiers—the oversized military arrow in the quiver—these tools are precisely what the government of the United States has often turned to in an attempt to resolve disputes overseas. Diplomacy has atrophied dramatically in recent years, with U.S. ambassadors and other diplomats declining in number and influence. As Richard N. Gardner notes, lawmakers have been willing to appropriate 16 percent of the annual budget on defense, but the percentage earmarked for international diplomacy has plummeted from 4 percent in the 1960s to only 1 percent today.[11] The United States currently spends $68 billion on weapons research alone, a figure greater than the entire defense budget of any other country in the world; and there are more people working in the Pentagon than for the whole government of Australia.[12]

Military power is a beguiling policy option for officials in Washington, DC, where the Pentagon steadily absorbs a large portion of the government's budget. America's profligate spending on the military is fueled by the sophisticated lobbying of generals, admirals, and veterans groups, joined by savvy bureaucrats in search of expanded programs, strategists in the White House, pork-minded lawmakers, munitions-makers like Boeing and Lockheed-Martin, and the national laboratories where many of the weapons are designed—the classic "iron triangle" of Political Science 101. Acts of violence by foreign nations and terrorist groups—notably the 9/11 attacks—feed the perception that the United States must maintain a colossal military force. So does the historical memory of the results of appeasement at Munich, the shock of bombs falling on Pearl Harbor, and the unsettling Soviet build-up of weapons during the Cold War. The latter, though frequently exaggerated by the Pentagon, guaranteed an American build-up as well, and these dynamics no doubt fueled the arms race on both sides.

The investment in conventional (nonnuclear) military forces during the Reagan administration rose to an 8 to 9 percent real growth rate per annum (in 1986 dollars), the highest since the Second World War. Annual military spending neared $400 billion in 1987, compared to $144 billion at the beginning of the Reagan years. Following the end of the Cold War in 1991, Presidents George H. W. Bush and Bill Clinton reduced U.S. defense expenditures as they searched for a "peace dividend" to spend on cash-starved domestic programs such as education and health care reform. In the aftermath of the 2001 attacks against the United States, however, President George W. Bush proposed a $379 billion defense budget in 2002, an increase of $48 billion over the previous year. By 2005, the

Pentagon budget had reached $444 billion, a growth of 41 percent since 2001—and those costs excluded the supplemental appropriations to finance the ongoing conflicts in Iraq and Afghanistan. From 2006 to 2011, the Pentagon planned to spend $2.3 trillion.[13] Just as Osama bin Laden and Al Qaeda had the effect of reviving the imperial presidency, so too terrorists managed to send the U.S. military budget spiraling upward again toward Reagan-era highs.

In terms of the percentage of gross domestic product (GDP) spent on the U.S. military, the United States doubtless could allocate substantially more public funds on armaments than it has, even during the record defense spending sprees of the Reagan and second Bush administrations. The Department of Defense spent at a GDP level of about 5 percent in 1980, approached 6 percent in 1983, and stayed close to that figure through 1987. The percentage then declined throughout the rest of the Cold War and afterward, reaching a low point of about 3 percent of GDP in 1999. Now the figure has risen above 4 percent and continues to climb, accelerated by the "supplemental" budgets for the wars in Afghanistan and Iraq. "Americans spend more on junk food every year than on defense," argues a colleague in belittling the notion that the United States spends too much on military programs.[14] While this observation is true, the more meaningful question is: how much does the United States really *need* to spend on defense to maintain its security? A related question is: to what extent do hugely expensive aircraft carriers and gold-plated fighter planes truly defend the nation against the likes of Al Qaeda and other terrorist organizations?

In recent years, the United States, courtesy of the American taxpayer—like it or not, has spent more on its military establishment than have virtually all the other nations of the world combined.[15]

The Pentagon has more than 750 military bases in 130 countries around the world, along with secretive Special Forces in 125 countries. Several of these bases are new and located in the Middle East and Southwest Asia, in places like Bahrain, Kyrgyzstan, United Arab Emirates, Qatar, and, of course, Afghanistan and Iraq.[16] The bases no doubt give the impression, however untrue, to many Muslims that the United States seeks a permanent military presence in their lands. Since the end of the Cold War, the American government has sought new basing opportunities in Eastern Europe as well, including in Bulgaria and in Romania near the Black Sea. In all of these cases, the bases have been useful as staging areas for U.S. troops and equipment bound for Iraq and Afghanistan, but they have had the side effects of costing a great deal of money and raising fears about American hegemonic expansion.

Cummings and Wise have commented on the domestic consequences of this global military network and its supporting infrastructure at home. "Billions of dollars that might, in part at least, have been used for education, housing, transportation, and similar programs were siphoned off into arms," they write. "Even when the United States lost its main adversary, with the disintegration of the Soviet Union, the vast defense and aerospace industries continued to flourish."[17]

Entry into war against Iraq in 2003 spurred a further increase in funding for the military. The spending spree began during the first year of the war, with a special appropriation outside the regular Defense Department budget of $87 billion. Most of the costs went toward trying to secure the peace after U.S. forces quickly overran the Iraqi Army and settled into a much more complicated war against urban guerillas ("insurgents") in the labyrinthine streets of Baghdad, Fallujah, Mosul, and other cities across the war-wrecked nation.

Defense scholar Donald Snow observed before America's entry into the second Iraq war that in modern guerrilla combat generals soon come to understand that "the situation is more intractable than we had realized, that our involvement is more open-ended than we had thought, and the long term success is much more difficult to attain than we had calculated."[18] So U.S. forces discovered in Afghanistan and Iraq. The pattern in recent U.S. military interventions has been to bomb targets within an enemy nation; then later, when it comes time to rebuild the nation after the war, Washington officials borrow more money to repair the destruction—a lethal and costly approach to urban renewal in the Balkans and now in Iraq and Afghanistan.

More complicated still is the creation of order, stability, and justice in the war zone—in a word, nation-building, a task that has proven enormously difficult and expensive in places like Kosovo, Afghanistan, and Iraq. One result has been a record $412 billion budget deficit for the United States in 2004, along with a steadily rising national debt. Coupled with the extensive tax cuts during the second Bush presidency (the first administration to adopt such a policy in a time of war), the costs of the war forced the government to enact the third major increase in federal borrowing since President Bush assumed office in 2001. This legislation allowed the administration to raise the federal debt limit by $800 billion to a new ceiling of $8.2 trillion, as the federal debt soared to $7.4 trillion in the president's first term in office—even though Bush inherited a comfortable budget surplus from the Clinton administration. Paradoxically, herein may lie a weakening, not a strengthening, of America's defense posture. As Professor Paul Kennedy of Yale University warned in 1987, "If . . . too large a proportion of the state's resources is diverted from wealth creation and allocated instead to military purposes, then that is likely to lead to a weakening of national power over the longer term."[19]

The costs of war extend beyond a disquieting drain on the nation's fiscal resources. In the early 1900s, a young Winston Churchill could participate, without fear of widespread carnage, in a British cavalry charge by the 21st Lancers against the fearsome, scimitar-wielding Dervish warriors in Egypt. "Nobody expected to be killed," he recalled in a memoir. "Here and there in every regiment or battalion, half a dozen, a score, at the worst thirty or forty, would pay the forfeit; but to the great mass of those who took part in the little wars of Britain in those vanished light-hearted days, this was only a sporting element in a splendid game."[20] Those days are gone.

In Iraq, insurgents cunningly use rocket-propelled grenades, hidden roadside bombs, and shape charges during the second Persian Gulf War, leading to mounting U.S. casualties. In November 2004 alone, 137 American troops died in Iraq; and just a single attack on December 21, 2004, killed 24 U.S. soldiers and wounded 60 more. By October 2005, over two thousand Americans had perished in Iraq. Some view these mounting casualties as a small price to pay for freedom in the region and the prevention of a possible attack by the Iraqis or terrorist allies against the United States.[21] But how real was the threat of an Iraqi attack against this nation? The lack of WMDs in Iraq offers a compelling answer to that question—one that could have been answered by a combination of UN inspectors on the ground in Iraq in 2003 and further patient intelligence work. Further, is it America's obligation to extend freedom by the point of a bayonet to despotic regimes around the globe? If so, at what price in U.S. blood and treasure?[22]

THE ARSENAL

The size and potency of America's weapons arsenal stands in silent testimony to the nation's fixation on the military instrument of foreign policy. The arsenal brims with strategic nuclear, tactical nuclear, and conventional weapons. Strategic nuclear weapons are lodged inside the nose caps of intercontinental ballistic missiles (ICBMs), based in silos in Nebraska and elsewhere. (Cornhuskers joke that their state is the world's premier nuclear power.) Other nuclear warheads lie within the bellies of slick, black submarines, atop submarine-launched ballistic missiles (SLBMs). Still more rest in the cargo hatches of long-range stealth bombers. Together, these three "platforms"—land, sea, and air—comprise the nuclear triad.

The ICBMs number about 1,700 in the United States and have the capacity to strike targets halfway around the world in thirty minutes with a high degree of accuracy. They can release sufficient energy to topple skyscrapers and vaporize the inhabitants of targeted cities, making the effects of atomic bombs dropped on Hiroshima or Nagasaki seem like antiquated bonfires. The SLBMs number about 3,100 and each submarine that carries them boasts more destructive power than the aggregate total of every weapon ever used in the previous history of warfare. The bomber leg of the triad, consisting of some 1,100 nuclear warheads, has an important advantage over the ground and sea legs: it is the only system that can be redirected, even recalled, after being set on its flight path. It also has, however, a major disadvantage: bombers are easier targets for enemies to spot and knock down.

Even though fewer in number now than during the peak years of the Cold War, the nearly six thousand warheads that make up the triad today reach far beyond the listing of targets the United States is likely to have if a nuclear war were to break out. As President Dwight D. Eisenhower once noted, the only conceivable purpose for such a large inventory of nuclear weapons is to have enough weapons to make the rubble bounce after the first wave of destruction— "overkill," in Pentagon parlance.

Moving down the weapons "food chain," tactical nuclear weapons have a more limited energy yield than strategic nuclear weapons and are designed to strike relatively small targets on a battlefield. The smallest can fit snugly into an infantry backpack. Some, though, carry the punch of a Hiroshima-sized bomb—some ten kilotons of TNT.

America's conventional arsenal is comprised of nonnuclear technology: everything from M-16 rifles to the blast effects of TNT and other chemical reactions. Sometimes the distinction between tactical nuclear and conventional weapons becomes meaningless, though, for all intents and purposes. The power of certain advanced, high-yield conventional weapons, such as the earth-penetrating "Daisy Cutter" bomb used against the Taliban regime in Afghanistan and the Iraqi regime, are barely distinguishable from low-yield tactical nuclear weapons in terms of their destructive effects.

The explosive power of high-yield nuclear weapons, if ever fired in warfare, would be catastrophic.[23] As psychologist Erik Erikson cautioned, Homo sapiens has become a species capable of exterminating itself. A nuclear blast produces intense heat, high winds, and severe atmospheric disturbances, as well as radiation that can last for thousands of years. The immediate area around ground zero would suffer massive destruction. In a nuclear attack against a city, about 50 percent of the deaths would come from the instant release of thermal energy, as if the city's inhabitants had been placed inside an oven set at fifty million degrees centigrade— equivalent to falling into the sun. Another 35 percent would die from the blast wave, and 15 percent from ionized radiation.[24] The larger the yield of the weapon, the more important the thermal effect becomes. The added radiation threat results from gamma rays emitted during the explosion—small particles that would rip apart the molecules of human tissue as they penetrated the body. That is, if anyone had managed to escape from the third-degree burns of the thermal energy. If striking the testes or ovaries, gamma rays could cause irreversible genetic alterations. The effects of gamma ray bombardments may be hidden and delayed, with cancers metastasizing in individuals five or even forty years after the initial exposure.

Another product of a nuclear explosion is the electromagnetic pulse, or EMP. "Gamma rays will cause electrons to be ejected from atoms in the air, thus ionizing the atmosphere around the burst," explains a weapons expert.[25] "This will result in disturbances of electromagnetic waves transmitted by radar and communications equipment." The end result: an inability to use a cell phone or computer. All communications and radar operations would cease within the vicinity of the bombing. Cars would not start either, since the microchips in automobile ignitions would be destroyed.

If several cities were targeted in a nuclear war—the bleak scenario that occupied the attention of strategists who faced the chilling prospect of a U.S.-Soviet showdown during the Cold War—the outcome could be nothing short of catastrophic for humanity, according to various computer models of a nuclear war. Under a heavy assault of nuclear warheads, cities would burn. Soot and smoke would rise into the atmosphere and block out the sun's rays, dropping temperatures to subfreezing levels for a meter or more into the ground. Burying the dead would be out of the question. Drinking water would be frozen, too, and food supplies would diminish as a result of wheat and other crops being deprived of the ability to photosynthesize. Looking into this "nuclear winter" scenario during the Cold War, a prominent research team concluded: "It is clear that the ecosystem effects *alone* resulting from a large-scale thermonuclear war could be enough to destroy the current civilization in at least the Northern Hemisphere. . . . The possibility of the extinction of Homo sapiens cannot be excluded."[26]

No one knows with certainty what the ecological effects of a nuclear war would be. Even without the onset of a nuclear winter, the postattack conditions would be decidedly grim. Antibodies and other medical supplies would be destroyed; physicians and nurses would be killed or incapacitated; radiation would linger. The distribution of food would be difficult and, in the garbage-strewn postattack environment, a recrudescence of the rat population would erupt. The targeted nation would be thrown back immediately into a "medieval setting."[27] As we know from Japan in 1945, even one small nuclear bomb dropped on a medium-sized city can lead to the sudden death of over a hundred thousand people. In a densely populated location like New York City or Chicago, the instant toll could be in the millions.

These potential calamities are widely understood yet nations around the world continue to pursue the development and stockpiling of nuclear weapons, with America's vast nuclear holdings a poor example for them to follow. Despite many years spent in negotiations over arms-control accords during and after the Cold War, the modest cutbacks in the number of nuclear weapons that have been achieved by Russia and the United States still leave both nations with staggering surpluses—much more than is reasonably required for purposes of deterrence (perhaps a few hundred warheads). Also, Russia's stockpiles of fissionable matériel are said to be poorly guarded against theft or sale, leading to the threat of "loose nukes."

STAR WARS

In hopes of thwarting a nuclear attack against the United States during the Cold War, the Reagan administration conceived of an imaginative proposal to shield the United States. The nation would be hermetically sealed from the deadly downward arc of enemy missiles by way of a protective ballistic missile defense (BMD) system, as if it the United States could be protected from the dangers of the world like a scene in a glass paperweight. The proposal, which envisioned knocking down incoming missiles with space- and ground-based laser technology, was known within the administration as the Strategic Defense Initiative (SDI). The media soon labeled the envisioned system "Star Wars," after the popular sci-fi film of the era.

Whether the BMD, whose variation in the second Bush administration was known as the ground-based interceptor, or GBI, would actually work remains a topic of lively debate among scientists, politicians, and academics. Many are skeptical, calculating that a well-armed adversary could overwhelm a GBI system by firing clusters of nuclear-tipped missiles at the United States accompanied by thousands of decoy missiles that would confuse the ground interceptors. Even if the purpose of a GBI system were less ambitious, say, limited to shooting down just one or a few missiles fired at the United States, critics argue that the enormous sums of money already spent on the early stages of the system—with much more to follow—are futile. The Al Qaeda terrorists who attacked the United States in September of 2001 were armed with knives and box cutters. Their next modus operandi may be the placement of a nuclear device on a cargo ship entering an American port, on a train passing through a city, or inside a van or SUV parked beneath a towering building. In the 1980s, the brilliant *Atlanta Journal Constitution* cartoonist Mike Luckovich drew a figure of Uncle Sam on guard, holding up a ballistic missile defense laser weapon designed to knock down any incoming enemy missiles. As he peered into the skies awaiting an attack, a terrorist sneaked up behind him and left a suitcase filled with an atomic bomb.

Moreover, a GBI system invites an arms race with Russia and China. Imagine if the United States were able to perfect a ballistic missile shield. It would continue to possess a massive nuclear offensive arsenal and would now be protected from retaliation by another nation, robbing other nations of their own nuclear deterrence. Officials in Washington could choose to annihilate the Russian or Chinese civilizations, without fear of a nuclear response that would destroy the United States. This is an unnerving scenario for someone living in Moscow or Beijing, even though we in the United States understand that the likelihood of a future U.S. policy of nuclear genocide is virtually zero. The probable response in Russia and China to the ongoing construction of a full-blown GBI system will be to build a new fleet of missiles of their own, to make the American shield obsolete even before it is completed. Perhaps they will choose to construct their own defensive shields, nullifying the American nuclear deterrent. President Vladimir V. Putin announced in November 2004 that Russia had developed a new nuclear missile—a "hypersonic flying vehicle"—designed apparently to elude the GBI and maintain the credibility of the Russian posture of deterrence.[28]

The Russian nuclear initiative may have been a response, as well, to the second Bush administration's evident interest in the creation of a new generation of nuclear weapons. The head of the National Nuclear Security Administration announced in 2003 that the United States would "explore a range of technical options that could strengthen our ability to deter, or respond to new or emerging threats."[29] Of particular note are low-yield nuclear weapons for use in the battlefield, seemingly an advanced notice to the world that America was prepared to use nuclear weapons to win battles in the twenty-first century.

THE MILITARY-INDUSTRIAL
COMPLEX

President Dwight D. Eisenhower offered the best explanation for America's excessively large nuclear and conventional arsenal: a military-industrial complex that had run amok in search of profits from weapons manufacturing. "This conjunction of an immense military establishment and a large arms industry is new in the

American experience," warned the president in his farewell address to the American people on January 17, 1961. He continued:

> The total influence—economic, political, even spiritual—is felt in every city, every statehouse, every office of the federal government. We recognize the imperative need for this development. Yet we must not fail to comprehend its grave implications. Our toil, resources, and livelihood are all involved; so is the very structure of our society. . . . The potential for the disastrous rise of misplaced power exists and will persist.[30]

The president might have added that, for the nation's weapons laboratories, there is also the added incentive of laboratory funding and the prestige that government contracts bring to scientists, along with the excitement of new scientific advances in weapons design— the sheer joy of the physics involved. He could have also pointed to another manifestation of the military-industrial complex: America's role as the world's biggest arms merchant. In recent years, the United States has sold over $14 billion worth of weaponry to other countries, a sum that exceeds the level of arms exports by all of the European nations combined.[31]

THE DEMISE OF DETERRENCE

Deterrence is the ability to convince an enemy not to attack, based on the certainty of a devastating retaliatory response. During the Cold War, the Soviet Union and the United States were like two scorpions in a jar: if one stung, the other would return the favor. Both would die. The suicidal consequences that would result from the failure of deterrence kept both sides at bay and discouraged the outbreak of World War III.

What if deterrence fails? If attacked by nuclear weapons, presumably the United States would respond with a cataclysmic counterattack using nuclear weapons of its own. Happily, this scenario has not become a reality. At the level of conventional weapons, though, history provides some recent examples of failed deterrence. Iraq's invasion of Kuwait in 1991 suggests that Saddam Hussein assumed the United States would not care enough to involve itself militarily in the protection of the small, oil-rich nation; and, again, in 2003 the Iraqi dictator gambled that the United States would not attack his country based on rumors and flimsy evidence that he possessed weapons of mass destruction. Saddam's mistaken assessments proved disastrous for Iraq in both cases, leading in December 2003 to his capture and imprisonment by U.S.-led forces, and the end of his regime.

Deterrence against Iraqi aggression failed because, in both instances, the nation's dictator refused to believe that America would take up arms against his country. Al Qaeda proved impervious to deterrence, as well, attacking the United States in 2001 regardless of the inevitable military response that would send CIA operatives, Special Forces, and Air Force bombers to Afghanistan in an effort to kill or capture the terrorist group's leaders and members. When deterrence fails at the conventional level and the United States feels that its interests have been affected, America's leaders have demonstrated their willingness to carry out a military response against the adversary.

The experiences with Saddam Hussein, the 9/11 attacks, and the potential danger that rogue nations or terrorists might acquire

WMDs—nuclear, chemical, biological, radiological—and use them against the American homeland, led President George W. Bush to conclude that deterrence might no longer be effective against potential enemies. He turned to an additional and more aggressive instrument to enhance U.S. security. On June 1, 2002, in a commencement address at the United States Military Academy, the president unveiled the outlines of a new defense strategy. He declared that, in the war against Al Qaeda and its allies, "deterrence—the promise of massive retaliation against nations—means nothing against shadowy terrorist networks with no nation or citizens to defend." Henceforth, the United States would "confront the worst threats before they emerge, relying on a policy of "preemption."

Three months later, the Bush administration formally changed U.S. defense policy to embrace this new doctrine.[32] The United States would "no longer solely rely on a reactive posture as we have in the past," said the president, ". . . We cannot let our enemies strike first. . . . As a matter of common sense and self-defense, America will act against emerging threats before they are fully formed."[33]

The administration and others often used the phrase "preemption" as though it were interchangeable with the idea of "preventive war," although the two are distinct strategic concepts. The doctrine of preventive war assumes that war with another nation is inevitable; therefore, it is better to begin the war oneself than to wait until the adversary grows stronger. This (mistaken) view led the Japanese to strike the United States at Pearl Harbor in 1941. Preemption refers, in contrast, to a nation's decision to conduct a quick strike against another threatening nation, based on reliable intelligence that the adversary is about to launch an immediate

attack. Despite its choice of the term preemption, the Bush administration seemed to be embracing a preventive war approach toward
adversaries like Iraq.

This departure from reliance on deterrence was legitimate,
claimed the Bush administration, because of the attacks against
the United States in 2001. Later in the year, both the president
and National Security Adviser Condoleezza Rice warned that the
United States might see a nuclear mushroom cloud rise up from an
American city, unless the nation acted in a "preemptive" manner
against rogue states and terrorist organizations.

Critics were quick to reject this approach to foreign threats.
They argued that deterrence had worked against most enemies,
and that Al Qaeda could be handled by tracking down the terrorists using the CIA and Special Forces. Opponents of the administration's new defense doctrine also feared that it opened a
Pandora's box in which a state could argue its right to use force
against any neighbor, simply by claiming that it had to resort to a
preemptive strike because the other side was supposedly planning
a surprise attack. Should Pakistan hit India preemptively with
nuclear weapons because the latter might attack it, or vice versa?
A world in which nations launched surprise attacks against other
nations, for fear that the same thing could happen to them, would
lead only to chaos. One could see the error of this thinking in
America's invasion of Iraq in 2003, which turned up no weapons
of mass destruction. As Louis Fisher has written, "The campaign
for war [against Iraq] was dominated more by fear than facts,
more by assertions of what might be, or could be, or used to be,
than by what actually existed."[34]

THE STRUGGLE OVER
THE WAR POWERS

The battle between the legislative and executive branches for control over the war power and the use of military force abroad reached a climax in 1973 with the passage of the War Powers Resolution. The statute placed obstacles in the way of presidential authority to commit American forces overseas without congressional approval.

As Pat Holt, a former Foreign Relations Committee staff director, has written, "Where to draw the line between the power of Congress to declare war and the power of the president as commander in chief is one of the most controversial issues relating to the Constitution." Articles I and II of the Constitution set up the perfect conditions for a tug of war between the branches over the war power. When the Vietnam War began to fail and the presidency was further weakened by the Watergate scandal, lawmakers tightened their grip on the rope and pulled hard. "The War Powers Resolution, in essence," concludes Holt, "is an effort by Congress to give itself more leverage in the tug of war with the executive branch."[35]

The War Powers Resolution requires that the president "in every possible instance shall consult with Congress" before introducing armed forces "into hostilities or into situations where imminent involvement in hostilities is clearly indicated by the circumstances." In addition, the Resolution requires the president to report to the Congress within forty-eight hours about the deployment of troops. If these troops face "hostilities," the presidential report starts a sixty-day clock, after which the White House has to obtain congressional approval for continuation of the military involvement. The Resolution stipulates, moreover, that if the Congress refuses to endorse the president's use of force within sixty days of the initial report, the U.S. troops *have* to be withdrawn. Lawmakers can grant a thirty-day extension if necessary, to assure an orderly and safe exit.

The proposed legislation was not perfect and had detractors across the political spectrum; but it passed nonetheless, because most members of Congress had grown sufficiently frustrated at presidents who used the military without congressional debate or authority. Senator Jacob Javits (R-NY), the chief architect of the legislation, explained after the vote: ". . . after 200 years, at least something will have been done about codifying the implementation of the most awesome power in the possession of any sovereignty and giving the broad representation of the people in Congress a voice in it. This is critically important, for we have just learned [with the war in Vietnam] the hard lesson that wars cannot be successfully fought except with the consent of the people and with their support." In Javits's opinion, "At long last . . . Congress is determined to recapture the awesome power to make war."[36]

The War Powers Resolution in practice has had a rocky history. Presidents of both parties have attempted to skirt its provisions through various methods, such as claiming that U.S. troops have been on rescue or peacekeeping missions abroad and were not in "zones of hostility."[37] For example, President Reagan sent 1,200 Marines to Lebanon, where a civil war was in progress. He refused to report to Congress under the War Powers Resolution, on vague grounds that the U.S. troops were in Lebanon to help the prospects for peace, but would stay away from the fighting in Beirut near where they were bivouacked. No hostilities, no report to Congress, and, thus, most importantly from his point of view, no sixty-day clock. In October 1983, a suicide truck filled with explosives rammed into the U.S. military headquarters, killing 241 Americans and shattering the notion that somehow our troops were outside the zone of hostilities.

Some have concluded that the Resolution has become an "irrelevancy."[38] Yet few lawmakers wish to discard the law, "if for no other reason," points out a study, "than it would symbolize to many in Congress a surrender of its role in war-making decisions."[39] Periodically scholars and others call upon Congress to honor its own statute and take steps to check presidents when they fail to seek formal congressional approval for armed intervention. "The war powers issue cries out for attention," writes Andrew J. Bacevich of Boston University. "In a post-9/11 world, what limits—if any—exist on the president's authority to use force?"[40] The apparent answer at this point is: few, if any.

THE DECLINE OF DIPLOMACY

America's enormous expenditures on weapons, the deployment of its soldiers around the globe, the establishment of bases in places like Saudi Arabia and Uzbekistan where the United States is not wanted—all are driven by a sense that U.S. security interests depend on an American military presence and intervention in locations far removed from our shores. But should not the United States be more circumspect about the costs that accompany playing the role of the world's sheriff?[41] Moreover, do Americans really wish to promote the impression that inevitably accompanies widespread armed intervention, namely, that the United States is an imperial power—a "hegemon," in the favored expression of those who choose to see the foreign policy of this nation in the worst possible light? Indeed, do we wish to give the impression that the United States is a power prepared to adopt a doctrine of preemptive strikes or preventive wars against any nation (Iraq at the moment) that either possesses or might want to possess WMDs that could be used against Americans? Has the United States become, as the counterterrorist expert Richard A. Clarke suggests, a nation that "apparently believes in imposing its ideology through the violence of war"?[42]

Before labeling nations part of an "axis of evil," as President George W. Bush called Iraq, Iran, and North Korea in 2002, should we not have had a better idea of what makes these countries tick and how much of an imminent danger they really are to the United States? On the first anniversary of the 9/11 terrorist attacks, as the president appealed to the American public and members of the UN for their support of military action against Iraq, government officials in Washington, DC, acknowledged that the intelligence agencies had yet to prepare a major assessment (a national intelligence estimate, or NIE) on Iraq's nuclear, chemical, and biological weapons capabilities.[43] When an NIE was finally produced by the intelligence agencies in October of 2002, it predicted the likelihood of WMDs in Iraq. Dismissing countervailing views in other parts of the government (notably, the Energy and State Departments), the administration used the estimate as a justification for invading Iraq, whether or not the UN Security Council thought war was justified. Diplomatic approaches to disarming Iraq were trumped by sketchy intelligence reports in the hands of U.S. policy officials eager to try an experiment in bringing democracy to the Middle East, not to mention settling the score with Saddam Hussein—still in place as Iraq's dictator despite the defeat American forces had dealt his country in the first Persian Gulf War.

Diplomacy was handicapped from the start. The State Department's budget is a pittance, while the Defense Department enjoys lavish funding. For example, funding for public diplomacy is presently at a modest $4.05 million. In the intelligence budget, some 85 percent of the $44 billion per annum is devoted to military purposes, in contrast to the gathering of information about political, economic, and social conditions around the world that might help diplomats ward off the outbreak of military conflict in the first place. Today, the U.S. military has supplanted, to a large degree, activities that used to be the domain of American diplomats: humanitarian relief, nation-building, bilateral negotiations with other nations, peacekeeping. As Dana Priest states, ". . . [there was an] imbalance of resources that began to grow. The military took on many of the jobs that the State Department had, and they still have them today."[44] An American historian observes that in the age of globalization, "American military proconsuls—generals with immense power and support staff larger than that of the White House—control the four corners of the world."[45]

It was telling when, in 2003, Secretary of Defense Donald H. Rumsfeld held a reception in Washington, DC, for representatives of the Coalition of the Willing (the label the Bush administration gave to the thirty-three, mostly small, nations that had consented to join the second U.S. war effort against Iraq). Missing on the invitation list: Secretary of State Colin Powell.[46] Rumsfeld would handle relations with America's allies, not the diplomats from Foggy Bottom. As an aide to Colin Powell would tell the public two years later, he was convinced that Rumsfeld and Vice President Cheney represented a powerful "cabal" against the State Department.[47] A similar theme runs through George Packer's study of the war in Iraq, entitled *The Assassins' Gate*: America's diplomats were regarded as the enemy; they had fouled up Bosnia and Kosovo and had to be kept away from the war in Iraq.[48]

In 2005, the Pentagon promoted a global counterterrorism plan that would permit Special Operations forces to move inside a foreign country for covert activities without informing the U.S. ambassador there, weakening the long-standing "chief of mission" authority given to State Department diplomats. Nor would the CIA be told about the secret military operations.[49] In the halls of the Pentagon, the State Department is referred to derisively as the Department of Nice. When it came to achieve America's foreign policy objectives, the tougher Defense Department would get the job done.

AMERICA STRETCHED THIN

The core problem with a U.S. military presence in locations around the globe has been well stated by historian Paul Kennedy. Great powers have declined through the centuries because they over-reached in their conduct of foreign affairs, what Kennedy refers to as "imperial overstretch." The costs of military projection around the globe become too great and undermine the home economy. "The sum total of the United States' global interests and obligations is nowadays," Kennedy writes, "far larger than the country's power to defend them all simultaneously."[50] Kennedy wrote those words *before* the second Bush administration embarked on wars in Afghanistan and Iraq, coupled with a global struggle against terrorists hiding out (according to the president) in sixty different nations.

In America's early history, John Quincy Adams sensed the risks inherent in extensive involvements overseas. As secretary of state, he cautioned on July 4, 1821, that America should avoid going abroad "in search of monsters to destroy." Entanglement in foreign wars would have a pernicious effect. "The fundamental maxims of [America's] policy would insensibly change from liberty to force," he continued, ". . . She might become the dictatress of the world: she would no longer be the ruler of her own spirit." Subsequently, as president, Adams declared in his inaugural address that "America is the friend of all the liberties in the world, [but] the guardian of only her own."[51]

The Bush administration takes quite a different tack. Defending Bush's strategy, historian Gaddis explains that "it's necessary now, as it has not been in the past, to go abroad in search of monsters to destroy," or else the United States might suffer a devastating hit from terrorists and rogue states armed with WMDs. He looks upon President George W. Bush as the "first great grand strategist of the 21st century" and applauds the current circumstances, stating that "with great power has come a great aspiration, which is to end tyranny throughout the world."[52]

No longer divided into two ideological Cold War camps, the world will experience extensive fragmentation, ethnic strife, human rights abuses, and violence for many years to come. If the world is lucky, the forces of political, economic, and cultural integration— often called "globalization"[53]—may draw nations together to a point where they will adopt more harmonious approaches to the settlement of international disputes. In the meantime, Americans would do well to be more discriminating in their decisions about whether to respond to world events with the introduction of troops.

Sometimes the United States has sagely avoided the temptation to rush in with warriors, as some advocated in response to the killing of American soldiers in Somalia in 1993 (the "Black Hawk down" incident[54]), or when the war escalated in the Balkans during the Clinton years. Sometimes Americans have failed to show the flag when a military presence from the United States and other nations might have prevented widespread killings, as in the Rwandan genocide of 1993.

As a rule of thumb, U.S. armed intervention abroad is appropriate to halt genocides, to counter the crossborder aggression of one nation against another, or to preempt a genuine threat of an imminent attack against the United States. In all possible circumstances, the U.S. response to these conditions should be carried out in the company of leading allies.

The use of external force to settle disputes within a sovereign nation is, however, a much more difficult proposition to justify. Particularly in this case, diplomatic and economic pressures on a repressive regime can have a chance of changing the state's behavior, as happened with respect to apartheid in South Africa without military intervention. All too often, though, diplomacy has been pushed aside by the precipitate use of military force. In recent years, examples include interventions in Grenada, Nicaragua, Panama, and the invasion of Iraq in 2003 before UN weapons inspectors had been given a reasonable chance to determine the true extent of the threat posed by the Hussein regime. That threat turned out to be a mirage, as a sufficient number of security advisers warned the Bush administration before its decision to invade—enough to have warranted a delay in invasion plans to acquire more information about the suspected WMDs.[55]

The United States obviously needs a strong military for its own self-defense and to protect its interests abroad. The objective, however, is to make sure that the military tail does not wag the rest of the government. Many of America's armed interventions could have been resolved with patient diplomacy and, if need be, strong economic sanctions and the building of global opprobrium aimed at the opposing regime. Cultural and moral norms can be more powerful than military interventions.[56] Nonmilitary approaches should be given an opportunity to succeed; if they fail, the military stands ready to move in, if necessary. As for the Bush doctrine of "preemption," the intelligence justification for such action needs to be much stronger than it was in the decision to invade Iraq in 2003. Here, again, diplomacy would have bought time to gather additional intelligence. Moreover, deterrence remains a persuasive counter to most foes, with the exception of those who are willing to commit suicide by attacking the United States. In this extreme case, America can still use the military option. We do not have to be merely reactive, though. We can do much to strengthen our intelligence shield and domestic security defenses. As well, we can search more energetically for ways to reduce the anger—of all but the most intractable foreign extremists—toward the United States.

Advocacy of greater discrimination in the use of U.S. military force should not be confused with a policy of appeasement. If attacked, the United States will respond with appropriate force, as Al Qaeda and the Taliban regime in Afghanistan discovered in 2001–02. When access to oil is threatened, the industrialized nations will not stand by idly; when modern-day autocratic imperialists, like Serbia's Slobodan Milosevic, permit mass rape and genocidal brutalities by their soldiers, America will help organize opposition through the United Nations and regional defense pacts. But for the United States to concern itself with all of the political and military eruptions that inevitably will occur around the globe is a sure prescription for sapping America's resources and energies, while presenting ourselves to the world as an international meddler of the first order.

NOTES

1. "Bush Seeks to Calm Afghan Anger," *International Herald Tribune* (July 6–7, 2002), p. 3.
2. BBC interview, National Public Radio (September 6, 2002).
3. Quoted in Norman J. Padelford and George A. Lincoln, *The Dynamics of International Politics* (New York: Macmillan, 1962), p. 340.
4. David D. Newsom, *Diplomacy and American Democracy* (Bloomington: Indiana University Press, 1988), p. 219.
5. Quoted in correspondence to the author from British scholar-researcher Frank Adams (December 21, 1988).
6. See Fred Kaplan, "All It Touched Off Was a Debate," *New York Times* (September 8, 2005), p. E5; "Diplomacy at Work," unsigned editorial, *New York Times* (September 20, 2005), p. A28.
7. David A. Baldwin, *Economic Statecraft* (Princeton: Princeton University Press, 1985), pp. 41–42.
8. Loch K. Johnson, *Secret Agencies: U.S. Intelligence in a Hostile World* (New Haven: Yale University Press, 1996).
9. Joseph S. Nye, Jr., *The Paradox of American Power* (New York: Oxford University Press, 2002), p. 9.
10. Correspondent Eric Severeid, interview with William O. Douglas, *CBS Evening News* (January 19, 1980).
11. Richard N. Gardner, "The One Percent Solution," *Foreign Affairs* (July–August 2000), p. 3. Of course, sometimes expenditures on the military can assist diplomacy, since a show of force might convince an adversary to negotiate differences rather than fight—an approach known as "coercive diplomacy" [see Alexander L. George and William E. Simons, eds., *The Limits of Coercive Diplomacy*, 2nd ed. (Boulder, CO: Westview, 1993)]. This occasional connection between the military and diplomacy does not negate the point, however, that the United States has placed an excessive emphasis on military budgets and the use of force.

12. Max Boot, remarks, Yale University (October 19, 2005).
13. Leslie Wayne, "White House Tries to Trim Military Cost," *New York Times* (December 6, 2005), pp. C1, C4.
14. Personal correspondence (April 25, 2005); the colleague prefers to remain anonymous.
15. Defense specialist Lawrence J. Korb, testimony, *Hearings*, Budget Committee, U.S. House of Representatives (February 12, 2002).
16. Eric Schmitt, "Pentagon Construction Boom Beefs Up Mideast Air Bases," *New York Times* (September 18, 2005), p. A10.
17. Milton C. Cummings, Jr., and David Wise, *Democracy Under Pressure*, 10th ed. (Belmont, CA: Thompson-Wadsworth, 2005), p. 581.
18. Donald M. Snow, *When America Fights: The Uses of U.S. Military Force* (Washington, DC: Congressional Quarterly Press, 2000), p. 112.
19. Paul Kennedy, *The Rise and Fall of Great Powers: Economic Change and Military Conflict from 1500 to 2000* (New York: Random House, 1987), p. xvi.
20. Winston S. Churchill, *My Early Life: A Roving Commission* (New York: Scribner's, 1930), p. 180.
21. See the comments of Douglas J. Feith, undersecretary of defense for policy in the second Bush administration, in Jeffrey Goldberg, "A Little Learning," *The New Yorker* (May 9, 2005), p. 39. Observes Max Boot: "After two years of fighting, the number [of U.S. casualties in Iraq] is less than those who died on one morning in America in September 2001 (remarks, Yale University, October 19, 2005).
22. On the difficulties of democratic nation-building, see Francis Fukuyama, *The End of History and the Last Man* (New York: Free Press, 1992); Samuel P. Huntington, *The Clash of Civilizations and the Remaking of World Order* (New York: Simon & Schuster, 1996); Walter Russell Mead, *Power, Terror, Peace, and War: America's Grand Strategy in a World at Risk* (New York: Knopf, 2004); and Fareed Zakaria, *The Future of Freedom: Illiberal Democracy at Home and Abroad* (New York: Norton, 2004).
23. See Graham Allison, *Nuclear Terrorism: The Ultimate Preventable Catastrophe* (New York: Henry Holt and Company, 2004); and Jonathan Schell, *The Fate of the Earth* (New York: Knopf, 1974).
24. L. W. McNaught, *Nuclear Weapons and Their Effects* (London: Brassey's, 1984), p. 27.
25. Ibid., pp. 30, 96.
26. P. R. Ehrlich et al., "The Long-Term Biological Consequences of Nuclear War," *Science* 222 (December 23, 1983), p. 12989, original emphasis.
27. Dr. Jennifer Leaning, remarks, Harvard-MIT Summer Program on Nuclear Weapons (June 17, 1985). See also, Allison, *Nuclear Terrorism; and* Schell, *The Fate of the Earth.*

28. Steven Lee Myers, "Putin Says New Missile Systems Will Give Russia a Nuclear Edge," *New York Times* (November 18, 2004), p. A3.

29. Linton F. Brooks, quoted by Ian Hoffman, *Oakland Tribune* (December 11, 2003), as cited by Steven Aftergood in *Secrecy News*, the electronic newsletter of the Federation of American Scientists (December 17, 2003).

30. *Public Papers of the Presidents*, Dwight D. Eisenhower, 1960–1961 (Washington, DC: Office of the Federal Register, National Archives, 1961), p. 1038.

31. Cited in Thom Shanker, "U.S. and Russia Still Dominate Arms Market, but World Total Falls," *New York Times* (August 30, 2004), p. A6.

32. See Ivo H. Daalder and James M. Lindsay, *America Unbound: The Bush Revolution in Foreign Policy* (Washington, DC: Brookings Institution, 2003).

33. Speech, U.S. Military Academy (June 1, 2002).

34. Louis Fisher, "Deciding on War against Iraq: Institutional Failures," *Political Science Quarterly* 118 (2003), p. 389.

35. Pat Holt, *The War Powers Resolution: The Role of Congress in U.S. Armed Intervention* (Washington, DC: American Enterprise for Public Policy Research, 1978), p. 39.

36. Quoted in "Congress Overrides Nixon's Veto of War Powers Bill," *Congressional Quarterly Weekly Report*, vol. 31 (November 10, 1973), p. 2985; and the *Congressional Record* (1973), p. 36187.

37. For examples, see Daniel S. Papp, Loch K. Johnson, and John E. Endicott, *American Foreign Policy: History, Politics, and Policy* (New York: Pearson-Longman, 2005), pp. 286–288.

38. For example, see Richard E. Cohen, "United Front on War Powers—For Now," *National Journal* (January 23, 1993), p. 208.

39. Robert A. Katzmann, "War Powers: Toward a New Accommodation," in Thomas E. Mann, ed., *A Question of Balance: The President, the Congress, and Foreign Policy* (Washington, DC: Brookings Institution, 1990), p. 67. On the War Powers Resolution, see also Harold Hongju Koh, *The National Security Constitution: Sharing Power after the Iran-Contra Affair* (New Haven: Yale University Press, 1990).

40. Andrew J. Bacevich, "War Powers in the Age of Terror," *New York Times* (October 31, 2005), p. A19.

41. See Richard N. Haass, *The Reluctant Sheriff: The United States After the Cold War* (New York: Council on Foreign Relations, 1997).

42. Richard A. Clarke, *Against All Enemies: Inside America's War on Terror* (New York: Free Press, 2004), p. 283. When the Pew Research Center asked people in other countries about their comfort level with the United States as the only superpower, the following percentage said they would prefer that Europe, China, or some other nation become as powerful as the Americans,

presumably to serve as a buffer against U.S. power: France (85 percent), Germany (73 percent), Spain (69 percent), Poland (68 percent), and Britain (58 percent). Sixty-three percent of Americans were happy with the way things are. See James Traub, "Their Highbrow Hatred of Us," *New York Times Magazine* (October 30, 2005), p. 15, based on the Pew Global Attitudes Project, June 2005.

43. Eric Schmitt and Alison Mitchell, "U.S. Lacks Up-to-Date Review of Iraqi Arms," *New York Times* (September 11, 2002), p. A23.

44. Dana Priest, comments, *Booknotes*, C-SPAN Television Network (March 9, 2003); see her *The Mission: Waging War and Keeping Peace with America's Military* (New York: W. W. Norton, 2003), as well as Chalmers Johnson, *The Sorrows of Empire: Militarism, Secrecy and the End of the Republic* (New York: Henry Holt, 2004).

45. Günter Bischof, "American Empire and Its Discontents: The United States and Europe Today," in Michael Gehler, Günter Bischof, Ludger Kühnhardt, and Rolf Steininger, eds., *Towards a European Constitution: A Historical and Political Comparison with the United States* (Wien: Böhlau Verlag, 2005), p. 191.

46. *New York Times* reporter Maureen Dowd, comment, *This Week with George Stephanopoulos*, ABC Television Network (November 21, 2004).

47. Col. Lawrence Wilkerson, USA (Ret.), former chief of staff, Department of State (2002–05), remarks, New America Foundation, American Strategy Program Policy Forum, Washington, DC (October 19, 2005).

48. Published by Farrar, Straus & Giroux (2005).

49. Ann Scott Tyson and Dana Priest, "Pentagon Seeking Leeway Overseas," *Washington Post* (February 24, 2005), p. A1.

50. Kennedy, *The Rise and Fall of Great Powers*, p. 515.

51. Delivered on March 4, 1825, and Adams delivered his inaugural address on March 4, 1825. On these speeches, see Samuel Flagg Bemis, *John Quincy Adams and the Foundations of American Foreign Policy* (New York: Knopf, 1949); Mary W. M. Hargreaves, *The Presidency of John Quincy Adams* (Lawrence, KS: University Press of Kansas, 1985); and Richard C. Rohrs, "John Quincy Adams," in Bruce W. Jentleson and Thomas G. Paterson, eds., *Encyclopedia of U.S. Foreign Relations*, vol. 1 (New York: Oxford University Press, 1997), p. 17. On foreign monsters, the German philospher Friedrich Nietzsche warned, too, that "he who fights with monsters should be careful lest he thereby become a monster" [from his *Beyond Good and Evil*, chapter IV, paragraph 146 (1886), translated by Helen Zimmern]. I am indebted to my colleague and friend Professor Eugene Miller for tracking down this Nietzsche citation for me.

52. Professor John Gaddis, "The Past and Future of American Grand Strategy," Charles S. Grant Lecture, Middlebury College (April 21, 2005).

53. See Thomas L. Friedman, *The World Is Flat* (New York: Simon & Schuster, 2004).
54. See Mark Bowden, *Black Hawk Down* (New York: Penguin, 1994).
55. See, for instance, Clarke, *Against All Enemies*; Bob Woodward, *Plan of Attack* (New York: Simon & Schuster, 2004).
56. For one illustration, see the approach of the Chinese Ming Dynasty to foreign affairs, examined by Williamson Murray and Mark Grimsley, "Introduction: On Strategy," in Williamson Murray, MacGregor Knox, and Alvin Bernstein, eds., *The Making of Strategy: Rulers, States, and War* (New York: Cambridge University Press, 1994), p. 17.

CHAPTER 4

Unilateralism

HOW TO LOSE FRIENDS
AND ALIENATE PEOPLE

This chapter and the next look at instances of America separating itself from other nations. The themes of "unilateralism" and "isolationism" (Chapter 5) have similarities. According to standard definitions, *isolationism* is a national policy of abstention from alliances and other relationships overseas; *unilateralism*, too, implies an inclination to seek one's own way in world affairs, free from alliance partnerships and cooperative international agreements. I have chosen, however, to separate the two concepts (with some inevitable dovetailing), because each points to a somewhat different set of attitudes and behavior.

I use the term "unilateralism" to focus on the tendency for nations to pursue independent action, without talking to or listening to other nations—reminiscent of a line from comedian Lily

152

Tomlin: "Together, we are in this alone."[1] By "isolationism," I have in mind a nation's desire to retreat from international responsibilities and mores, concentrating instead on its domestic problems. Unilateralism: acting alone; isolationism: retreating from the world.[2] The overlap comes from the fact that acting alone can be interpreted as a way of retreating from the world; yet, I think the terms are sufficiently distinct to stand as separate "sins."

Nothing has so alarmed and disheartened America's allies as the recent unwillingness of the United States to work in harness, or even consult meaningfully, with them before carrying out important foreign-policy initiatives.[3] This does not mean, of course, that America must straitjacket itself into inaction whenever other nations prove unwilling to join in international activities officials in Washington, DC, view as vital. It may be, from time to time, that U.S. national security interests require this nation to move forward alone. It does mean, however, that in all but the most extraordinary circumstances the United States ought to try its best to join with other nations in a collective response to global challenges. Otherwise, the United States leaves the impression that its citizens don't care what others think.

One of America's friends, then–German Chancellor Gerhard Schröder, learned through newspaper accounts in August 2002 about the second Bush administration's new policy of a possible preemptive military strike against Iraq. "Consultation cannot mean that I get a phone call two hours in advance only to be told, 'We're going in,'" the chancellor complained. "Consultation among grown-up nations has to mean not just consultation about the how and the when, but also about the whether."[4] Arguably America's best friend among foreign leaders, British Prime Minister Tony Blair,

had this to say regarding America's minimal interest in the 2005
World Economic Forum in Davos, Switzerland: "If America wants
the rest of the world to be part of the agenda it has set, it must be
part of their agenda, too." He added: "What people want is not for
America to concede, but for America to engage."[5]

In another example of American unilateralism, when Donald H.
Rumsfeld, the secretary of defense in the second Bush administration, referred in August 2002 to any renewal of weapons inspections
in Iraq as a "sham," he undercut multilateral efforts by the United
Nations to negotiate a resumption of the search for WMDs.[6] The
administration reversed itself the next month and sought UN
approval for more weapons inspections; yet, when Iraq agreed, the
United States continued to push for a resolution that threatened
the use of force if the Iraqis reneged, even though most members of
the UN were prepared to see how the inspections unfolded before
escalating to a vote in favor of carrying out, or even threatening,
military intervention. The United States was once again out of step
with the world, even with some of its most reliable allies. This "go it
alone" attitude raised questions about whether the United States
itself had become a "rogue nation" intent on having its own way in
the world, ignoring existing treaties and alliances.[7]

Granted, taking a unilateral approach to foreign affairs is
easier than linking up with others. Ultimately, though, success in
the international arena is more likely through collective action,
since the globe is too large, complex, and perilous for the United
States to cope with by itself. Moreover, when it comes to the loss
of life in the name of peacekeeping, is it not better for the civilized
community of nations to share this burden, rather than have
American troops make most of the sacrifices?

THE LIMITS OF ACTING ALONE

The inadvisability of unilateralism becomes clear when one considers the reasons why America has a foreign policy in the first place. Clearly, in its relationships abroad the United States enjoys certain advantages. "Not since Rome has one nation loomed so large above the others," writes Joseph S. Nye, Jr., who cites an observation from Hubert Vedrine that "U.S. supremacy today extends to the economy, currency, military areas, lifestyle, language and the products of mass culture that inundate the world, forming thought and fascinating even enemies of the United States."[8] However preeminent the United States may be, the nation still faces severe limitations on its ability to act as it wishes on the world stage. When asked in 1988 what U.S. strategy should be toward assisting the Soviet Union revamp its crumbling economic system, a State Department official replied sagaciously: "I don't think we should have a strategy, frankly, because most things we do we make such a mess of. Our ability to influence things diminishes greatly the farther we get from our shores."[9] One does not have to embrace Lord Salisbury's extreme philosophy: "Whatever happens will be for the worse," he is reputed to have said, "and therefore it is in our interests that as little should happen as possible." It is prudent, though, to maintain a realistic view of America's limited ability, by itself, to transform events around the globe.

An appreciation for these limitations ought to be the most important lesson for Americans to have learned from more than two hundred years of experience in dealing with other nations. The largely unilateral involvement of the United States in the Vietnamese civil war from 1964–75 offers a poignant chapter from this lesson book. That intervention cost Americans more than 58,000 lives, hundreds of thousands wounded, and hundreds of billions of dollars, along with the pain at home of disruptive political unrest, economic stagnation, and disregard of pressing social needs at home (including President Johnson's tabled "war against poverty"). More recently, despite the further expenditure of billions of dollars, America's influence remains minimal outside of Kabul after the U.S. invasion of Afghanistan in 2001; and the U.S.-led invasion of Iraq in 2003 has produced not the flowering of representative government in that divided and artificial nation-state, but rather continuing warfare, civil disruption, and economic chaos, punctuated by a couple of ambiguous elections that have had the effect of advancing Iraq closer to a Shiite-led fundamentalist theocracy. Only a Pollyanna would view these events as harbingers of a liberal democracy in the Middle East.

Even closer to these shores, the success of the United States in controlling events in Central and South America has proved limited. In the 1960s, pressure from the United States—including multiple assassination plots—failed to oust the communist leader of Cuba, Fidel Castro. In the 1980s, America attempted to dictate the outcome of the Nicaraguan civil war, in which once again, as in Vietnam, we backed a losing faction, the contras (from the Spanish *contrarevolucionarios*), against a weak Marxist regime led by the Sandinistas. Only in tiny Grenada—one-fifteenth the size of Delaware—was a large U.S. invasion force able, in 1983, to overcome a ragtag band of Marxist resisters; and in Panama, in 1989, to overthrow the dictator (and former CIA asset), General Manuel Antonio Noriega. While some of these military interventions had a modest multilateral component, all were essentially

U.S. operations, with the White House and the Pentagon calling the shots—the fig leaf of pseudomultilateralism.

Closer still to home, America's own defenses against threats from abroad have been highly porous. The 9/11 terrorist attacks against New York City and Washington, DC, are the most shocking examples, but illegal aliens and dangerous drugs also flow into the United States like water through fingers. Only about 30 percent of all the cocaine and heroin smuggled into this country from abroad is intercepted by U.S. government authorities. The rest makes it into the nation's back alleys and affluent suburbs alike, in an insidious attack on American society.[10]

Each year, some five to six hundred tons of cocaine are produced in Peru, Bolivia, and Colombia, of which three hundred tons are shipped to the United States and the rest chiefly to Europe. Some three hundred tons of heroin are refined from opium, mainly in Burma and Afghanistan (where production is spiraling upward), with ten tons shipped into the United States and much of the rest going to Russia and Eastern Europe.[11] This losing effort has led experts to conclude that success against the illegal drug flow does not lie in unilateral American attempts to seal its borders; after all, intercepting drugs is like searching for the proverbial needle in a haystack, given the thousands of ships, airplanes, and motorized vehicles that enter the United States each year. More promising are joint operations with other nations to stop production at its sources and close down money laundering in international banks, coupled with a more extensive education program aimed at drug consumers and graphically spelling out the physiological dangers of narcotics use. Vital, too, are better international programs to assist nations in their efforts to grow legitimate crops for sale abroad.

THE SEARCH FOR PEACE
AND SECURITY

At the top of the list of America's foreign policy objectives is the safety of the United States, its citizens, and its friends. During the Carter administration, the director of the influential Policy Planning Staff in the Department of State noted that "our first and most important foreign policy priority is peace—for ourselves and for others." Similarly, during the Reagan years, the State Department emphasized the importance of "seeking to protect the security of our nation and its institutions, as well as those of our allies and friends."[12] So far, though, humanity's record for peace and security has been, to say the least, less than one would like. It is true (and often overlooked) that, most of the time, most nations have been at peace with one another—no small accomplishment given the bitter animosities that so often arise between countries. Still, a striking fact is that during the fifty-five hundred years of recorded history, the world has enjoyed only some three hundred years (off and on) in which no nation has been at war anywhere on the globe. In the twentieth century, one hundred sixty million people died in violent conflict. Dictators like Adolf Hitler of Germany, Joseph Stalin of Russia, Pol Pot of Cambodia, and Mao Tse-tung of China killed millions more in internal pogroms. During the Second World War alone, over sixty million people lost their lives, and more than twenty-five million have died in armed conflict since then.

In 1986, heralded by the United Nations as the "Year of Peace," five million combatants in forty-one nations engaged in armed conflict. As the Cold War neared an end in 1989, one out of every four countries was at war. In 1989 alone, some five hundred thousand people lost their lives in violent struggles in Central America, Sudan, Eritrea, the Middle East, Northern Ireland, South Africa, and Sri Lanka.[13] Around the globe, nations purchase weapons—chiefly from the United States—at the cost of about $1 million every minute; collectively, they spent about $800 billion on their militaries in 2002, compared to $56 billion in development assistance to help the poor nations of the world.[14] Today, U.S. troops and enemy insurgents are killing each other at an alarming rate in Iraq, along with untold numbers of civilian bystanders.

Dr. Bernard Lown, a Nobel Peace Prize recipient from the United States, has observed that "no diseases, no pestilence, no plagues have claimed as many lives as war."[15] How has this happened? How can this earth—so beautiful in its lakes and mountains, a paradise among the barren planets of the solar system—be so wracked with hostility and bloodshed, when its inhabitants long for peace, when few people of any race or nationality wish to die prematurely on a killing field? What is the best pathway for the United States to follow in its search for peace and security? Answers to these questions are vital, for the core objective of protecting the security of the United States can be achieved only if this nation and others prove able to resolve their international disputes through nonviolent means.

The peaceful resolution of international disputes demands attention even more in the twenty-first century, as nuclear, chemical, and biological weapons spread around the planet at an accelerated rate. Nuclear weapons are now openly in the hands of eight nations: the United States, Great Britain, France, China, Russia, India, Pakistan, and North Korea. Israel is also thought to have enough nuclear warheads to annihilate every major Arab city; and

Iran is widely suspected to be in hot pursuit of its own nuclear weapons, produced clandestinely under the camouflage of a peaceful nuclear reactor program. Further, some fifteen developing nations possess ballistic missiles. These rockets are capable of reaching far beyond the confines of a local battlefield and can be equipped with nuclear, chemical, or biological warheads. According to the CIA, twenty countries are developing chemical warheads and ten countries are producing biological warheads; moreover, states the Agency, "*every* nation in the Middle East has a chemical weapons program."[16]

As the United States knows from the experience of the outbreak of global war in 1914, and again in 1939, limited regional conflicts can spread quickly to engulf the major powers. The second Persian Gulf War in 2003 became a target for Al Qaeda sympathizers and others attracted to a jihad against Americans. According to reporters on the scene, each week the war spawns new anti-U.S. insurgents (many from Afghanistan, Pakistan, Saudi Arabia, Syria, and other terrorist hideouts) as destruction and carnage spread from city to village across Iraq.

The end of the Cold War provided an optimistic counterpoint to the violence that afflicted so many parts of the globe. On this "good news" front, Eastern Europe found liberation from the stifling suppression of communism and, in the process, Germans abandoned the artificial and incongruous division of their nation into two countries in favor of reunification. Moreover, nations around the world began experimenting enthusiastically with democracy as a form of government. In Latin America, for example, juntas have been largely replaced by openly elected regimes. The result is a paradox. On the one hand, the world looks in some respects much like it did during the Cold War, with many nations and terrorist organizations, as well as ethnic and tribal factions, still prone to use force in the pursuit of their international objectives. On the other hand, peace and democracy have taken root in places where two decades ago no one would have imagined the possibility. This condition has produced feelings of uncertainty and insecurity about the future of the world, and America's role as a global power.

For some, the best pathway toward a more peaceful world lies in solitary action taken by the United States. "The form of realism that I am arguing for—call it new unilateralism—is clear in its determination to self-consciously and confidently deploy American power in pursuit of . . . global ends," writes the columnist Charles Krauthammer, expressing a viewpoint widely shared by so-called neoconservatives ("neocons"). He continues: ". . . the new unilateralism defines American interests far beyond narrow self-defense. In particular, it identifies two other major interests, both global: extending the peace by advancing democracy and preserving the peace by acting as balancer of last resort." Krauthammer concludes that "unipolarity, managed benignly, is far more likely to keep the peace . . . [than is] building an entangling web of interdependence." Interdependence—that is, working with other nations toward peace, prosperity, and justice through the creation of global and regional institutions—translates, in Krauthammer's worldview, into being "held hostage to others."[17]

Krauthammer and other neoconservatives view military force as a highly effective tool of foreign policy. While that is sometimes true, the neocons have a proclivity to underestimate the costs of war. With respect to the latest conflict in Iraq, for example, they failed to appreciate the ironic truth that it is often easier and requires fewer troops to win a war than it does to secure the peace. John J. Mearsheimer also advocates the imperative of acting alone against threats from abroad. He notes approvingly that, "the great powers do not merely strive to be the strongest great power . . . their ultimate aim is to be the hegemon—the only great power in the [international] system." He offers this blunt policy prescription: "In the anarchical world of international politics, it is better to be Godzilla than Bambi."[18] Niall Ferguson, a British historian (now at Harvard University) critical of Britain's fall from global power, likewise advocates the proud and energetic pursuit of an American global empire. The world needs adult supervision and his candidate for supervisor is the United States.[19]

In sharp contrast, Nye places a premium on multilateralism.[20] He sees cooperation with other nations through international institutions as the best way to reduce animosity toward America's global pursuit of security and commercial interests. Further, multilateralism may be the only way to prevent the emergence of balancing actions taken against the United States by wary powers with smaller military establishments, such as the nations of Europe uniting against what they might perceive to be a headstrong and self-absorbed United States. Historian Arthur M. Schlesinger, Jr., argues that "unilateralism rose to crescendo in the Bush Doctrine of the right to wage preventive war [in Iraq], a right reserved exclusively for the United States."[21] Indeed, preventive war and unilateralism go hand in hand, bound together by a willingness to use military force without consulting, let alone seeking the support of, any other nation—a guaranteed prescription for the loss of legitimacy in the world community of nations.[22]

This is not to say that the Bush administration has rejected all forms of multilateralism. In the United States, policy and politics at home or abroad is usually more a matter of tendencies and centers of gravity than stark ideological extremes. President George W. Bush managed to rally a majority of European nations, including Britain, Italy, Spain, and Poland, behind its war with Iraq in 2003. The administration has also used a multilateral approach for some aspects of the global war against terrorism, including military operations against Al Qaeda and the Taliban regime in Afghanistan following the 9/11 attacks. Further, it has wisely adopted a cautious multilateral approach toward curbing nuclear weapons programs in Iran and North Korea. Unlike the Clinton administration, President Bush has taken the issue of global terrorism to the United Nations and other international organizations; and his administration has aggressively sought out arrangements for intelligence-sharing related to terrorist activities, strengthening liaison relationships with several foreign espionage services. Among them: the French, the Germans, the Russians, and the Chinese.

The historical record suggests that all administrations engage in selective multilateralism, confronting international challenges either through a coalition of nations or solitary action based on more narrow national interests. Yet the absence of such major powers as France, Germany, and Russia in the "coalition of the willing" for the war in Iraq severely eroded the international legitimacy of that intervention. And since the war began, the resolve of Spain, Italy, and some other members of the coalition has weakened as the U.S. objective has moved from deposing Saddam's regime to bringing democracy to Iraq. The central point, though, is that the second Bush administration has been far less willing, generally, than its recent predecessors to recognize the constraints imposed by a unilateral approach to foreign policy objectives.

The arguments for and against unilateralism affect other U.S. foreign-policy pursuits. Among them are the fostering of commercial ties with other nations, improvements in the quality of life on this planet, and the quest for universal human rights.

ECONOMIC PROSPERITY

The second highest priority of U.S. foreign policy is the economic security of the American people. "Aside from war and preparations for war, and occasionally aside from migration," writes economist Thomas C. Schelling, "trade is the most important relationship that most countries have with each other."[23] During the Clinton administration, Secretary of State Warren M. Christopher stated during his Senate confirmation hearings: "Practitioners of statecraft [must not] forget that their ultimate goal is to improve the daily lives of the American people."[24] This bread-and-butter dimension of foreign policy relies on effective trading relations between the United States and the rest of the world. As a report from the Carnegie Endowment for International Peace concluded, "Today foreign policy can also raise or lower the cost of your home mortgage, create a new job or cause you to lose the one you've got."[25]

The success of U.S. commodities in foreign markets translates into jobs for American workers. Rising oil import costs mean inflation at home—indeed, a hemorrhaging of U.S. national wealth to oil-rich sheikdoms in the Middle East (like Saudi Arabia, supposedly an American ally yet, ironically, the homeland of fourteen of the nineteen Al Qaeda terrorists who struck the United States on 9/11, each funded in part by "charities" supported by the Saudi royal family). A rupture in U.S. relations with Russia and the former Soviet Republics can cost the American farmer dearly in the loss of grain sales abroad. Economic woes in Brasília and Caracas can lead to defaults on international loans financed by the American banking community.

A range of unilateral foreign-policy instruments are available to the United States in pursuit of global economic goals. For example, America's large navy exists in part to keep the world's sea-lanes open for U.S. commercial shipping. The CIA has been called upon by presidents to help protect American business interests overseas, as it did in Guatemala (1954), and in Chile (1970). Mostly, though, the United States has had to rely on multilateral diplomacy to develop a worldwide network of trading partners. The largest two-way commercial relationship in the world is between the United States and Canada, accounting for 20 percent of all American exports. Mexico, China, the European Union, and Japan rank next in trading relationships with the United States. The developing world, home of three-fourths of the world's population, is a significant and growing region of commerce for America as well.

The importance of multilateral economic cooperation can be seen, as well, in the efforts by the United States to punish nations who have violated international norms of decent behavior. When the Soviet military invaded Afghanistan in 1979, President Carter instituted a grain embargo (a prohibition against exports) against the U.S.S.R. The embargo failed, though, as Canada and Argentina gladly stepped forward to fill the demand. American farmers— reluctant to lose sales, even to communists—clamored to have the

U.S. sanctions removed and the Reagan administration soon complied. Iraq's invasion of Kuwait in 1991 provoked a worldwide boycott (a prohibition against imports) of Iraqi oil sales, depriving Iraqi dictator Saddam Hussein of an estimated $17 billion a year in revenues. This action was accompanied by a general trade embargo against Iraq, though one that was only partially successful because neighboring Jordan refused to curb illegal goods moving across its borders and into Baghdad. The record indicates that economic inducements like embargoes and boycotts have had only modest success over the years, and are guaranteed to fail if attempted unilaterally.[26]

One of the most blatant forms of unilateralism in the international economic domain is the practice of protectionism, that is, the use of government tariffs and quotas against imports to shield U.S. industries from foreign competitors.[27] While espousing free trade principles in public speeches, behind the scenes President George W. Bush (like many presidents of both parties before him) responded to pressure from U.S. steel companies by imposing tariffs on imported steel. Among other nations, Brazil complained about the tariffs as a contradiction of the goal to enhance free trade in the Western Hemisphere. Rising above the complaint threshold, Russia retaliated by banning its sizable import of poultry from the United States—vital to the economy of states like Georgia and Alabama. The World Trade Organization weighed in with a ruling against the steel tariffs; and, in 2003, much to the displeasure of the U.S. steel lobby in the nation's capital, the Bush administration responded to the growing international criticism by lifting the tariffs.

Proponents of unilateralism may wish otherwise, but the fact is that the economy of the United States is deeply interwoven into the economies of other nations—the essence of the popular expression "globalization," a one-word attempt to capture the idea of the world's deepening economic interdependence. America relies on the rest of the world especially for consumer goods, automobiles, and fuel. In some years, petroleum imports have accounted for as much as one-third of America's total imports—the largest single deficit commodity in U.S. trade. Other significant imports include clothing; iron and steel; consumer electronics; nonferrous metals; footwear; coffee; tea and spices; natural gas; diamonds; paper; telecommunications equipment; alcoholic beverages; toys and sporting goods; and fish. On the other side of the ledger, America exports chiefly food, chemicals, and machinery. Among the most conspicuous U.S. export successes have been cereals and grains; aircraft equipment and spacecraft; music CDs; films; computers; coal; skateboards and snowboards; military arms and vehicles; construction equipment; plastic and rubber; animal feed; cotton; tobacco; pharmaceutical products; and power-generating equipment.

Despite some strong showings, in the commodities mentioned above this nation suffered record trade imbalances of over $725 billion in 2005, particularly in commercial transactions with China.[28] Contributing to the trade imbalance has been the decline in America's merchandise trade performance, along with rising oil import costs. Even agricultural exports—once America's strongest suit—have fallen into decline, with the United States in recent months sometimes importing more food than it has exported. The imbalance also reflects the weakened state of diplomacy in the United States, with too few diplomats pursuing trade deals overseas, as well as the lack of U.S. businesspeople overseas who are fluent in foreign languages. This condition has been exacerbated by the insistence of the second Bush administration on fighting a war in Iraq and its refusal to embrace widely supported treaties on the environment and other global issues. As nations become more skeptical about the United States as a responsible world leader, they sour on trade agreements with us. Weakened diplomacy and a lack of fluent business professionals are hardly the only reasons why the United States suffers an imbalance in world trade; international commerce is a thickly woven plait. They are, however, two important strands.

QUALITY OF LIFE

A third goal of American foreign policy, though one less uniformly supported by American citizens than the primary objectives of military and economic security, has been to find solutions to a cluster of lifestyle problems that threaten the future of the United States and the rest of the world. For most people around the globe, adequate health care, housing, and education are sadly lacking. Just a short distance from the United States, more people in Belize, Guatemala, Honduras, and Nicaragua die from enteritis and diarrheal disorders (which stem from bacteria in polluted water) than from any other cause.

Moreover, the world's rain forests face widespread destruction. Nearly two-thirds of these forests have disappeared already in Central America. In Costa Rica, the rain forests are vanishing at a rate of three hundred sixty square miles annually. Farther south, in Brazil, the Amazon—the world's most magnificent rain forest—has shrunk from one hundred forty thousand to just four thousand square miles in the past two centuries. Worldwide, urban growth has swallowed up over a million acres of forested land in just the past ten years. Today, the rate of rain forest decline around the world is estimated at fifty thousand square miles per year, an expanse larger than the state of Pennsylvania. Trees act as sponges to absorb carbon dioxide (CO_2) and other greenhouse gas emissions, thereby slowing global warming—crucial to the survival of life on this planet.

Yet America's attitude at the Earth Summit meeting in 1992 (the UN Conference on Environment and Development, held in Rio de Janeiro) displayed no sense of urgency. Every major industrial country, except the United States, expressed support for targets and timetables to limit greenhouse gas emissions, even though Americans are responsible for producing more than a quarter of these emissions. Remarked a Japanese diplomat at the meeting: "If the U.S. cannot commit itself to stabilize CO_2 emissions, then developing countries like China, India, Brazil, and Mexico won't make commitments, either. We need a strong CO_2 convention—one with teeth in it."[29]

In 2005, eight leading industrial nations (the G-8) convened in Gleneagles, Scotland, to address quality-of-life issues. The participants agreed on useful measures to reduce global poverty and disease, but deep fissures appeared between the United States and the other seven nations (Canada, France, Germany, Italy, Japan, Russia, and the United Kingdom) over the issue of greenhouse gas emissions and global warming. President Bush acknowledged in the language of the final communiqué on climate change that the burning of fossil fuels adds to global warning, as he had often refused to concede in the past; nonetheless, he then blocked efforts by Tony Blair, the British prime minister and host of the conference, to have the G-8 agree on specific targets for reducing gas emissions.[30] The Bush administration has long opposed caps on carbon dioxide emissions and prefers to seek voluntary reductions by industries, on grounds that formal caps would jeopardize the American economy. This argument holds no water for other nations, however, since their economies would take a hit, too. They are willing to make the sacrifice, until new technologies are able to reduce emission levels, for the sake of a higher goal: protecting the planet from dangerous overheating.

Before he became vice president in the Clinton administration, Al Gore explained on the floor of the Senate the multiple risks posed by vanishing forests. "Around the world we lose between 1 and 1.5 acres of forest every second," he said. "With this loss, plant and animal species are disappearing from the face of the Earth at a rate that is 1,000 times faster than at any point in the previous 65 million years." His conclusion: for all the nations of the world, working together, "the effort to save the global environment must become the central organizing principle in the post-Cold War world."[31]

Among the lost flora in the forests may be yet undiscovered plants that contain wondrous cures for human disease. For example, the Madagascar periwinkle, discovered by botanists not long ago in the rain forests of this large African island, contains a substance that has been remarkably successful in treating leukemia in young children. The Pacific yew in Oregon yields a drug called taxol, shown to be valuable in the treatment of ovarian cancer. Only about 30 percent of the flora in the world has been studied by botanists and other scientists; how many yet-to-be-studied plants might be beneficial to humans? How many plants will be destroyed by loggers who clear-cut the forests before scientists have been able to tap their miracle cures? "We've been saying for some time that the ancient forest may hold answers to questions that nobody has yet to ask," observes an American ecologist.[32] Moreover, the buildup of chemical pollutants in the atmosphere that contributes to the greenhouse effect also retards the production of farm crops in every country. Still another ecological challenge is the suffocation of arable land in North Africa by spreading deserts.

Troubling, as well, is the accelerated disappearance of the planet's animal species. From 1987 through 1992, the endangered species list in the United States alone jumped from 451 to 617 species—a 37 percent increase. As Jared Diamond notes in *Collapse: How Societies Choose to Fail or Succeed*, a nation's decline is often a result of biological suicide through the unthinking devastation of its ecological support system.[33] As with flora, so are fauna essential to the ecological balance that supports humankind. Neither will be saved by America on its own.

As scientists have slowly begun to appreciate, the world's environment does not respond to the wishes of any single nation; its connections are global. Coal-burning in Asia can affect the quality of air in the Karwendel in the Austrian Alps or Deer Valley in the Wasatch region of the Rocky Mountains.

Again, the solutions lie in multilateral, not unilateral, action. Over a decade ago, historian Paul Kennedy stressed that for a better quality of life in the world, "environmental pacts, increases in overseas aid from today's pitifully low percentages, the maintenance of open access to the third world's exports, and reduction of fuel use and greenhouse emissions is a fundamental requirement."[34] Much of what Americans can accomplish in tandem with other nations and international organizations does not demand great expense. One illustration is related to the need for fertilizer plants in poor nations. The red acidic soil of Africa requires additives; yet, in all of sub-Saharan Africa, there are only two major fertilizer plants, both in Nigeria.[35] Wealthier nations, working together, can assist agricultural production throughout Africa with small investments in the local production of fertilizer. The technical know-how of the industrialized nations and their experience with market economies are valuable assets, too, that can be shared through cooperative enterprises involving rich and poor nations working together.

HUMAN DIGNITY

A fourth objective of American foreign policy, which also lacks the public consensus accorded the goals of physical and economic security, has been efforts to eliminate global injustices, especially the violation of human rights around the world. The Carter administration elevated this concern to a high position on America's foreign policy agenda; and, in a list of international objectives issued by the Reagan administration during its last year in office, at the top stood a commitment to "uphold the principles of freedom, the rule of law, and the observance of fundamental human rights."[36]

The nurturing of an expanding community of liberal democracies is, in itself, a monumental challenge, far beyond the capacity of any single nation to deal with alone.[37] During the end stages of the Cold War—not much over a decade ago—fewer than twenty nations out of the total of about one hundred ninety were generally considered legitimate democracies, with a high regard for fair elections, a media free of government censorship, and robust civil liberties.[38] Even now, as many nations try their hand at this form of government, few have achieved a level of success comparable to the Western democracies. Little wonder why: democracies take time to mature. In the United States, it took one hundred years of "democracy" to integrate black citizens into American society. Today the full integration of women and minorities continues to lag behind white males. In the Philippines, democracy took some eighty-five years to mature.

The idea, popular in the second Bush administration, that democracy can be installed in Iraq at the point of a gun remains a chimera. Had President George W. Bush taken the time to consult with leading comparative politics scholars in the nation's universities, he would have received a large dose of realism about the difficulties of introducing representative government into places with a long history of autocratic rule—especially in Iraq, where the effort is being led essentially by just one nation, the United States, and in the middle of a war. Nor do Americans have much of a record for patient dedication to nation-building overseas; and, until the ongoing war in Iraq, President Bush exhibited no interest whatsoever in nation-building. Perhaps he was guided early in his presidency by a more traditional view of conservative foreign policy. Commenting on nation-building and the war in Iraq, the father of modern conservatism, journalist William F. Buckley, Jr., has said: "It's anything but conservative. It's not conservative at all, inasmuch as conservatism doesn't invite unnecessary challenges. It insists on coming to terms with the world as it is. . . . "[39]

Despite the difficulties of establishing liberal democratic regimes around the world, most Americans would probably endorse a viewpoint advanced by an official in the Carter administration: "There is a simple moral imperative at the heart of our national identity," he said, ". . . every individual has inherent rights and a special dignity. This belief has shaped our national purposes throughout our history."[40] In the United States and around the globe, freedom from tyranny and a guarantee of democratic safeguards—above all, reliance on the rule of law, as well as open and competitive elections—rank high in the hierarchy of human aspirations.

This feeling was vividly displayed in China, in May of 1989, when over one million people (mainly students) flooded Beijing's Tiananmen Square in a mass demonstration of fervor for democratic reform—the largest public protest in the history of modern China. The old-guard Chinese leaders quickly crushed the democracy movement with tanks and soldiers. Nonetheless, the quest for greater political freedom continues among Chinese political refugees abroad and a courageous underground within the world's most populous nation.

Six months after the inspiring events in Tiananmen Square, another celebration of freedom burst out. Germans on both sides of the Berlin Wall, which had divided East and West Berlin since 1961, rejoiced together at its surprise opening by East German communist leaders intimidated by the rising demands in their country for more openness and freedom to travel, even migrate. This fresh surge for liberty was stimulated in part by the relaxation of the Soviet grip on Eastern Europe and, no doubt, by the alluring television images of the good material life in the West. In a gross miscalculation, East German leaders reasoned that if they opened the wall the political pressures resulting from a gathering tide of would-be emigrants seeking escape from East Germany through Czechoslovakia and Hungary would diminish. Those wishing to leave the communist regime could now simply walk across the once heavily guarded "no-man's zone" between East and West Berlin. What the communist leaders failed to anticipate was that, in place of the expected trickle, a deluge of frustrated East Germans streamed through the new opening. The result was a media spectacle that revealed, for the entire world to see, the illegitimacy of the communist regime, hammering the final nail in the coffin of a hated and dying government, and symbolically signaling the end of the long Cold War.

This fresh spirit favoring liberalism, capitalism, and democracy seemed to infect much of the world. Within a year, it spread across the Soviet Union, splintering this erstwhile superpower into fifteen separate republics, most (to one degree or another) experimenting with democratic forms of government—the most important global event since the end of the Second World War. Tyranny and totalitarianism seemed to be in full retreat in places where, once, they had reigned supreme. It soon became clear, however, that in spite of this widespread enthusiasm for reform, people across large portions of the globe would remain victims of old style repression. For every Estonia (one of the freed Soviet Republics), there was a Somalia; and for every Poland, an Iraq. Moreover, some communist regimes continued to survive, perpetuating an often cruel and stifling rule over citizens, including China (with one-fifth of the world's population), Cuba, and North Korea; and many of the former Soviet republics, although no longer communist, remain nondemocratic.

Even in countries newly released from communist bondage, ancient animosities among ethnic groups brought about fierce internecine fighting. In the former nation of Yugoslavia, civil war broke out in 1991, with Serbian nationalists proclaiming (in a phrase reminiscent of the Nazi Third Reich) their intention to pursue a policy of "ethnic cleansing" against Muslims and other factions in Bosnia-Herzegovina.[41] Serbian soldiers reportedly engaged in widespread rape of Muslim women in Bosnia-Herzegovina. In an all-too-typical event in 1992, Serbian troops removed two hundred hospitalized Croat soldiers from their beds and shot them, while Serbian snipers fired against civilians (including international news reporters, several of whom died from their wounds). In retaliation, Bosnian Muslims attacked Serbian civilians in villages close to the Bosnian town of Bratunac. Instead of peace after the end of the Cold War, impassioned ethnic warfare soon consumed thousands of Muslims, Serbs, and Croats. A trail of refugees numbering over 1.6 million fled to safer places in Europe, the largest exodus of war victims in the region since the Second World War.

In light of the fragmentation of the world into many independent nations in place of the two chief ideological encampments of the Cold War, the human rights question becomes: how can these nations be moved toward a form of representative government? By all indications, success will require the cooperation of the world's existing strong democracies. For example, only with the intervention of NATO forces—a true collective military response by the United States, Canada, and major European nations—was peace finally restored in the Balkans.

Less successful was America's intervention into Somalia in 1992. That year, upward of two thousand Somalians were perishing each day from lack of food and water. Nearly every night during the month of November, television news shows brought to America's living rooms emotionally wrenching images of children lying dead from starvation in the streets of Mogadishu and Somalia's other cities and villages, or so near death that their fly-covered eyes stared blankly into the cameras, uncaring, the shriveled skin on their bodies draped against the bony outlines of ribs and hips. The tragic conditions touched the hearts of Americans and their opinion leaders. Television and newspaper commentators urged the first Bush administration to assist the humanitarian efforts of the UN in Somalia by providing military protection for relief workers, who were under constant threat from marauding bands of tribal gunmen engaged in the theft of food and medical supplies from the international organization.

Under these pressures—and perhaps shocked himself by the television pictures of the dead and dying children of Somalia—President George H. W. Bush requested UN support to lead a military coalition, comprised mainly of U.S. troops, into Somalia. As Steel notes, the United States probably would never have responded to the crisis in Somalia "were it not for the power of television to bring the most horrifying images into the American living room."[42]

The objectives of America's Operation Restore Hope in Somalia were, first, to secure the nation's seaports, airports, and cities for the safe delivery of food and medicine and, second, to establish a "secure environment" where UN peacekeeping forces ("blue helmets") could operate. In the largest purely humanitarian intervention in America's history, the Marines—operating without significant assistance from other nations—took over the streets of Mogadishu and other locales, chasing away or disarming tribal extortionists and bullies. Food at last flowed unimpeded to the needy, at least within the regions where the Marines were stationed. Children played in the streets again, instead of sitting listlessly on stoops and in gutters. It appeared a triumph for American foreign policy.

Then, things fell apart. In the waning months of the first Bush administration, acting Secretary of State Lawrence S. Eagleburger wisely cautioned against efforts by America to change conditions in places like Somalia virtually by itself. "The United States cannot have its own way simply by snapping fingers," he said.[43] His replacement in the incoming Clinton administration seemed to agree. During his confirmation hearings in 1993, Warren M. Christopher emphasized his belief in the "discreet and careful" use of force by the United States, noting that "we cannot respond to every alarm."[44] Yet respond the Clinton administration did in 1993, by sending American troops back into Somalia, this time with a more difficult goal: to capture the leading Somalian warlord, General Mohamed Aidid. The outcome, vividly recorded in the best-selling book *Black Hawk Down*,[45] was the killing of eighteen U.S. troops in Mogadishu—some of whom were shot, stripped of their clothing, and dragged through the dirt streets of the city. The insurgents, operating on their home turf, routed the Marines and Special Forces with rocket-propelled grenades and urban guerrilla tactics. Even though the intervention in Somalia enjoyed international backing through a UN Security Council resolution, and some UN blue-helmet troops fought and died there in early skirmishes with warlords, at the operational level (Task Force Ranger) the Americans took on the warlords and their guerrilla fighters single-handedly in 1993. The risks of an intervention that relied too heavily on American forces alone became clearer and President Clinton ordered the remaining troops home.

Altruism is a deep-seated and noble sentiment in American foreign policy. Nevertheless, pleas to help those in distress around the world are easy to dismiss—especially after experiences like those suffered by U.S. troops acting alone in Somalia. As Nicholas D. Kristof notes with respect to Bosnia and Rwanda, "the pattern was repeated over and over: a slaughter unfolded in a distant part of the world, but we had other priorities and it was always simplest for the American government to look away."[46] When the United States and other nations ignored the slaughter in Rwanda in 1994, over a half million people died in an act of Hutu genocide against the Tutsi minority. Today, new slaughters are underway in the Darfur province of Sudan. In the extreme cases of genocide, even a unilateral intervention by the United States (or some capable power) would be better than nothing; but the most effective approach, and one entirely manageable with the right diplomatic skills, patience, and determination—hallmarks of the foreign policy team during the first Bush administration—is for the United States to rally the armed forces of civilized nations to stop the genocidal bloodshed.

Americans have a clear stake in the advancement of democracy and human dignity around the globe, since democratic regimes are far less likely to become enemies of the United States. The so-called democratic peace hypothesis, central to recent political science research on international conflict, posits the idea that democracies rarely if ever go to war against other democracies.[47]

It should have been clear even before the tragedy in Somalia that America can never achieve peace and democracy abroad simply by wielding its own bayonets. That objective requires collective political and economic diplomacy, involving the major democracies working together and without false hopes of instant success, as they did in response to the death and havoc brought to nations on the Indian Ocean by the earthquake-spawned tsunamis of December 26, 2004.

If these diplomatic efforts fail, collective military operations may then be necessary and can be successful, as shown by the actions of NATO in the Balkans during the 1990s.

SAYING NO TO THE ROLE
OF LONE RANGER

"The course of this nation does not depend on the decisions of others," said President George W. Bush proudly in his State of the Union address in 2003. Naturally, the United States will never allow itself to be dictated to by other nations against its own vital security interests; but the most important interests of Americans (as of everyone else in the world)—world peace, economic opportunities abroad, quality of life, human dignity for all—can only be met through the joint efforts of all the world's civilized nations. To reach these worthy objectives, decisions must be made collectively, not just by one nation—even a superpower. As Adam Cohen has pointed out, when the president stated in his State of the Union address in 2004 that he did not need a "permission slip" to defend the United States, it had the effect of weakening the principle of multilateralism, a widely accepted approach to American foreign policy since the end of the Second World War.[48]

In place of having the world dial 911 in expectation of reaching the U.S. Marine Corps, developing effective emergency military teams formed by nations working together in various regions of the world, under the auspices of the UN—say, a well-trained, professional African Emergency Military Team—is a laudable goal for dealing with Rwanda-like situations in the future.[49] The United States could help with such collective arrangements by supplying its fair share of personnel, funding, and expertise. Some may wince at the thought of Americans lining up for more assignments abroad, but these would be supportive in nature and limited in scope. As we are beginning to understand in Iraq (and should have remembered from Vietnam), far more wrenching is the prospect of America continuing to play the role of the Lone Ranger, trying to solve the world's problems largely by itself and running up a horrendous debt in blood and treasure. Real multilateralism—NATO, GATT, WTO—works; unilateralism and pseudomultilateralism do not.

In her confirmation hearings for secretary of state on January 18, 2005, Condoleezza Rice said, "Our interaction with the rest of the world must be a conversation, not a monologue." Here, at last, was the right approach. Was it only nice-sounding rhetoric to impress senators on the Foreign Relations Committee?

NOTES

1. My thanks to political scientist Robert Pastor for reminding me of this line.
2. See Daniel S. Papp, Loch K. Johnson, and John E. Endicott, *American Foreign Policy: History, Politics, and Policy* (New York: Pearson-Longman, 2005).
3. See Julia Preston, "U.N. Delegates Wait for Bush to Make Case Against Iraq," *New York Times* (September 11, 2002), p. A22.
4. Quoted by Steven Erlanger, "German Leader's Warning: War Plan Is a Huge Mistake," *New York Times* (September 5, 2002), p. A1.
5. Quoted by Floyd Norris, "Watching America: Will It Listen to Foreigners, or Do as It Pleases?" *New York Times* (January 28, 2005), p. C1.
6. Edward Alden and Carola Hoyos, "A Loose Cannon," *Financial Times* (August 10–11, 2002), p. 7.
7. See, for example, Clyde Prestowitz, *Rogue Nations: America's Unilateralism and the Failure of Good Intentions* (New York: Basic Books, 2003).
8. Joseph S. Nye, Jr., *The Paradox of American Power* (New York: Oxford University Press, 2002), p. 1.
9. Quoted by Daniel Ford, "A Report at Large: Perestroika," *The New Yorker* (March 28, 1988), p. 80.

10. See Loch K. Johnson, *Bombs, Bugs, Drugs, and Thugs: Intelligence and America's Quest for Security* (New York: New York University Press, 2000).

11. Ibid.

12. See, respectively, Anthony Lake, *Managing Complexity in U.S. Foreign Policy*, U.S. Department of State, Bureau of Public Affairs (March 14, 1978), p. 1; and *Fundamentals of U.S. Foreign Policy*, U.S. Department of State, Bureau of Public Affairs (March 1988), p. 1.

13. The Stockholm International Peace Research Institute, cited in "Institute Issues Tally of World Conflicts," *Boston Globe* (June 18, 1987), quoted by Joseph S. Nye, Jr., "International Security Studies," in Joseph Kruzel, ed., *American Defense Annual, 1988–1989* (Lexington, MA: Lexington Books, 1988), p. 242.

14. World Bank President James Wolfensohn, *The NewsHour with Jim Lehrer*, PBS (January 2, 2005).

15. Public address, "Beyond War" Convocation, San Francisco (September 12, 1985).

16. William H. Webster, director of central intelligence, speech, Council on Foreign Relations, Washington, DC (December 12, 1988); and Loch K. Johnson, "Smart Intelligence," *Foreign Policy* 89 (Winter 1992–1993), p. 56, original emphasis.

17. Charles Krauthammer, "The Unipolar Moment Revisited," *The National Interest* 70 (Winter 2002–2003), pp. 12–14, 17.

18. John J. Mearsheimer, "Better to Be Godzilla than Bambi," *Foreign Policy* 134 (January/February 2005), p. 48.

19. Niall Ferguson, *Empire: The Rise and Demise of the British World Order and the Lessons from Global Power* (New York: Basic Books, 2003), and *Colossus: The Price of American Empire* (New York: Penguin, 2004).

20. Nye, *The Paradox of American Power*, pp. 10, 171. See also Ralph G. Carter, "Leadership at Risk: The Perils of Unilateralism," *PS: Political Science and Politics* 36 (2003), pp. 17–22.

21. Arthur M. Schlesinger, Jr., *War and the American Presidency* (New York: Norton, 2002), p. 18.

22. See Benjamin R. Barber, *Fear's Empire: War, Terrorism, and Democracy* (New York: Norton, 2003), p. 28.

23. Thomas C. Schelling, "National Security Considerations Affecting Trade Policy," *Report*, Williams Commission, vol. I (1974), p. 737.

24. Committee on Foreign Relations, U.S. Senate (January 1993).

25. Carnegie Endowment for International Peace, National Commission on America and the World, *Changing Our Ways: America and the New World* (Washington, DC: The Brookings Institution, 1992), p. 2.

26. See David A. Baldwin, *Economic Statecraft* (Princeton: Princeton University Press, 1985).

27. See Papp, Johnson, and Endicott, *American Foreign Policy*, pp. 324–325.
28. David Armstrong, "U.S. Racks Up Record Trade Deficit," *San Francisco Chronicle* (February 11, 2006), p. C1.
29. Quoted by John Newhouse, "The Diplomatic Round: Earth Summit," *The New Yorker* (June 1, 1992), p. 78.
30. Richard W. Stevenson, "G-8 Claims Some Progress on Aid and Global Warming," *International Herald Tribune* (July 9–10, 2005), p. 1.
31. Senator Al Gore (D-TN), remarks, *Congressional Record* (April 7, 1992), pp. S4872, S4874. See also Al Gore, *Earth in the Balance: Ecology and the Human Spirit* (New York: Penguin-Plume, 1993).
32. Wendell Wood, Oregon National Resources Council, quoted in Timothy Egan, "Trees That Yield a Drug for Cancer Are Wasted," *New York Times* (January 29, 1992), p. A9.
33. New York: Viking, 2005.
34. Paul Kennedy, "True Leadership for the Next Millennium," *New York Times* (January 3, 1993), p. E11.
35. Richard Critchfield, "Bring the Green Revolution to Africa," *New York Times* (September 14, 1992), p. A19.
36. *Fundamentals of U.S. Foreign Policy.*
37. On the important distinction between liberal and illiberal democracies, see Fareed Zakaria, *The Future of Freedom: Illiberal Democracy at Home and Abroad* (New York: Norton, 2004).
38. Arend Lijphart, *Democracies* (New Haven: Yale University Press, 1984), p. 8.
39. Interviewed by George Will, *This Week*, ABC News (October 9, 2005).
40. Lake, *Managing Complexity*, p. 6.
41. See Sabrina Petra Ramet, "War in the Balkans," *Foreign Affairs* 71 (Fall 1992), pp. 174–181; and Steven L. Burg and Paul S. Shoup, *The War in Bosnia-Herzegovina: Ethnic Conflict and International Intervention* (Armonk, NY: M. E. Sharpe, 1999).
42. Ronald Steel, *Temptations of a Superpower* (Cambridge, MA: Harvard University Press, 1995), p. 103.
43. Lawrence S. Eagleburger, remarks, C-SPAN Television (August 15, 1992).
44. Committee on Foreign Relations, U.S. Senate (January 1993).
45. Mark Bowden, *Black Hawk Down: A Story of Modern War* (New York: Penguin, 2000).
46. Nicholas D. Kristof, "Mr. Bush, Take a Look At MTV," *New York Times* (April 17, 2005), p. A15, citing the pattern discerned by Samantha Power, *A Problem From Hell: America and the Age of Genocide* (New York: Basic Books, 2002).
47. Michael E. Brown, Sean M. Lynn-Jones, and Steven E. Miller, eds., *Debating the Democratic Peace* (Cambridge, MA: MIT Press, 1997).

48. Adam Cohen, "Why the Democrats Need to Stop Thinking About Elephants," *New York Times* (November 15, 2004), p. A22. David Skidmore notes that unilateralism is hardly just a Republican phenomenon. "Under both presidents [Clinton and the second Bush]," he writes, "U.S. behavior was strongly unilateralist" ["Understanding the Unilateralist Turn in U.S. Foreign Policy," *Foreign Policy Analysis* 1 (July 2005), p. 223].

49. On some of the problems faced by Africa in attempting to provide its own emergency army through an African Union, established in 2002, to deal with situations like Somalia and Rwanda, see Bruce Jentleson, *American Foreign Policy: The Dynamics of Choice in the 21st Century*, 2nd ed. (New York: Norton, 2004), pp. 448–49.

CHAPTER 5

Isolationism

LEADING WITH ONE'S HEAD
IN THE SAND

Instead of conducting foreign affairs unilaterally or, for that matter, even reaching out a hand to work with other democracies, the United States could simply turn its back on the rest of the world altogether, savoring America's prosperity in splendid isolation, refusing to enter into agreements with other countries, pouring resources into a ballistic missile defense, sealing the borders, constructing a Fortress America designed to barricade the United States against the forces of chaos beyond the Atlantic and Pacific moats. For some, it is tempting to pretend Americans can exist apart from other nations, shutting out of our lives those people overseas who dislike us or raise troubling questions about policies fashioned in Washington, DC, and those who write unsettling slogans like one scrawled in black paint on a piazza wall in Venice recently by an anonymous America-hater:

I wanna see the Constitution burn

Wanna watch the White House overturn

Isolationism, recall, was America's initial response to the wrangling world and remained so throughout most of the nation's history. "Steer clear of permanent alliances with any portion of the foreign world," George Washington warned in his Farewell Address. "Peace, commerce and honest friendship with all nations, entangling alliances with none," Thomas Jefferson prescribed in his first inaugural address. These cautionary speeches made sense at the time, when a weak America could ill-afford to slip into the vortex of Continental wars. Even in those days, however, the founders understood how important it was to maintain trade relations abroad that would enhance the economic growth of the new nation; therefore, isolationist rhetoric aside, they sought commercial ties wherever feasible. Today, as modern communications and transportation have shrunk the world, America's economic prosperity has become even more closely tied to international trade and business transactions.

Despite the increasing commercial interdependence of nations, coupled with signs of growing political and cultural integration, the isolationist instinct lives on in America. One can see it in letters-to-the-editor columns, or even in the ruminations of some presidential candidates. "To apply the Founders' principle today, the U.S. government should bring ALL military forces home from foreign bases," reads a citizen's letter to a newspaper in the rural South, "and stop playing diplomatic footsy with ALL governments, but especially those in the Mideast."[1] Recommending withdrawal of U.S. forces from South Korea and Europe, along with an end to America's participation in foreign aid programs, a GOP presidential candidate, Pat Buchanan, wrote in 1991: "All that buncombe about history 'placed on our shoulders' sucked the Brits into two wars, and left them living off Uncle Sam's food stamps. If America does not wish to end her days in the same nursing home as Britannia, she had best can Beltway geo-babble about 'unipolarity' and 'our responsibilities to lead.'"[2]

According to polling data, Americans support a limited degree of international involvement, such as fighting world hunger and taking steps to clean up the global environment.[3] Moreover, large percentages normally respond favorably to questions about the need to protect the jobs of American workers and U.S. business interests abroad (twin commercial objectives that usually elicit the highest approval responses), secure adequate energy supplies, prevent the spread of nuclear and other weapons of mass destruction, and continue to contain communism.[4]

Nevertheless, polls have indicated weak support among Americans for several aspects of international involvement by the United States. For example, in 1991 a national poll conducted by the Chicago Council on Foreign Relations indicated that the nation's leaders—the decision-makers—exhibited even weaker support than the general public for certain foreign-policy objectives (see Figure 5.1).[5]

In this poll, the views of leaders and the general public on the question of "helping to improve the standard of living of less developed nations" were about the same: both less than a majority, at 42 percent for the leaders and 41 percent for the public.

FIGURE 5.1
U.S. Attitudes Toward Foreign Policy Objectives

Question posed: Do you think the following foreign policy objectives are very important?

FOREIGN POLICY OBJECTIVES	SUPPORT FROM LEADERS*	SUPPORT FROM PUBLIC
Protecting U.S. jobs	39%	65%
Protecting U.S. business abroad	27%	63%
Promoting global human rights	45 %	58 %
Protecting weaker nations	28 %	57%
Containing communism	10 %	56%
Strengthening the United Nations	39%	44%
Spreading democracy to other nations	26%	28%

*Individuals in government, business, academe, media, unions, churches, and volunteer groups.

In 1995, a *Times-Mirror* survey found that about 80 percent of the public did not place a high priority on the protection of weaker nations against foreign aggression; the promotion and defense of human rights in other countries; the improvement of living standards in developing nations; or the advancement of democracy in other nations.[6] A sizable majority (69 percent) thought that strengthening the United Nations should be a low priority, even though the UN's budget is just $1.3 billion a year compared, for example, to the program costs of $38.1 billion for the Defense Department's crash-prone V-22 Osprey aircraft, the $40 billion for development of the F/A-22 Raptor fighter jet (and another $78.1 billion earmarked to build 277 of the aircraft), or the $4.4 billion monthly costs of military operations in Iraq in 2004. In the poll, few saw much need to promote political and economic stability in

Mexico, or democracy in Russia. Referring to a recent Pew poll, Fukuyama notes that not since the end of the Vietnam War in 1975 have so many Americans endorsed the statement that the United States "should mind its own business" when it comes to world affairs.[7]

One of the nation's leading experts on public opinion and American foreign policy is Professor Ole R. Holsti of Duke University. He sees in recent polls indications that "a consistently strong majority of Americans accept an active American role across a broad spectrum of issues, but not without some important reservations." Holsti continues: "Public enthusiasm for efforts to remake the world in America's image—through promotion of democratic institutions, human rights, market economies, and the like—has consistently been quite limited, especially if such endeavors are undertaken by means of military interventions."[8] Along some dimensions of foreign policy,

---

FIGURE 5.2
U.S. Attitudes Toward Selected Foreign Policy Goals

SELECTED FOREIGN POLICY GOALS	LEADERSHIP SUPPORT	PUBLIC SUPPORT
Strengthening the United Nations	40%	38%
Protecting weaker nations	33%	18%
Combating world hunger	67%	43%
Improving the global environment	61%	47%
Helping overcome poverty in poor nations	64%	18%
Protecting U.S. business interests abroad	22%	32%
Spreading democracy	29%	14%

U.S. leaders and the general public alike display limited support for internationalism, as shown by the figures from polling in 2004, presented in Figure 5.2.[9]

ISOLATIONISM AND THE BRICKER MOVEMENT

Admittedly, the world may appear more benign when, in the manner of the ostrich, one's head is in the sand but this is a vulnerable posture. The Second World War taught many Americans about the danger of ignoring the rest of the world. Still, the isolationist instinct has proved resilient. As early as 1943, in the middle of the Second World War, isolationists on Capitol Hill began to speak out against the idea of creating a United Nations at war's end. Senator Arthur Vandenberg (R-MI) complained that the draft proposal for such a world organization "pledged our total resources to whatever illimitable scheme for relief and rehabilitation all around the world our New Deal crystal gazers might desire to pursue . . . "[10] The isolationists failed to stop the establishment of the UN but their attack against a wider role for America in the world soon refocused, in the 1950s, on efforts to trim President Eisenhower's sails as the nation's diplomat in chief. Led by Senator John W. Bricker (R-OH), lawmakers sought an amendment to the Constitution that would advance their isolationist agenda by limiting the president's authority to enter into international commitments on behalf of the United States. They intended, as well, to dilute the effect of any such commitments on U.S. domestic laws. The "Bricker Revolt" was underway.[11] While lawmakers were wise to have concerns about presidents gathering too much power over foreign affairs—sin number 2—beneath the surface of the Bricker movement lurked a more troubling philosophy: a distrust of U.S. involvement in international agreements altogether.[12]

Most upsetting to Senator Bricker and his supporters was Article VI, Clause 2, of the Constitution:

> This Constitution, and the Laws of the United States which shall be made in Pursuance thereof; and all Treaties made, or which shall be made, under the Authority of the United States, shall be the supreme Law of the land; and the Judges in every State shall be bound thereby, any Thing in the Constitution or Laws of any State to the Contrary notwithstanding.

To the Brickerites, this passage allowed the president, in effect, to enter into treaties and other agreements "under the authority of the United States" that would be binding on federal and state law. By international agreement, the president or his subordinates might impose upon the nation legal obligations that would invade the domain of power reserved to the states and, thereby, argued the Brickerites, deprive the people of rights guaranteed under the Constitution. The Bricker movement was, in a nutshell, a thinly disguised defense of states' rights, a concept dear to conservative isolationists.

Disturbing to the Brickerites were proposals before the United Nations to advance an antigenocide convention, a declaration of human rights, and other proposals, which, if adopted as treaties by the United States, would have pledged—or at least, so they feared—the United States to endless interference in the domestic affairs of other countries, and, more important still, invited *their* interference in America's domestic affairs. According to a student of the Bricker era, some southern senators dreaded the possibility that the federal government might declare an end to segregation in the United Sates by means of an executive agreement with an African ally.[13]

Behind their ardent defense of states' rights and their distaste for New Dealers stood another bugbear that alarmed the Brickerites: the White House's use of secret executive agreements to end America's happy isolation from the world and its woes. The memory of President Franklin Delano Roosevelt's hidden agreements with the Soviets during the Second World War remained fresh in the minds of Republican Party leaders still fuming over the "loss" of Eastern Europe to the U.S.S.R. as a result of secret negotiations by Roosevelt with Joseph Stalin. "The power of the executive agreements has resulted in such catastrophes as Yalta, Potsdam, and Tehran," bemoaned a statement from the Wisconsin State Republican Party in 1953.[14] The merits or demerits of these particular Second World War summits aside, this time the fears of the Brickerites were more defensible; in the modern era the executive branch would often go on to misuse the executive agreement authority, entering the United States into questionable commitments abroad (such as secret assurances during the Johnson administration that the United States would defend Thailand) without congressional debate, or sometimes without even awareness among lawmakers of significant negotiations conducted by the executive branch with other nations.[15]

Bricker initially introduced his key amendment to curb the president's agreement powers in 1951, but not until 1954 did Senate conservatives settle on compromise language they thought would have a chance of passing. Critics of the Bricker Amendment, including President Eisenhower and Secretary of State John Foster Dulles, were appalled by the possibility that the measure might actually become law. For journalist Walter Lippmann, efforts to improve the wording of the Amendment had led to several renditions that were "one and all . . . unwashed, unpeeled, uncooked, and not yet fit to be eaten."[16] The constitutional authority Professor Edward S. Corwin concluded magisterially:

> No such act of mayhem on the Constitution is required to meet existing perils. The Anti-Genocide Convention, the proposed Convention on Human Rights and the like are undoubtedly ill-considered proposals, but the Senate itself has the power, has it but the intestinal fortitude to use it, to administer the *congé* to all such utopian projects. Can it be that some Senators prefer to be able to invoke the Constitution as a reason for doing the sensible thing rather than face up to certain pressure groups? The Bricker proposal is really a vote of lack of confidence in the political courage and integrity of the body from which it emanates.[17]

The Brickerities, though, were not easily dissuaded. On February 26, 1954, they rallied behind a substitute amendment offered by Senator Walter George (D-GA), after Bricker's own tougher amendment was defeated. It required implementing legislation by *state* legislatures for all international agreements touching on questions of states' rights! The George Amendment, if successful, would still have represented a major victory for the isolationists. The Amendment read:

> Section 1. A provision of a treaty or other international agreement which conflicts with this Constitution shall not be of any force or effect.

Section 2. An international agreement other than a treaty shall become effective as internal law in the United States only by an act of Congress.[18]

Begrudgingly, the Brickerites accepted this language as a final refuge. As one study has concluded, the George Amendment drew "great appeal from the fact that it avoided the radicalism of the Bricker proposal while at the same time it satisfied the desire of many senators for greater control over the drawing up of executive agreements."[19]

At last came the day the Brickerites had labored toward for three years. It was now or never. All their chips were on the George substitute amendment. "The last moments of the debate were both bitter and emotional," reported the *New York Times*.[20] The clerk began the slow calling of the roll. Thirty minutes later, the vote was yeas 60, nays 31. The George Amendment—and Bricker's isolationist movement—had failed by a single vote.

"Spurred by the success of the Twenty-Second Amendment [limiting a president to two terms], the foes of Presidential power launched the Bricker Amendment," reflects presidential scholar Louis W. Koenig.[21] Even more, beyond their fear of presidential autocracy, the Brickerites—isolationists all—were worried about the consequences of what they referred to as the pernicious "new internationalism." During a hearing on the Bricker proposal, Senator Pat McCarran (D-NV) burst out: "I voted for what I consider now to be a bad treaty that I will regret probably all the days of my life . . . the United Nations."[22] For the Brickerites, diplomacy by way of treaties and other international agreements had become, as one of their witnesses put it during hearings into the Bricker

Amendment, "a kind of 'Frankenstein' instrumentality, which can change and even destroy the liberties of the American people and their form of government."[23]

THE REJECTION OF
CONTEMPORARY TREATIES

The role of the United States in the world, internationalism versus isolationism, is tightly wrapped around the means by which the nation pursues its foreign policy: multilateralism versus unilateralism. In an echo of the Bricker Amendment era, America in more recent years has displayed, once again, a suspicion toward international diplomacy. This time the revolt has been led not by southern and midwestern conservative lawmakers, but by the executive branch under President George W. Bush in alliance with neoconservative political thinkers and activists.[24] His administration has rejected a number of treaties widely supported by the international community. On occasion, credible arguments can be advanced by the United States for refusing to sign on with other nations in an international agreement; just because a majority of the world's governments may agree among themselves does not mean that the United States must tag along, against its own self-interests. However, when we have a persistent pattern of rejecting agreements that most of the world finds beneficial, we ought to be considering more seriously why we are usually out of step and if it is truly imperative to alienate so many friends overseas by our solitary behavior. While this behavior provides an illustration of unilateralism as well, the rejection of international pacts are examined more closely in this chapter because they suggest an American retreat from global responsibilities adopted by previous administration—a form of isolationism from the world's expanding network of international agreements.

For example, inside the Vienna-based Organization for Security and Cooperation in Europe (OSCE), the second Bush administration displayed hostility toward the principle of multilateral diplomacy in 2002 by attempting to impose a 15 percent reduction in OSCE's already thin budget, despite the important work this organization performs to reduce tensions and advance human rights in turbulent regions of Eastern Europe.[25] Further, the administration decided early in 2001 to abrogate an important arms agreement with the Soviet Union—the 1972 Anti-Ballistic Missile Treaty—so that the United States could move forward on the construction of a ballistic-missile defensive shield. This was a bilateral and not a multilateral treaty, and both parties had a right to abrogate with six-months notice under the terms of the pact; nevertheless, America's decision to dissolve this tie with another important military nation—a major treaty entered into by the Nixon administration and the Senate in 1972—further revealed the proclivity of the Bush administration to set the United States apart from partnerships with other nations.

Among the international agreements both Presidents Clinton and the second Bush have refused to submit to the Senate for approval are the 1997 Kyoto Protocol on Climate Change and the 1997 International Land Mine Treaty. The second Bush administration has also stalled on U.S. entry into the Rome Statute of the International Criminal Court (ICC); the Comprehensive Nuclear Test Ban Treaty; a program to curb trafficking in small arms; an agreement to improve primary education in poor nations; the Anti-Ballistic Missile Treaty; a new convention on cultural diversity; and a verification protocol supporting the Biological Weapons Convention. The United States remains the only developed nation that has failed to ratify the Basel Convention, a UN treaty intended to limit the trade of hazardous waste; and the Bush administration declined to join an international plan, sponsored by Britain, France, Spain, Italy, and Sweden, to raise $4 billion on the bond markets for expanding the use of vaccines across the developing world.[26] The United States has pressured some poor countries (Niger, for example) to join in its opposition to certain international agreements, like the ICC pact, by threatening to cut off development assistance.[27]

The Kyoto Accord provides an illustration of the United States as the odd man out. In December 2004, delegates from over 190 nations gathered in Buenos Aires at a UN conference to toast the passage of the Kyoto Protocol, which went into effect on February 16, 2005. It is the first treaty to mandate reductions in the greenhouse gases that scientists blame for global warming. Though an imperfect instrument (for example, it exempts major polluters like China and India on grounds that they are developing countries), the protocol is generally considered an important step toward improving the earth's environment. One of the treaty's central provisions requires industrialized nations to reduce their emissions of carbon dioxide gases in 2012 by at least 5 percent below 1990 levels. Europe and Japan have been especially enthusiastic about the environmental pact; and, after waffling for years, even Russia signed the treaty in hopes of improving trade relations with the European Union. The United States refuses, however, to accept the underlying scientific premise of the treaty, even though the science has been endorsed by virtually all other nations of the world, namely, that the earth is approaching a dangerous level of warming. Many American experts, including members of the Union of Concerned Scientists, have regularly sounded an alarm that humans are responsible for introducing a clear pattern of climate change that is likely to increase global warming. An increase in greenhouse emissions is associated with more frequent and severe global flooding, heat waves, and hurricanes. Rejection of the protocol made the United States an object of derision among the delegates at the Kyoto Protocol celebration in Buenos Aires. "It all underscores the necessity of all the communities of the world to work together to solve the world's worst problems," said a Pacific-island delegate at the conference.[28]

Less tactfully, Jeff Fiedler, an American observer representing the Washington-based Natural Resources Defense Council, declared that "this is a new low for the United States, not just to pull out, but to block other countries from moving ahead on their own path." He added: "It's almost spiteful to say, 'You can't move ahead without us.' If you're not going to lead, then get out of the way."[29] Dismissive of the criticism, U.S. delegates continued maneuvers at the session to block attempts that would have begun discussions about more detailed ways to slow down global warming. Had the United States offered a reasoned critique of the treaty (which is hardly perfect) and worked more closely with other nations in an attempt to modify its provisions, the rest of the world may have been less upset; instead, the American delegation managed to alienate other delegates with their dismissive attitude.

Most of the world, too, rejects the use of land mines, which have killed or maimed thousands around the world. Again, the United States refuses to enter into an international treaty banning land mines because the Pentagon finds them useful in some instances, especially on the Korean Peninsula as a deterrent against a North

Korean invasion of South Korea. Experts outside the Pentagon find it unlikely that land mines would stop North Korea, with its million-man army and nuclear weapons, if Pyongyang really wished to go to war. A stronger deterrent are the thirty-five thousand U.S. troops stationed in the Demilitarized Zone (DMZ) separating the two Koreas, along with America's own overwhelming nuclear deterrent. In the meantime, land mines take their daily toll of civilian casualties, often children, who play soccer on the fields or walk the pathways where the explosive devises have been laid over the years in Cambodia, Vietnam, and many other nations.

In 1998, another UN conference negotiated a treaty to establish an International Criminal Court.[30] If ratified by sixty nations, it would have jurisdiction over war crimes, crimes against humanity, and genocide. By 2002, more than enough nations (seventy-eight) had ratified the accord and the ICC is now operational. The United States has not ratified the agreement, fearful that America's enemies might try to use the Court to prosecute U.S. soldiers involved in peacekeeping operations abroad or in "legitimate" wars like the effort begun in 2003 to replace the dictatorship in Iraq with a democratic regime. President Clinton signed the treaty in 2000, but did not submit the document to a hostile Senate. Upon entering office in 2001, President George W. Bush renounced the treaty out of hand, drawing sharp criticism from the European Union, Amnesty International, and others. As Fukuyama puts it, "The United States was seeking to pass judgment on others while being unwilling to have its own conduct questioned in places like International Criminal Court."[31]

In March of 2005, Secretary of State Condoleezza Rice sent UN Secretary General Kofi Annan a letter that informed him the

United States had withdrawn from still another international agreement. This time the Bush administration objected to the jurisdiction of an international court over the claims of foreigners held in American jails.[32]

An American historian and Europeanist friendly toward the United States, Günter Bischof worries about "the willful destruction of the cooperative global system of alliances and international organizations that [George W. Bush's] father's generation had built after World War II."[33] Often forgotten in this rush to reject treaties and other international agreements are the advantages that can accrue to the United States from involvement with the rest of the world. The creation of an effective North Atlantic Treaty Organization (NATO) in 1949 is one of the most well-known examples. Another illustration, closer to home, of how Americans have benefited from international agreements is the North American Free Trade Agreement (NAFTA).[34] Implemented in 1994, the commercial pact has improved the flow of goods, services, and investments among the three signatory nations: Canada, the United States, and Mexico. NAFTA created the largest free-trade area in the world in terms of gross product, with commercial transactions in the region expanding dramatically by a factor of three. Today, trade among the three nations accounts for 86 percent of the gross product of the Americas; and trade between the United States and the two other nations is twice that of with Western Europe. NAFTA is not perfect and, above all, lacks a workable infrastructure—or hardly any infrastructure at all—to smooth out disagreements and misunderstandings among the three trading partners. Still, much of the horror predicted by NAFTA opponents never materialized, such as the substantial loss of American jobs to Mexico.

GUIDING PRINCIPLES FOR
AMERICAN FOREIGN POLICY

Despite the globalization of the world, isolationists have not gone the way of the dinosaurs. On the contrary, as Professor Schlesinger writes, "The collapse of the Soviet threat revived the prospect that haunted [Franklin] Roosevelt over half a century ago—a return to isolationism."[35] Nye notes, too, that since the terrorist attacks against the United States in 2001, ". . . isolationist and unilateral temptations remain."[36]

Mossbacked isolationism—a head-in-the-sand approach to world affairs—makes no sense in the present world of interdependent nations. Moreover, it harms the interests of the United States to reject out of hand treaties that the rest of the world finds important. It is not only a matter of unilateralism—preferring to act on one's own; it is a matter, as well, of isolationism from the sensibilities of people in other countries. A good example is the recent controversy over application of language from the Geneva Conventions in the adoption of U.S. detention rules for captured terrorists. The second Bush administration evidently wishes to avoid the Geneva Convention framework, arguing that torture should be allowed by American interrogators in the military and the intelligence agencies to extract information from enemies in order to try to prevent another 9/11 disaster. Virtually everyone agrees that in a "ticking bomb" scenario, it may be necessary to resort to torture. Yet to apply that standard to 99 percent of the other interrogation settings has the result of alienating other nations upon whom we must depend to work with us in the war against terrorism. As an anonymous administration official who opposes U.S. exception from the Geneva Conventions told the *New York Times*, the fight against terrorism relies upon "creating alliances," and America's abandonment of the Conventions has just the opposite effect.[37]

Despite the desirability of joining international coalitions for some purposes, prudence for Americans lies as well in honoring the instinct of caution that has been a part of America's heritage in foreign policy since the nation's earliest days: a wariness about becoming overcommitted abroad. Some of the most distinguished statesmen, scholars, and journalists in the United States have provided valuable counsel over the years about the danger of unnecessary interventions and entanglements abroad, without eschewing America's responsibilities as a leading power—navigating a course between the extremes of isolationism, on the one hand, and compulsive intervention (of the kind discussed in Chapter 3), on the other hand. Their collective wisdom on how to steer such a course is worth examing here.

Henry Kissinger, secretary of state for Presidents Nixon and Ford, has outlined three broad questions to guide the rational planning and "grand strategy" for America's external affairs:

What global changes is the United States prepared to resist?
What are this nation's goals?
What resources does the nation have to pursue these goals?[38]

Another of America's top scholars on foreign policy, political scientist Hans J. Morgenthau, gave nine sensible guideposts for U.S. diplomacy. He divided them into "rules of diplomacy" and "prerequisites of compromise":

Rules of Diplomacy

Diplomacy must be divested of the crusading spirit.

The objectives of foreign policy must be defined in terms of the national interest and must be supported with adequate power.

Diplomacy must look at the political scene from the point of view of other nations

Nations must be willing to compromise on all issues that are not vital to them.

Prerequisites of Compromise

Give up the shadow of worthless rights for the substance of real advantage.

Never put yourself in a position from which you cannot retreat without losing face and from which you cannot advance without grave risks.

Never allow a weak ally to make decisions for you. The armed forces are the instrument of foreign policy, not its master.

The government is the leader of public opinion, not its slave.[39]

Focusing more specifically on the military side of foreign affairs, President Reagan's Secretary of Defense Casper W. Weinberger laid out a widely discussed and generally accepted litany of restraints. Recalling the disaster of America's intervention in Vietnam, he proposed "six commandments" for war-fighting, known as the Weinberger Doctrine. According to Weinberger:

- The military action had to involve vital national interests;
- The United States must intend to win;

- The operation had to have clear-cut political-military objectives;
- These objective had to be subjected to a continual reassessment;
- The American people had to be in support; and,
- All alternatives to the use of overt force had to have been tried first and found wanting.[40]

However much politicians and experts alike endorsed these principles when they were first presented in 1987, few of them have been followed in America's intervention into Iraq in 2003.

Army General Colin L. Powell, later secretary of state in the second Bush administration, added two corollaries to the Weinberger Doctrine: the United States should use overwhelming force to achieve its objectives, and it should have a clear exit strategy. Powell's advocacy of overwhelming force raised serious questions since it is widely accepted that military arms ought to be applied only in a manner proportionate to the degree of military opposition one faces—part of the "just war" theory.[41] Critics, though, widely accepted the need for a good exit strategy in any military conflict—again, missing in the second Persian Gulf War. With respect to the use of secret paramilitary warfare by the CIA, another secretary of state, Cyrus Vance of the Carter administration, proposed this core guideline: "It should be the policy of the United States to engage in covert actions only when they are *absolutely essential* to the national security."[42]

Much sagacity lies in these prescriptions advanced by some of America's most experienced foreign policy officials and experts, speaking at the height of their careers. The earlier, but prescient, ruminations of journalist Walter Lippmann, set down in the middle of the Second World War, provide a thoughtful capstone to their counsel. Foreign policy success, Lippmann argued, depends upon a nation balancing its international commitments with its power. If a nation reaches beyond its means, it increases the probability of failure.[43] A modern-day expression of this grand strategy rule of thumb comes from historian John Lewis Gaddis, who advises that interests should not exceed actual capabilities.[44]

If anything should be self-evident from these insights, as well as from our foreign-policy experiences since the beginning of the twentieth century, it is that the United States is unable to shape the world to its liking. Yet, during the Cold War, leaders of the United States often acted otherwise. Operating at the opposite extreme from isolationism, some officials believed that America should have a presence practically everywhere around the globe, as a means of countering a possible Soviet presence—however remote a locale might be from the United States and its core interests. Here were the "zero-sum" advocates, who saw the world in black-and-white terms, as if the planet were merely an arena for mortal combat between the United States and the U.S.S.R. For those who shared this stark view of the world, every tremor of revolution in Chad, Grenada, or Nicaragua required a U.S. response, regardless of how small the nation, how large the loss of American lives, or how extensive the drain on the federal treasury. Little wonder the German Nobel Laureate for literature, Günter Grass, asked in anguish (with Nicaragua in mind): "How impoverished must a country be before it is not a threat to the U.S. government."[45]

If the United States is to restore its financial solvency and improve its sagging position in the global trading markets; if Americans are to regain the respect and devotion around the world that we once enjoyed following the Second World War; if we are to care for our own people—with one in eight Americans living in poverty, with America's population centers facing traffic gridlock, its lakes and rivers filled with pollutants, its teenage pregnancies and suicide rates still too high (though declining), its cities and byways plagued by illegal narcotics, and social security and health care begging for reform—then surely this nation must adopt a more discriminating approach to foreign intervention.

This is by no means an argument for a return to isolationism, but rather for a more thoughtful debate in the nation about how far America's commitments should extend overseas, especially in the light of so many pressing needs at home. The sin of isolationism is not the longing to return America from an overextended world posture; it is to adopt a policy of self-absorption at the expense of being a good global neighbor, such as supporting a worldwide effort to ban land mines and multilateral efforts to protect the global environment, while also being a good provider at home. Unilateralism means a failure to consult with and listen to other nations—to go it alone; isolationism means to go even further than that by withdrawing from, or eschewing, existing international institutions, agreements, responsibilities, and norms. They are twin evils that dismiss the possibilities of international cooperation.

Only the foolhardy would embrace a policy of neoisolationism in today's close-knit world, but consider these conditions inside the United States that cry out for attention. Since the end of the Cold War, federal spending has declined for job training, employment programs, and low-income housing. Moreover, five juveniles are murdered each day in this nation; 8.5 million American children (11.6 percent) are without health insurance; one-third of the young people who enter high schools never graduate. In some states, the graduation rate from high school for African Americans is less than 30 percent, and for Hispanics even lower. In the United States, 35.9 million people live below the poverty threshold. Consider Manhattan. The top fifth of income earners there make fifty-two times more than the lowest fifth: $465,826 compared with $7,047—the latter an income roughly equivalent to what one would find in Namibia.[46] Former President Jimmy Carter has reported that 45 percent of African Americans and other minorities in the United States live in poverty. He adds: "Forty percent of black males are functionally illiterate, and among younger adults, one-fourth are now in prison or on probation. Their chance of being killed by violence is greater than it was for the average soldier who went to Vietnam." The former president notes further that "twenty percent of the babies born at Grady Hospital in Atlanta, Georgia, are already addicted to crack cocaine."[47]

The $1.1 billion spent by the United States each week in Iraq during the second Persian Gulf War could have been spent in the United States, enabling 1.5 million students to attend college, providing 5.4 million poor children with meals for a year, and contributing to pressing homeland security needs such as influencing port and railroad defenses. "The sooner we learn to impose some reasonable restraint on our own tendency to intervene too much in other people's affairs," urged a member of the Senate Foreign Relations Committee some years ago, "the happier land we will have and the less burden we will place upon our own people to undertake sacrifices that are not really related to their own good or the good of their country."[48]

Beyond the financial costs lies the immutable fact that the Untied States can exercise only a limited influence over the affairs of other nations. America's experience in Indochina should have seared that lesson into the nation's memory. Despite an enormous commitment of resources to South Vietnam—the more than 58,000 GIs killed, the three hundred thousand injured, the untold number who continue to suffer from the effects of Agent Orange and other chemical defoliants used during the war, the soldiers with lasting psychiatric and drug disturbances[49]—a wide range of overt and covert force used by the United States proved unable to curb the internal corruption of the South Vietnamese government or unite its army into an effective fighting force. Now, History— the sternest of taskmasters—is repeating the lesson in Iraq.

Nevertheless, concern about America's overreach abroad should not lead the United States back to isolationism and a narrow concentration on domestic affairs. Two world wars have driven home the point that Americans cannot escape from the world, however much we may wish to at times. Instead, the concern should lead the nation toward a more discriminating foreign policy, one that will allow the United States to spend less on military operations abroad and more on foreign development and humanitarian assistance for poor nations. Less unwarranted involvement abroad would provide Americans, too, with the resources to address social problems at home, as well as strengthen the nation's harbors, railways, water supplies, crops, and nuclear reactors against terrorists, without continuing the dangerous pattern of cutting taxes—always politically popular but not necessarily fiscally sound—and borrowing money to pay for basic government services that citizens need, want, and deserve.

Wouldn't it make more sense for the United States to "intervene" abroad first with brigades of school, church, and home builders; with nurses, physicians, dentists, and other health care specialists; with teachers, farmers, economists, investment bankers, experts in governance, and technicians; with Foreign Service diplomats, Peace Corps volunteers, and nongovernment service agencies; and—only in the most pressing circumstances—with the CIA, the Marine Corps, or the Special Forces? Let America's guiding standard be the Marshall Plan—a mutually beneficial program that helped future allies find their economic legs again while, at the same time, opening markets for the United States. In union with every other civilized nation, let America answer the call from those in distress overseas from the threat of genocide. Let the wealthy nations respond to natural disasters, as Americans—in and out of the government—did so generously for the victims caught in the path of the terrible tsunamis that struck the Indian Ocean in the waning days of 2004. Let America's overarching objective be collective action with the other nations of the world in the support of a flourishing international commerce and liberal democratic institutions.

NOTES

1. Letter to the editor, *Athens Banner-Herald*, Athens, Georgia (September 10, 2002), p. A6, original emphasis. More recently, another writer rues the "billions [of U.S. dollars] given in the last half-century to ungrateful foreign aid recipients," letter to the editor, *Atlanta Journal Constitution* (March 1, 2006), p. A12.
2. Pat Buchanan, "Now that Red Is Dead, Come Home America," *Washington Post* (September 8, 1991), p. C1; see also Patrick J. Buchanan, *The Great Betrayal: How American Sovereignty and Social Justice Are Being Sacrificed to the Gods of the Global Economy* (Boston: Little, Brown, 1998).
3. Mary McGrory, "Americans Care about Combating Hunger," *International Herald Tribune* (August 2, 2002), p. 4; Alvin Richman, "American and

Russian Publics View Global Issues as Top Foreign Policy Goals," *U.S. Information Agency Report* (August 2, 1996), p. 1.

4. Bruce W. Jentleson, *American Foreign Policy: The Dynamics of Choice in the 21st Century*, 2nd ed. (New York: Norton, 2004).

5. John E. Rielly, ed., *American Public Opinion and U.S. Foreign Policy 1991* (Chicago: Chicago Council on Foreign Relations, 1991), p. 15, based on a December 1990 Gallup survey.

6. Richman, "American and Russian Publics," p. 1.

7. Francis Fukuyama, "After Neoconservatism," *New York Times Magazine* (February 19, 2006), p. 63.

8. Ole R. Holsti, "American Public Opinion and Foreign Policy: Did the September 11 Attacks Change Everything?" paper presented at the Hendricks Conference on "U.S. Foreign Policy in a Divided World," University of Nebraska, Lincoln, Nebraska (April 7–8, 2005), p. 13.

9. These figures are drawn by Holsti from *Global Views: American Public Opinion and Foreign Policy*, 2004 (Chicago: Chicago Council on Foreign Relations, 2004), Table 3.

10. Arthur H. Vandenberg, Jr., ed., *The Private Papers of Senator Vandenberg* (Boston: Houghton Mifflin, 1952), p. 67.

11. See Loch K. Johnson, *The Making of International Agreements: Congress Confronts the Executive* (New York: New York University Press, 1984); Henry Steele Commager, "The Perilous Folly of Senator Bricker," *The Reporter 9* (October 13, 1953), pp. 12–17.

12. The Bricker movement provides an illustration of how the "sins" examined in this volume can overlap and intertwine. The case is examined in some length here because it is a classic illustration of isolationism since the end of the Second World War, at a very high level of government.

13. Author's interview with Professor Francis M. Carney, University of California, Riverside, California (May 21, 1968). On the key Bricker Amendment vote in Congress, all but three of the twenty-two southern senators supported Senator Bricker. In 1984, conservative senators would again express their concern about an antigenocide treaty that might serve as a "pretext for foreign meddling in United States domestic affairs" [Martin Tolchin, "Senate Surprised on Genocide Pact," *New York Times* (September 14, 1984), p. A4].

14. Quoted in Henry Steele Commager, "The Perilous Folly of Senator Bricker," p. 15.

15. Johnson, *The Making of International Agreements*.

16. Walter Lippmann, "Today and Tomorrow," *Washington Post* (February 4, 1954), cited in the *Congressional Record*, 83d Cong., 2d Sess. (February 2, 1954), p. 1325.

17. Edwin S. Corwin, "The President's Treaty-Making Power," *Think* 19 (July 1953), p. 6.

18. *Congressional Record*, 83d Cong., 2d Sess. (February 2, 1954), p. 1103.
19. Stephen A. Garrett, "Foreign Policy and the American Constitution: The Bricker Amendment in Contemporary Perspective," *International Studies Quarterly* 16 (June 1972), pp. 198–199.
20. William S. White, "Senate Defeats All Plans to Check Treaty Powers, Final Vote Margin Is One Vote," *New York Times* (February 27, 1964), p. A15.
21. Louis W. Koenig, *The Chief Executive* (New York: Harcourt, Brace & World, 1964), p. 7.
22. Remarks, *Hearings*, Committee on the Judiciary, U.S. Senate, 82d Cong., 1st Sess., p. 145.
23. Testimony of Frank Holman, *Hearings*, Committee on the Judiciary, U.S. Senate, 85th Cong., 1st Sess., p. 423.
24. A point made by Fukuyama, "After Neoconservatism," pp. 62–67.
25. Author's interviews with OSCE senior officials, Vienna (July 9, 2002).
26. Celia W. Dugger, "Billions for Vaccines for the Poor to Be Raised in Bond Markets," *New York Times* (September 9, 2005), p. A10.
27. Nicholas D. Kristof, "Schoolyard Bully Diplomacy," *New York Times* (October 16, 2005), p. E13.
28. Quoted by Larry Rohter and Andrew C. Revkin, "Cheers, and Concern for New Climate Pact," *New York Times* (December 13, 2004), p. A6.
29. Quoted by Larry Rohter, "U.S. Waters Down Global Commitment to Curb Greenhouse Gases," *New York Times* (December 19, 2004), p. A6.
30. See Donald W. Jackson and Ralph G. Carter, "The International Criminal Court: Present at the Creation," in Ralph G. Carter, *Cases in U.S. Foreign Policy*, 2nd ed. (Washington, DC: CQ Press, 2005), pp. 363–388.
31. "After Neoconservatism," p. 66.
32. Samantha Power, "Boltonism: A Comment," *The New Yorker* (March 21, 2005), p. 24.
33. "American Empire and Its Discontents: The United States and Europe Today," in Michael Gehler, Günter Bischof, Ludger Kühnhardt, and Rolf Steininger, eds., *Towards a European Constitution: A Historical and Political Comparison with the United States* (Wien: Böhlau Verlag, 2005), p. 198.
34. These observations draw upon Robert Pastor, public lecture, Yale University (November 3, 2005).
35. Arthur M. Schlesinger, Jr., *War and the American Presidency* (New York: Norton, 2004), p. 15.
36. Joseph S. Nye, Jr., *The Paradox of American Power: Why the World's Only Superpower Can't Go It Alone* (New York: Oxford University Press, 2002), p. 135.
37. Tim Golden and Eric Schmitt, "Detainee Policy Sharply Divides Bush Officials," *New York Times* (November 2, 2005), p. A1.

38. Henry A. Kissinger, "Dealing from Reality," *Los Angeles Times* (November 22, 1987), sec. 5, p. 1.

39. Hans J. Morgenthau, *Politics among Nations: The Struggle for Power and Peace*, 4th ed. (New York: Knopf, 1967; first published in 1949), pp. 540–548.

40. See Bernard E. Trainor, "Weinberger on Persian Gulf: Cap the Chameleon," *New York Times* (October 9, 1987), p. A20; Thomas A. G. Patterson et al., *American Foreign Relations: A History Since 1985*, vol. 2 (Lexington, MA: D. C. Heath, 1995), p. 511.

41. See Joseph S. Nye, Jr., *Ethics and Foreign Policy: An Occasional Paper* (Wye Plantation, MD: Aspen Institute for Humanistic Studies, 1985); John Rawls, *A Theory of Justice* (Cambridge, MA: Harvard University Press, 1971).

42. Cyrus Vance, testimony, "Covert Action," *Hearings*, Select Committee to Study Governmental Operations with Respect to Intelligence Activities, U.S. Senate (December 4, 1975), emphasis added.

43. See, for example, Walter Lippmann, *U.S. Foreign Policy: Shield of the Republic* (Boston: Little, Brown, 1943), pp. 7–8.

44. John Lewis Gaddis, *Surprise, Security, and the American Experience* (Cambridge, MA: Harvard University Press, 2004).

45. Quoted in *The Nation* (March 12, 1983), p. 301.

46. Sam Roberts, "In Manhattan, Poor Make 2 Cents for Each Dollar to the Rich," *New York Times* (September 4, 2005), p. 33 (Metro Section).

47. Jimmy Carter, State of Human Rights Address 1991, a paper delivered by the former president (December 8, 1991), Carter-Menil Human Rights Prize ceremony, Houston, Texas, reprinted in the *Georgia Review* 46 (Spring 1992), p. 4.

48. Senator Frank Church (D-ID), public address, Boise, Idaho (August 6, 1972).

49. See Charles Figley and Seymour Levintman, eds., *Strangers at Home: Vietnam Veterans Since the War* (New York: Praeger, 1980), pp. 213–228; Loch K. Johnson, "Political Alienation Among Vietnam Veterans," *Western Political Quarterly* 29 (September 1976), pp. 398–409; Daniel A. Pollock, Philip Rhodes, Colleen A. Boyle, Pierre Decoufle, and Daniel L. McGee, "Estimating the Number of Suicides among Vietnam Veterans," *American Journal of Psychiatry*, 147 (June 1990), pp. 772–776.

CHAPTER 6

Lack of Empathy

A WORLD OF DISEASE
AND DEPRIVATION

Former president Jimmy Carter cautioned Americans in 1988 about "the increasing disharmony and lack of understanding between rich and poor nations."[1] The disparity is increasing, as lamented in opening speeches by several world leaders at the UN World Summit on Sustainable Development held in Johannesburg in 2002. Beneath the anguished rhetoric heard at the Summit lies the harsh reality of a skewed income distribution among the inhabitants of this planet. Among the indicators: the world's wealthiest five hundred individuals have the same combined income as the world's poorest 416 million people.[2]

Five billion of the world's six billion people live in developing nations. The statistics on their lives are grim. A UN study released in 2002 reported that 2.8 billion live on less than $2 a day. That figure includes half the women of the world: 1.5 billion individuals. As many as 1.2 billion men and women eke out an existence on just $1 a day.[3] In comparison, a cow in the European Union receives a daily government subsidy greater than what the world's poor live on ($2.20 a day) and the American government paid more in farm subsidies to its twenty thousand cotton growers in 2005 ($4.7 billion) than the total amount of U.S. aid to Africa.[4] Many women in poor countries are forced into prostitution as the only hope of earning money to feed their children.[5]

Many people around the globe lack much formal education. In countries such as Benin, Guatemala, Haiti, Morocco, Pakistan, and Uganda, less than 30 percent of adults age 25 and over have completed primary school.[6]

Disease in poor nations is rampant.[7] Malaria, a mosquito-borne disease, kills anywhere from 1 to 2.2 million people a year—most of them children—and is the number-one killer in sub-Saharan Africa.[8] Each day, some two thousand children under the age of five succumb to the disease—40 children each half hour.[9] In the Democratic Republic of Congo alone, some one thousand people die every day of preventable diseases like malaria and diarrhea.[10] The second Bush administration has received high marks among malaria-watchers for proposing to spend $1.2 billion over five years to fight malaria in fifteen African countries, chiefly for treated nets, indoor spraying, and a combination of drugs; still, the Roll Back Malaria campaign initiated by the World Health Organization (WHO) and other international health and development agencies in 1998 has proved sluggish. Indeed, more people are suffering from the disease now than when the campaign began.[11]

Almost three million people, mostly in the developing world, died of tuberculosis in 1995, surpassing the worst years of the tuberculosis epidemic that swept the earth at the beginning of the twentieth century. In sub-Saharan Africa, a region raked with tetanus, whooping cough, and measles—diseases all but unknown in wealthy nations—20 percent of all children never reach their fifth birthday. Acute respiratory infections also stalk the young; and polio, stamped out in the United States, is responsible for crippling some two hundred thousand children a year in the poorer nations. Just in 2000, 11.1 million children under the age of five died from preventable diseases.[12]

The AIDS epidemic has claimed about as many victims—almost forty million[13]—as the Black Death in Europe in the mid-fourteenth century. Five million people died of the disease in 2004. Around 95 percent of AIDS-infected individuals live in the developing world. As reported by UNAIDS (an arm of the World Health Organization), each day HIV strikes about six thousand young people between the ages of 15 and 24, along with two thousand children under 15.[14] "Every minute of every day a child dies of an AIDS-related illness," reports Celia W. Dugger of the *New York Times*.[15] According to UN documentation, AIDS has undergone a "feminization" in recent years, with women and girls now comprising just under half of the 40 million people around the world currently infected with HIV.[16]

Sub-Saharan Africa is the home of 28.1 million people with the HIV/AIDS virus. In the Sauri region of western Kenya, AIDS has stricken fully 30 percent of the population.[17] Upon returning from a trip to Zambia in 1991, former President Jimmy Carter reported that in the city of Janeiro "twenty-three percent of the babies are born with the AIDS virus."[18] In South Africa, an estimated seven hundred thousand children have become orphans as a result of their parents dying from AIDS.[19] The Caribbean is the location of the world's second-highest HIV infection rate; in 2000, half a million children in this part of the world died from AIDS, while another half-million became newly infected (primarily from mother-to-child transmissions).[20]

The HIV virus undermines resistance to infections. Within eight years, those initially infected with HIV/AIDS in 2004 will succumb to the disease's terrible, debilitating effects. That year, 2012, a "tidal wave of illness and death" is expected to sweep across sub-Saharan Africa.[21] In locations where treatment for AIDS is unavailable, the infection-to-death cycle can be as short as three years.

Nor is the more developed world immune from this pandemic, with the incidence of HIV/AIDS climbing rapidly in Asia, India, and Russia. Once a country inches up to a level of 1.0 percent AIDS in its adult population, it reaches a tipping point. The infection rate then accelerates quickly, in a logarithmic increase, to engulf 25 percent of the population—the fate that Asia, India, and Russia now face.[22] For example, a decade ago, South Africa took about six years to go from a 0.5 to a 1.0 percent HIV infection in the adult population. Once arriving at the 1.0 percent threshold, the disease rapidly shot up to infect a quarter of the population. China is also moving along the lines of the South African experience. By 2010, it is expected to have ten million HIV cases, unless it takes dramatic action to stem the tide through prevention methods.[23] North America has had more success in combating AIDS, thanks both to its affluence and its state-of-the-art pharmaceutical companies. However, this region, too, has over a million people with the disease, which is especially prevalent in black communities.[24]

These statistics can be numbing. They coldly reflect enormous human suffering that can be understood only by departing from the aggregate numbers and peering into the lives of specific individuals who have suffered from AIDS. One of the most well-known was twelve-year-old Nkosi Johnson, an eloquent, intelligent young man from KwaZulu-Natal in South Africa. Nkosi died of AIDS in 2001. The year before his death, he spoke movingly of his struggle against the disease at the International AIDS Conference in Durban. His words and his courage inspired millions in Africa and across the continents to take up the fight he eventually lost.[25]

Among the more than two million children stricken with HIV is eleven-year-old Ntokozo, who lives in Lavumisa, Swaziland. He should be attending school in the third grade. Instead, as the *New York Times* reports,

> . . . he lies on the floor of his one-room hut, his knees swollen like baseballs and his mouth pitted with sores. His mother, who died in May, infected him with H.I.V., either during her pregnancy or later as he helped tend her oozing sores. His sister, Nkululeko Masimula, 26, wanted a job. "I wanted to have my own business; to be a hairdresser or a wholesaler," she said. Instead, she tends her brother and their 61-year-old grandmother. She sells the family's chickens to raise money for food. Finding the $20 a month required to take her brother to the nearest anti-retroviral drug site, 60 miles away, is a pipe dream.[26]

Slowing and then reversing the HIV/AIDS rates worldwide will take bold international leadership, better access to antiretroviral drugs and microbicides (vaginal gels and creams that can prevent infection), more health workers, and, of course, money to pay for health care. Currently about $6 billion is spent around the globe combating this disease, a remarkable amount; however, double that funding is deemed necessary to achieve success.[27] In 2004, the United States contributed the most to the fund for emergency AIDS relief (a $1.2 billion pledge), twice as much as all the rest of the donor governments combined. The $200 million proposed by the Bush administration for 2005, though, represents a sharp decline in U.S. support and is widely viewed as a disappointing contribution from the world's wealthiest nation, sending the wrong signal to other potential donors.[28]

Malnutrition, too, is a constant specter that haunts the planet. In the 1980s, ABC Television's "Evening News" reported on the frequency of death among children as a result of inadequate nutrition.[29] According to these figures, in the minute it will take to read this paragraph, twenty-eight children will die somewhere in the world from a combination of malnutrition and disease—a shocking roster of forty thousand deaths of the young every day. These statistics have failed to improve in the intervening years.[30] Much of this tragic loss—about 80 percent—can be traced to a simple lack of clean drinking water.[31] More than a billion people have no access to clean water, leading to the deaths of six thousand children each day from diarrhea and other water-related diseases.[32] In Southern Africa, between 12 and 14 million people are at risk of serious illness because of malnutrition.[33] Famine continues to plague Africa, most recently in the war-torn Darfur region of Sudan.

Moreover, childbearing presents a great danger to mothers in the developing world, with a woman in Africa having a one-in-three to one-in-eighteen chance of dying (the statistics vary, depending upon where the woman lives in Africa) during pregnancy and child-birth, compared to one-in-2,400 in Europe.[34] Around the world, half a million women unnecessarily perish each year in childbirth.[35]

As one would anticipate from these statistics, life expectancy is substantially lower in poor nations; for instance, only 39 years in Sierra Leone.[36] In Swaziland, a kingdom in the northeast of South Africa, life expectancy averages 34.4 years and experts predict that by 2010 the average will be 30 years. In Zimbabwe, the average is only 33.1 years, and in Zambia, 32.4 years.[37] According to UN estimates, in six sub-Saharan nations, most individuals will never live long enough to celebrate their fortieth birthday.[38]

There *are* solutions to many of the world's health-related problems. "It's not as though there is nothing to be done about it," writes Tom Teepen, an Atlanta-based newspaper editorialist who has examined the challenge of disease and hunger in the developing world. "An easily used oral rehydration packet can end diarrhea for just 10 cents. Imagine that. Saving a child's life for a lousy dime. Children can be immunized against the standard menu of preventable diseases for just $5 each. The price of a movie ticket can buy life and a healthy childhood."[39] The director of the Earth Institute at Columbia University, Jeffrey Sachs, points out that the use of mosquito bed nets impregnated with insecticide would prevent over a million children from dying of malaria each year. The cost: about $2 to 3 billion per annum, or approximately $2–3 per person from the rich nations.[40]

The Carter Center in Atlanta has demonstrated how dramatic improvements can be made in the well–being of poor people over-seas. In Ghana and Nigeria, the microscopic larvae of a worm often present in drinking water can infect humans. A year after ingesting the parasite, a worm up to a yard long emerges through the victim's skin, bringing about great discomfort and debilitating sores. Former President Carter turned to the U.S. company DuPont and Precision Fabrics for help. The company agreed to manufacture thousands of yards of filters to strain the guinea-worm larvae from ponds, producing a pure drinking water. The filters and related programs have reduced the cases of guinea-worm disease by more than 30 percent. One of the outcomes of the project is that farmers and workers in the two African nations are now much more productive.[41]

In addition to innovative programs like this one, slowing the world's population explosion would greatly ease the problems of world hunger and the sense of desperation that overshadows poor countries. Currently, world population is growing at a rate of one billion people every eleven years! The developing nations—those in the worst shape to deal with burgeoning population growth— will see the most alarming increases in birth rates. As historian Paul Kennedy notes, 95 percent of the projected doubling of the world's total population between now and the middle of the next century "will take place in developing lands."[42]

CATTLE CARS AND
FIRST-CLASS COACHES

While the poor nations of the world are locked in a vise of poverty and poor health, television saturates the globe with images of a luxurious lifestyle in the rich nations. Smiling American families are shown at home in their comfortable suburban dwellings with well-trimmed lawns. In the driveways are oversized vans, SUVs, and pickup trucks. The media carry reports across the world's latitudes about the luxurious lifestyle enjoyed by Western elites—rooms in Las

Vegas hotels that cost $1,500 a night or more; parties in New York City with corporate tables selling for $150,000; galas in Washington, DC, where maids fill toilet bowls with freshly chopped carnations after every flush; high schoolers in Long Island, New York, shelling out $20,000 to rent a house in the Hamptons for a post-prom party.[43] "We can't realistically hope to achieve security and stability in a world where more than half a billion people exist in poverty and hunger," declared Representative Mickey Leland (D-TX), when he served as chair of the U.S. House Select Committee on Hunger.[44] It is not difficult to understand why resentment and envy churn among the world's have-nots.

Economist Robert L. Heilbroner once compared the planet to "an immense train, in which a few passengers, mainly in the advanced capitalist world, ride in first-class coaches, in conditions of comfort unimaginable to the enormously greater numbers jammed into the cattle cars that make up the bulk of the train's carriages."[45] Too often, selfish elites within the developing world itself contribute to this alienation, such as Mobuto Sese Seko of Zaire, who pick-pocketed billions of dollars in foreign aid from his national treasury.

The widening divide between the haves and the have-nots has spawned a generation of underprivileged, resentful young men and women angered by the squalid lives their families or their fellow countrymen must endure—a prime reservoir for the recruitment of terrorists.[46] By addressing more resolutely the underlying conditions of poverty and disease in the developing nations, the affluent nations can help to excise the cancer of despair in the developing countries before it metastasizes into acts of violence. Thomas L. Friedman vividly states the case for being empathetic: "In today's globalized world, if you don't visit a bad neighborhood, it will visit you."[47]

Native Americans speak of walking in another person's moccasins, visualizing life from that individual's point of view. As a nation, the United States must exhibit greater empathy toward the woeful situation faced by others around the world—not in the sense of feeling a condescending sympathy, but rather by striving to understand better their hopes and fears, and by offering a helping hand. America's remarkable secretary of state after the Second World War, George C. Marshall, brought to his job an admirable capacity for empathy. In preparation for his 1947 Harvard University commencement address announcing the European Recovery Program (later known as the Marshall Plan), he crossed out a reference to "the Communist threat," a phrase which an aide had placed in a draft of the speech. Instead, the global enemies Marshall chose to list were "hunger, poverty, desperation, and chaos."[48] Yet his sage approach to foreign affairs has been shunted aside, as funding for international assistance has dwindled in most of the developed world. With the exception of Denmark, "there isn't a country in the world that devotes even 1.0 percent of its gross domestic product to helping poor countries," reported Michael Ignatieff in 2002, "—the U.S. is nearly at the bottom of the pile, spending a derisory 0.1 percent of GDP."[49] Since then, even Denmark has slipped below the 1.0 percent threshold.[50] The rich nations have been stingy.

For many decades, the United States has sold more weapons abroad than any other country. Yet President George W. Bush has pointed to literacy and learning as "the foundation of democracy and development."[51] Rather than being the premier salesman of weapons, what if America was better known for assisting other nations in building schools and libraries? Hospitals and health clinics? Churches and mosques? What about securing clean water for villages across Africa and Asia? Or building highways in Afghanistan, with construction projects that would pay local tribesmen a decent salary for a day's work and give them something more to do than shoot at each other (not to mention international aid workers and U.S. troops), while at the same time knitting together the geographical regions of a fragmented nation? America's military services are important instruments of foreign policy; but, for different reasons, so is the diplomatic corps. And so are U.S. businesspeople who, ideally in joint ventures with indigenous entrepreneurs, can provide jobs and hope for laborers in developing countries. The news of activities like these would spread throughout the developing world, doing more to win adherents to democracy and the United States than all the "democracy promotion" PR campaigns the government can devise.

TUNNEL VISION

Over the years, the United States has tended to ignore most of the world and its conditions of poverty while focusing on one or two primary threats. At times this has been sensible, in fact mandatory, for the security of the nation. In the early days of the Cold War, for instance, the Soviet Union and China—behemoth communist powers—bore all the hallmarks of highly threatening adversaries to America and its allies, with burgeoning stockpiles of WMDs, large armies, and harsh anti-American rhetoric. By the 1970s, however, the world no longer reflected the same zero-sum qualities: that either the communists or the capitalists would lose the Cold War with no possibility for coexistence. A policy of détente between the superpowers looked promising and was advocated by President Richard M. Nixon, renowned for his staunch anti-communist views throughout his earlier political career. The time seemed propitious for the peaceful settlement of America's differences with the Soviet Union and China.

This thaw in U.S.-Communist relations provided an opportunity for U.S. government officials to confront more directly the problem of disparities in wealth and health between the rich and poor nations, rather than viewing the developing world as chiefly a superpower battleground where U.S. security assistance to prop up anti-communist autocrats trumped development assistance for the poor. The Reagan administration took some steps in this direction, as the United States pushed the Uruguay Round of GATT talks in 1986 and promoted the Montreal Protocols on the global environment in 1987.

Yet even into the 1980s, many Americans remained mired in the Cold War, still viewing every manifestation of unrest and change in the world through a zero-sum lens. For example, during the 1980s, a right-wing organization in Oklahoma filled the radio airwaves with attacks against Representative James R. Jones (D-OK). The lawmaker's transgression: he had raised doubts about U.S. support to the contras, a ragtag army of mainly former indigenous security forces trying to overthrow the Marxist-leaning government in Nicaragua. "President Reagan's exactly right," said the ads, "... but your Congressman, Jim Jones, doesn't see the consequences of having a communist regime only two days' driving time from Texas. . . . For America's sake, call Congressman Jones right now."[52]

A 1988 fund-raising letter from President Reagan's Political Victory Fund praised conservative senators as "the few who are strong enough to stand up to the threat of Communism and say 'No Further!'" The letter claimed that, in contrast, "liberals" offered only "appeasement for the Communists" and a "crippled, weakened defense."[53] The rhetoric came straight out of the 1950s—an ongoing canonical obsession with the dangers of Soviet world conquest. Even though the world had changed dramatically from that era, the belief persisted that the Red Army, like nature, abhorred a vacuum and would seek to fill every global nook and cranny if the United States failed to check its aggression.

This obsession was hardly limited to extremist groups on the fringe right. America "cannot relax for a minute," warned Caspar W. Weinberger, President Reagan's secretary of defense. The United States had to guard against Soviet advances in every corner of the globe. "If you don't deal with it, they get a foothold."[54] Troops in Lebanon, the Grenada invasion, an American armada in the Persian Gulf without strategy or timetable—practically all forms of foreign intervention during the Reagan years became justified as part of a renewed Cold War crusade against the Soviet Union and other communist states.

In reality, communism was fading as an imminent threat to the United States. In 1986, Daniel Patrick Moynihan (D-NY), a member of the Senate Foreign Relations Committee, noted that "the one enormous fact of the third quarter of the 20th century [is] the near complete collapse of Marxism as an ideological force in the world."[55] A Democratic candidate for president in 1988, former Arizona governor Bruce Babbitt, stressed in his campaign speeches that "Marxism as an economic theory has been a total, unqualified flop everywhere."[56] Even President Reagan came to accept this view near the end of his presidency, after slipping in the public opinion polls as a result of the Iran-contra scandal. In 1988, he retracted his characterization of the Soviet Union as an "evil empire"[57] and pursued better relations between the superpowers, beginning with an agreement to eliminate intermediate-range nuclear weapons in Europe.

The Soviet Union had experienced only limited success abroad over the years since its consolidation of power in Eastern Europe. The only time since 1945 that the Kremlin sent troops directly into another nation outside of its established empire—Afghanistan—was a stunning failure. In 1989, after a decade of warfare, the Soviet Union finally abandoned its "pacification campaign"—the most costly Soviet military operation since the Second World War—following extensive losses in the field in battles against local mujahedeen guerrilla forces.[58] A CIA paramilitary operation to supply weapons, especially sophisticated Stinger and Blowpipe handheld antiaircraft missiles, to the mujahedeen probably accelerated the Soviet withdrawal; still, even without these modern weapons in the hands of Afghan warriors, the war had become a Vietnam-like quagmire for the Red Army, holding little prospect for victory.

In the decades following the Second World War, the Soviet "empire" had remained relatively static. Its domination was limited to the Eastern European bloc and Mongolia; within this domain, nations such as Poland and Yugoslavia—and even the tiny Baltic states of Estonia, Latvia, and Lithuania—sorely tested the Kremlin's ability to hold together its existing territories, let alone succeed in other foreign ventures. The once obedient Cuba also drifted farther and farther away from Soviet influence during the 1980s. The Kremlin faced a bleak reality during the Cold War: the U.S.S.R. was bordered not by a Canada or a Mexico, but rather by thirteen hostile nations, along with several antagonistic "republics" (states) and ethnic groups within its own borders.

During the long period of Soviet stasis, followed by decline, the United States could have shifted more of its attention, resources, and energy away from an overwhelming fixation on anti-communism and toward such important global issues as international trade, world health, global environmental pollution, refugee migration, food supplies, and population control. "The struggle between the Soviet Union and the West may become less central," predicted diplomat David D. Newsom before the Soviet breakup, "as both camps look over their shoulders at circumstances outside their experience."[59] Tunnel vision, coupled with a tendency in some quarters to demonize the communist threat even after its early virulent phases, prevented officials in Washington, DC (and Moscow, which suffered from its own bouts of worst-case scenarios regarding the West) from taking serious steps toward a lasting détente between the superpowers and reaching out to the forgotten parts of the world.

SEPARATING THE REAL DEMONS
FROM THE IMAGINED

Of course, even today the lingering capacity of the Russian republic to destroy the United States in a thirty-minute hailstorm of long-range missiles can hardly be ignored. That is one of the reasons America must maintain a nuclear and conventional deterrent, although not at the towering levels of weapons currently in the stockpile. The post-Cold War era, however, requires a new definition of national security, nothing less than a redrawing of the blueprint for U.S. relations abroad that goes beyond a simplistic concentration on global terrorism. Naturally, the new approach must maintain a prudent military shield; but it should reach out more energetically and sincerely for closer ties to other nations, particularly those in the developing world. The United States must practice a diplomacy that places empathy, in the sense of both sympathy and understanding, at the center of its outlook on the rest of the globe, a diplomacy that searches for partnerships in the common battle against Secretary Marshall's four dark horsemen of international despair: hunger, poverty, desperation, and chaos.

The first step is for the United States to slough off the siege mentality that characterized the Cold War and is beginning to grip Americans again in the struggle against international terrorism. Post-9/11 tunnel vision—looking upon the whole world as mainly a battleground against Al Qaeda—can once more diminish the chances for fresh approaches to foreign policy. Americans must try harder to comprehend the historical experiences, cultures, and world views of other peoples. Al Qaeda leads the list of major threats facing the United States but, for the people of Africa, AIDS and hunger loom much larger. Even America's close friends, the Canadians, are more concerned about improving health care in their country than about the war in Iraq—which, in fact, the government of Canada openly opposed. Citizens of the United States must appreciate these differences in perspectives and not reject them out of hand, just because they fail to align neatly with our own.

Consider the failures of Washington and Moscow to empathize with one another during the Cold War,[60] at least until Presidents Reagan and Mikhail Gorbachev finally decided to make peace. Had we pondered the staggering loss of life suffered by Soviet citizens during the Second World War—upward of 27 million fatalities—the United States might have appreciated better the concern of Russian citizens for the future defense of their borders. If one minute of silence were observed for each Russian killed in that war, the silence would last for over forty years. While this in no way excuses the brutality inflicted upon the Baltic states, Eastern Europe, and other Russian neighbors by Joseph Stalin and the Red Army after the Second World War (not to mention their own citizens), it does underscore the magnitude of the Russian suffering caused by Hitler and the predictably paranoid response of the Kremlin to the growing military might of NATO in Europe. Americans might have considered the likely effect of the anti-Soviet rhetoric that so often came out of Washington during the Cold War; and the worry that the Strategic Defense Initiative might instill in the minds of Russians, who could easily misinterpret a ballistic-missile defense system as a component of a U.S. first-strike strategy.

Conversely, Soviet citizens and their leaders might have considered more seriously the effect on Americans of the Kremlin's own hostile rhetoric, along with its vigorous arms build-up, the billions of rubles worth of weaponry provided to Cuba and Nicaragua (among other nations), a ballistic missile defense system of its own that in some aspects violated the 1972 Anti-Ballistic Missile Treaty, and an extensive system of civil defense facilities in Moscow—underground bomb shelters—that could have been interpreted by some in the United States as a preparation for nuclear war. The Soviet Union did represent a potential threat to the United States and had to be taken seriously throughout the Cold War but the added dimension of demonizing on both sides of the "iron curtain" contributed unnecessarily to an exaggerated fear of one another.[61]

In what ways today is the United States inflating the threats posed by other nations (China, for example), at the expense of foreign-policy initiatives to help poor nations? How well do Americans really understand the motivations of Islamic fundamentalism? Israel is a close friend and ally of the United States and always will be (it is the only liberal democracy in the Middle East); but, do we adequately comprehend how America's lopsided support for the Israelis incites distrust and anger among Arabs, especially when the weapons the United States sells to Israel are used to bomb Palestinian neighborhoods? Can we appreciate why religious fundamentalists in Saudi Arabia might balk at the stationing of U.S. military forces so near to their holy cities of Mecca and Medina? To what extent did we try—really try—to seek diplomatic negotiations between Kuwait and Iraq before the first Persian Gulf War? What if a UN peacekeeping force had set up camp along the Kuwaiti border before the war; would Iraq still have attacked? It seems unlikely. What if the United States had been more patient in 2003, giving UN weapons inspectors time—say, nine months—to find out if Iraq really did possess unconventional weapons?

Empathetic diplomacy, not noisy saber-rattling, ought to be the hallmark of America's foreign relations in the twenty-first century. The handshake of the economic deal and the diplomatic agreement must replace the mailed fist—here is the thread that runs through the chapters of this book.

Unfortunately, some violence-prone dictators and terrorist leaders will continue to understand only the use of force. The Serbian aggression against its neighbors in the 1990s is an illustration, properly thwarted by the United States, the UN, and NATO. For the despoilers of the international peace who attack sovereign nations, the civilized world must learn to respond bravely, promptly, and cohesively to restore order. Neither *Anschluss* nor invasion can be tolerated, since history has taught us how they lead only to further aggression and widening chaos. Severe economic sanctions should be the first step against a rogue nation or group. If such measures fail, the international community, working together through the auspices of the United Nations and legitimate regional authorities, will have to apply increasing levels of punishment—and military force, as a last measure—until the pariah is brought to justice. This will take hard work, diplomatic skill, patience, and, above all, a willingness to consult with, listen to, and accommodate our friends and allies as best we can, without jeopardizing America's own security. Adlai Stevenson's observation in the 1950s is just as valid today: the item of technology most needed by the United States is a hearing aid.

REACHING OUT

One important way of reaching out to the world's poor nations is to help them develop their economies. "The total cost in tax dollars for all our security and economic assistance programs in the developing countries is $43.91 per person," noted Secretary of State George P. Schulz during the Reagan administration. "In contrast," he continued, "we Americans spend $104 per person a year for TV and radio sets, $35 per person per year for barbershops and beauty parlors, $97 per person per year for soap and cleaning supplies, and $21 per person per year for flowers and potted plants."[62] A big part of the problem is that America's leaders have done a poor job explaining to the American people the good reasons for higher levels of foreign aid. Public opinion polls indicate that when Americans are informed about how little the nation spends on development assistance, they say they would support increased amounts.[63]

The United States is the richest nation in the world, but ranks with Japan as among the least generous donors to development assistance, at 0.16 of its gross domestic product (GDP).[64] (For the Marshall Plan, the United States appropriated funds equivalent to about 2.0 percent of GDP to rebuild Europe.) Only Italy is ranked lower than the United States among the industrialized nations. The U.S. government donates only about $16 billion each year for development assistance, compared to the $450 billion that it appropriates for the military—or compared to the $11 billion Americans spend on their pets.[65] This 28-to-1 ratio of military to foreign aid spending by the United States has led Jeffrey D. Sachs, an American economist appointed by the UN as head of its antipoverty Millennium Project, to lament that Americans have become "all war and no peace in our foreign policy."[66]

The second Bush administration has provided more foreign aid annually than did the Clinton administration; indeed, the amount of money the United States gave to developing countries plunged to its lowest levels in a generation during the Clinton years.[67] The Bush administration spent 16 cents for foreign aid out of every $100 of GDP versus 10 cents in the final months of the Clinton administration. Under President Bush, U.S. aid to Africa has almost tripled. Moreover, the Bush administration took steps to ease the burden of debt in Africa, eliminating $40 billion of debt owed by eighteen of the world's poorest nations (including fourteen in Africa), and it has done more than any of its predecessors to fight sex trafficking.[68] Still, the Bush administration exaggerates the degree of America's generosity by trying to cast the discussion of foreign aid in terms of the aggregate amount of funds spent worldwide each year. From this vantage point, the United States rises to the top of the list of international donors, simply because even its anemic 0.16 percent of GDP is a considerable amount of money compared to other nations, because of America's great wealth.

In 2002, the Bush administration pledged a 50 percent increase in foreign aid by 2006, embodied in a new initiative called the Millennium Challenge Account (MCA). Moreover, the administration has said it will spend another $15 billion to fight AIDS in Africa and the Caribbean. Based on these programs and aggregate figures, Secretary of State Colin L. Powell was able to argue that the United States alone accounted for more than 65 percent of all the economic development activities carried out by the Group of Seven (G-7, which is the G-8 minus Russia), and that America leads the world in the struggle against AIDS by spending twice as much as the rest of the world's donor governments.[69]

A third of the way into the MCA program, however, the United States had contributed only 0.16 percent of its national income (with Great Britain at 0.34, France at 0.41, Sweden at 0.79, and Norway at 0.92). Similarly, the Bush administration earned praise for trying to get a portion of American food aid to starving people more rapidly and efficiently (an initiative rejected by the Congress in 2005) but, at the same time, the United States reneged on its levels of commitment to food aid programs.[70] Most distressing of all, though, is the fact that not a single penny of the funding targeted for Africa by the MCA program in 2002 has been spent.[71] Even though the second Bush administration kept its promise to increase U.S. aid by a half (from 0.1 to 0.16 of GDP), that remains the smallest percentage among major donor nations.[72]

Few economists and certainly few nations around the world put as much stock in the aggregate aid expenditures as does the Bush administration; the more meaningful figure is considered the percentage of GDP. As the *New York Times* observes, ". . . no one is impressed when a billionaire writes a $50 check for a needy family."[73] More telling is how much a nation spends as a function of what it can afford to spend. This is where the United States falters. This is not to say that Americans are lacking in generosity. The outpouring of private and public funds from across the United States to help the victims of the December 2004 tsunami disaster belies that conclusion. It does mean, however, that as a nation we lag significantly behind the target of spending set for governments in the UN's Millennium Development Goals and endorsed by leading development specialists around the world, namely: 0.7 percent of GDP for aid to poor countries. This recommended goal for the well-to-do nations is estimated to be enough to cut global poverty in half over the next decade.[74]

Currently, the United States spends the equivalent of about 16 cents out of every $100 of income on development assistance; meeting the 0.7 goal would require a still reasonable spending level of about 50 cents per every $100 of income.[75] Looked at from another vantage point, the United States could meet the goal of the UN antipoverty plan if each American contributed "less than the cost of buying a cappuccino from Starbucks once a week."[76] The question is: are Americans willing to sacrifice what amounts to a cup of coffee in order to save the lives of the 20,000 individuals who currently perish from extreme poverty each day?[77] The failure of President Bush to even mention specifically development aid to Africa in his 2005 or 2006 State of the Union address is not a hopeful sign.

Some argue that if you add aid from nongovernmental organizations based in the United States, Americans rise much higher on the list of donors to international development. Not true, according to economist Jeffrey Sachs. The overall level of U.S. development assistance—public plus private—is about 20 cents out of every $100, leaving the United States on the next-to-lowest rung among industrialized nations, with only Italy ranking lower.[78] As sometimes happens in government and media reports, it is misleading as well to fold in—as part of the aggregate American development assistance figures—military aid, assistance to nondeveloping nations, and remittances sent to poor nations from people who come to the United States to work, thereby inflating the true level of aid dispensed by the United States to the low-income countries of the world.

THE UPS AND DOWNS OF U.S. FOREIGN AID

A sense of humanitarianism—a willingness to help those in the world who are less fortunate—has long been an important strand in the American religious tradition and has fortified proponents of a robust foreign aid program. Important, too, is a more self-interested motivation. As part of the containment doctrine designed to contain international communism, Washington officials decided early in the Cold War that the United States would need to strengthen governments around the world to make them more pro-West and less vulnerable to Soviet influence. In reference to America's own neighborhood, diplomatic historian Dana G. Monro observes: "We were interested in economic development in the Caribbean because the poorer countries were not likely to have better governments [that is, pro-West democracies] so long as the masses of the people lived in ignorance and poverty."[79] In this spirit, President Lyndon B. Johnson once declared that foreign aid was "the best weapon we have to ensure that our own men in uniform need not go into combat."[80] Another leading objective was to gain access to overseas markets through the admission ticket of foreign assistance—a prominent selling point for the Marshall Plan among lawmakers in 1947.

Driven by these goals, U.S. foreign aid went from primarily private and missionary donations before the Second World War to an expanding program that aimed to reconstruct the war-torn nations allied with the United States, strengthen other non-communist states, and encourage development of the poor nations as viable markets and buffers against communist expansion. The underlying political assumption was that economic development would nurture the seeds of democracy and, once established, the world's democracies could stand united against communism. From 1947 through 1950, U.S. officials earmarked most foreign aid (about $26 billion) for economic development. During the 1950s, however, officials discarded as simplistic the formula that correlated economic aid and the successful exercise of containment. Democracy had failed to take root with the alacrity planners had hoped. Recall that, throughout the Cold War, only some twenty nations were acknowledged to have truly democratic forms of government.[81] So the United States turned increasingly toward military defense assistance for countries like South Korea, South Vietnam, Taiwan, and the Philippines.

Guatemala offers an illustration. The entire U.S. military assistance program in Guatemala during the decade from 1944 to 1953 was only $600,000. Then, in 1954, in the wake of a successful CIA covert action to remove a president with suspected Marxist leanings (and someone whom the United Fruit Company, an American corporation, feared might nationalize its banana plantations), the funding for the military assistance program soared virtually overnight to $45 million.[82]

As America's aid program unfolded during the Cold War, its key early intiatives included the Truman Doctrine and the Marshall Plan; the China Aid Act of 1948, followed by economic aid to other Asian nations in 1949 (South Korea, Indonesia, Burma, Indochina, Thailand, and the Philippines); the Point Four technical assistance program for Asia, Africa, and Latin America, also in 1949, along with the Mutual Defense Assistance Act for Europe that same year; the Mutual Security Act for the Third World in 1951; and the Agricultural Trade Development and Assistance Act in 1954, better known as Public Law 480 or the "Food for Peace" Act. Between 1948 and 1952, the United States spent over $13 billion via the Marshall Plan to revive the economies of Europe (a comparable program today would cost about $90 billion). The result was a quick recovery from the devastation of the Second World War. Planners hoped this approach could become a model for American aid directed toward other parts of the world. According to Senator J. William Fulbright, the Marshall Plan "created a false impression that we could solve any problem by throwing money at it."[83] Unfortunately, few locations in the world had the prerequisites for success that Europe enjoyed, among them a skilled and experienced work force, strong productive potential, a common culture, and a readiness among leaders to work with one another.[84]

While in the 1950s the United States had turned more toward military assistance, during the 1960s it swung back again to a concentration on economic assistance. Economic aid was twice the amount of military aid from 1960 through 1965; the reverse of the previous decade. The new and more altruistic emphasis was on soft loans over direct grants and technical aid. These loans came at a lower interest rate with longer repayment schedules, and repayment was allowed in local currencies. Bickerton reports that, by 1960, soft loans had become "the single most important tool employed in the U.S. foreign aid program."[85] Among the landmarks of this period was the creation of the Agency for International Development (AID) in 1961, which provided better organizational focus within the state department to America's foreign assistance programs. That same year, the U.S. government established the Peace Corps and the Alliance for Progress, the latter designed to bolster the U.S. economic aid package for Latin America.

The Peace Corps stands as one of the most noteworthy expressions of international empathy exhibited by the government of the United States. It is not officially a part of the U.S. aid programs, but it has done wonders to win friends for America while helping poor people in other lands. Secretary of State Dean Rusk remembers traveling to a remote African village during the Kennedy administration. On the wall of the hut hung a photograph of President John F. Kennedy. A villager beamed at the president's image and explained to Rusk, through a translator, why the president was such a beloved figure: he had created the Peace Corps and its volunteers had helped the village with educational programs and irrigation projects.[86]

Diplomat David Newsom tells of a similar experience:

> Some years ago, I was at the opening of a six-kilometer road from a village in a West African country to a main road. Before the road was built, all the products of the village had to be portaged over a narrow path fording two streams. The road was made possible because an American technician, in this case a 61-year-old former telephone lineman from Chicago, had discovered a field of castaway truck chassis

and had shown how, by welding the chassis together, small bridges could be built. His was the ingenuity and the motivation. The work was that of the villagers.[87]

By the mid-1970s, however, pessimism about the usefulness of foreign aid had spread among officials in Washington, DC. Development assistance had long had its critics—"the greatest give-away in history," perennially grumbled Representative Otto Passman (D-LA), the powerful chairman of the House Appropriations Subcommittee on Foreign Assistance during the 1950s.[88] (Passman hailed from a small town in Louisiana and rarely traveled abroad.) During the Ford and Carter administrations, opposition to America's aid program became far more pervasive on Capitol Hill. The failure to achieve success in South Vietnam, despite the billions of dollars worth of U.S. assistance pumped into the country, cast a pall over the aid program soon after America's retreat from Saigon in 1973. Also, with the coming of détente in 1973–74, the need to shore up the developing world against the Soviets seemed less urgent.

Moreover, all too often aid seemed merely to prop up dictators who siphoned off the funds for their personal aggrandizement. In 1974, liberals in Congress decided, through the Harkin Amendment, sponsored by Thomas Harkin (D-IA) and narrowly approved by lawmakers, to put a halt to aid for unsavory regimes that tortured dissidents and otherwise violated human rights. Later in the decade, critics pointed to the large foreign bank accounts held by Somoza of Nicaragua, Mobutu of Zaire, and other U.S. cronies in the Third World. In 1986, photographs of three thousand pairs of shoes purchased by Imelda Marcos, the wife of the deposed Philippine dictator, Ferdinand Marcos—a recipient of enormous sums of U.S.

aid—further soured critics on development assistance programs. "Compared to Imelda, Marie Antoinette was a bag-lady," complained a leading member of Congress.[89]

Most significant, though, were the lingering doubts about whether aid had much effect on a poor nation's development. According to World Bank economist William Easterly, Chad, Ghana, Zambia, and Zimbabwe have all received large amounts of aid, but their economies have been stagnant or even in decline, while Hong Kong, Malaysia, and Singapore have experienced economic expansion without much aid.[90] Indeed, some critics argued that U.S. assistance might actually retard, rather than accelerate, a nation's economic progress by establishing an unhealthy dependency among recipients. Further, many countries that received aid showed no compunction whatsoever against voting in opposition to the United States at the UN and in other international forums.

Was foreign aid worth the cost, especially when the United States had its own pockets of poverty where the finite resources of the taxpayer could be spent? Many a lawmaker remained skeptical. "I go home and see farmers' wives cry in front of me," said a Midwestern lawmaker, who also happened to be chair of the Appropriations Subcommittee on Foreign Operations (the key House panel on foreign aid). Underscoring his primary concern for problems in his home district, not overseas, he concluded: "Don't tell me about the Philippines."[91] Other members of Congress have joined the anti-aid chorus. The House notable Tom Delay (R-TX) vowed that you would not find him "putting Ghana over Grandma"; and Jesse Helms (R-NC), then chair of the august Senate Foreign Relations Committee, said during the 1970s that foreign aid was equivalent to throwing "money down a rat hole."[92]

There appear to be few firm answers about the results of America's expensive investment in foreign aid since the end of the Second World War. One 1970s scholarly review of the U.S. aid program concluded: "The impact of foreign aid remains obscure and perplexing."[93] Another, more recent commentary concludes that "looking at the overall record, there appears to be no statistical correlation between aid and growth."[94]

With the debate about the benefits of foreign aid ongoing, during the 1980s Congress began to slash assistance for some nations by over 50 percent. (Those countries with effective lobbies in Washington, such as Israel, Turkey, and Greece, managed to avoid the ax.) Regardless of the skepticism, foreign aid expenditures actually increased during the Reagan years. The rise in spending resulted in part from the administration's emphasis on expensive military hardware sales and grants to developing nations, as it heated up the Cold War conflict again with the Soviet Union. The funding request for military grant assistance in 1988, for example, climbed to 47.7 percent over the previous year, from $900 million to $1.3 billion.[95] The increased spending also reflected a renewal of interest in the use of economic aid as a deterrent to the spread of communism. In 1984, members of the Kissinger Commission, chaired by former Secretary of State Henry Kissinger, recommended an $8 billion economic aid program for Latin America to thwart communist takeovers. The Commission was less interested in promoting democracy, à la Wilson and (with guns) the second Bush; it settled for a policy of promoting ABC regimes (anybody but communists) that would ensure stability and pro-Americanism. What the dictators did within their own borders was their business, as long as they didn't try to nationalize or otherwise interfere with U.S. business interests.

In spite of the Reagan administration's renewed interest in foreign assistance in the name of anti-communism, followed two decades later by zeal in the second Bush administration for democracy promotion in Iraq and Afghanistan, criticism of the U.S. aid program continues to be intense and pervasive. A widespread pessimism infuses the policymaking and academic communities about the level of global development once thought possible in the heyday of the Kennedy and Johnson years. Yet can the United States afford to turn a cold shoulder to the needs of the developing world, where most of the planet's population resides?

SEARCHING FOR GLOBAL PARTNERSHIPS TO COUNTER GLOBAL POVERTY

It would be wise to heed the guidance of the American journalist and diplomat Carl Rowen. "We need officials who care about these poor, weak nations and their peoples," he advised, "officials who show up occasionally to ask, 'What are your special problems? What can we buy from you, and what can we sell? What is it in medicine, food, education, technology that we can provide?'"[96] Here are expressions of empathy that can attract allies—and open markets—for the United States throughout the world.

Of course, foreign assistance and trade are not the only ways for Americans to display empathy for the less advantaged. Opportunities for acts of friendship are often at hand. For example, Americans can win friends for our nation as they travel abroad. Most U.S. students backpacking and studying abroad are outstanding "ambassadors." A small percentage, though, come across as boors, drinking excessively in *Gasthause*s and pubs, treating dining cars on intercontinental trains as their own personal rec rooms, and even engaging in brawls in watering holes around the world. Unfortunately, these few can spoil the good impressions made by the majority of students. Treating international students and other visitors to the United States as welcomed guests is another way we can improve our relations with other countries. Yet, how many have invited foreign visitors into their homes, for Thanksgiving or on some other occasion? Some have, but not enough. Further, learning about other nations—their languages, histories, and cultures—is an appreciated compliment toward the people of other countries; and it accrues benefits to the United States, stemming from improvements in international commercial and diplomatic relations. Again, many Americans have taken an interest in international studies—indeed, a rising number since 9/11—but still too few.

Ambassador Rowan understood the importance of paying attention to the hopes and concerns of citizens in other lands. "The lesson of Afghanistan [for the Soviets in the 1980s]—and Vietnam [for the Americans from 1964–75]—is that no foreign policy can succeed in these times if it does not contain a large element of diplomacy," he wrote, adding: ". . . and a credible expression of compassion for the needs of people in the most wretched reaches of Afghanistan, Angola, Cambodia, Mozambique and similar societies." Rowan concluded: "This is a lesson not easily learned by people who think that by spending $300 billion or more a year on weapons, they have made themselves 'super' and bought control of the rest of this fragile planet."[97]

NOTES

1. Jimmy Carter, "The United States Must Guide Third World towards Self-Sufficiency," *Atlanta Journal and Constitution* (December 3, 1988), p. A23.
2. Nicholas D. Kristof, "Meet the Fakers," *New York Times* (September 13, 2005), p. A31.
3. Barry James, "Summit Aims, Again, for a Better World," *International Herald Tribune* (August 8, 2002), p. 1.
4. "Cow Politics," an unsigned editorial citing the Australian trade minister, Mark Vaile, *New York Times* (October 27, 2005), p. A30; Celia W. Dugger, "U.N. Report Cites U.S. and Japan as the 'Least Generous Donors,'" *New York Times* (September 8, 2005), p. A6.
5. Remarks, Dr. Peter Piot, executive director, UNAIDS, "Women and AIDS," *The NewsHour with Jim Lehrer*, PBS (December 1, 2004).
6. U.S. Agency for International Development, *Child Survival and Disease Programs Fund Progress Report* (2001).
7. U.S. Agency for International Development, *Global Health: Confronting the Challenges*, www.usaid.gov (2002); U.S. Agency for International Development, *USAID Highlights* 4 (Summer 1987), p. 2.; and U.S. Agency for International Development, *USAID Highlights* 3 (Winter 1986), p. 2.
8. Donald G. McNeil, Jr., "Plant Shortage Leaves Campaigns Against Malaria at Risk," *New York Times* (November 14, 2004), p. A6, for the one million figure; "America, the Indifferent," unsigned editorial, *New York Times* (December 23, 2004), p. A12, for the 2.2 million figure. See also Amir Attaran, "Necessary Measures," *New York Times* (September 13, 2005), p. A31, for the number-one killer statistic.
9. ABC News report (October 31, 2005).
10. "Thousands Died in Africa Yesterday," unsigned editorial, *New York Times* (February 27, 2005), p. A12.
11. See "How Not to Roll Back Malaria," unsigned editorial, *New York Times* (October 16, 2005), p. E11.
12. U.S. Agency for International Development, *Global Health*.
13. Report, *All Things Considered*, National Public Radio (December 1, 2004). Adults account for about 37.2 million of the victims, and children, 2.2 million.
14. World Health Organization, "WHO and the Humanitarian Crisis in Southern Africa," WHO Press Release (August 2, 2002).
15. "U.N. Puts Children in Forefront of AIDS Effort," *New York Times* (October 26, 2005), p. A11.
16. Remarks, Susan Dentzer, PBS health correspondent, "Women and AIDS," *The NewsHour with Jim Lehrer*, PBS (December 1, 2004).
17. John Cassidy, "Always with Us?" *The New Yorker* (April 8, 2005), p. 75.

18. Jimmy Carter, State of Human Rights Address, Atlanta (1991), p. 5.
19. *World News Tonight,* ABC (January 6, 2005).
20. Sheryl Gay Stolberg, "With Convert's Zeal, Congress Awakens to AIDS," *New York Times* (May 12, 2002), p. A1; U.S. Agency for International Development, *Child Survival.*
21. Michael Wines and Sharon LaFraniere, "Hut by Hut, AIDS Steals Life in a Southern Africa Town," *New York Times* (November 28, 2004), p. A15.
22. Dr. Peter Piot, "Women and AIDS."
23. Ibid.
24. Ibid.
25. See Jim Wooten, *We Are All the Same: A Story of a Boy's Courage and a Mother's Love* (New York: Penguin, 2004).
26. Wines and LaFraniere, "Hut by Hut," p. A14.
27. Ibid.
28. See "Global Fight," *The NewsHour with Jim Lehrer,* PBS (July 15, 2004).
29. Report, *Evening News with Peter Jennings,* ABC (December 11, 1986); see, also, U.S. Agency for International Development, *USAID Highlights* 3 (Winter 1986), p. 2, and U.S. Agency for International Development, *USAID Highlights* 4 (Summer 1978), p. 1.
30. U.S. Agency for International Development, *Child Survival.*
31. Report on the Conference of Soviet-American Physicians, WETA Public Television (December 21, 1984).
32. UN Children's Fund estimates, cited by Colin L. Powell, "No Country Left Behind," *Foreign Policy* (January/February 2005), pp. 31–32.
33. World Health Organization, "WHO and the Humanitarian Crisis."
34. U.S. Agency for International Development, *Child Survival*; and Sharon LaFraniere, "Nightmare for African Women: Birthing Injury and Little Help," *New York Times* (September 28, 2005), p. A1.
35. Nicholas D. Kristof, "Bleeding Hearts of the World, Unite!" *New York Times* (November 6, 2005), p. E13.
36. James, "Summit Aims," p. 1.
37. Wines and LaFraniere, "Hut by Hut," pp. A1, A14.
38. Ibid., p. A1.
39. Tom Teepen, "The Third World Is Fighting Many Plagues," *Atlanta Journal and Constitution* (February 5, 1989), p. B7.
40. Jeffrey D. Sachs, interviewed by Margaret Warner, *The NewsHour with Jim Lehrer,* PBS (January 17, 2005). For Sachs's general views on global poverty, see his *The End of Poverty: Economic Possibilities for Our Time* (New York: Penguin, 2005).
41. The Carter Center, *The Carter Center News,* Atlanta (Fall 1991), p. 14.
42. Paul Kennedy, "True Leadership for the Next Millennium," *New York Times* (January 3, 1993), p. E11.

43. See Lisa Kalis, "The Cost of Heavenly Sleep Can Be Sky High," *New York Times* (December 12, 2004), p. B13; Amy Larocca, "The Charity Ball Game," *New York Times* (May 9, 2005), p. 37; Haynes Johnson, "Let Them Eat Flowers," *Washington Post*, National Weekly Edition (March 12, 1984), p. A25; and Associated Press Report, "L.I. High School Cancels Prom Over 'Financial Decadence,'" *New Haven Register* (October 17, 2005), p. B4.

44. Quoted in George D. Moffett III, "Cuts in US Development Aid Protested," *Christian Science Monitor* (September 12, 1986), p. 8.

45. Robert L. Heilbroner, *An Inquiry into the Human Prospect* (New York: Norton, 1975), p. 39.

46. James A. Thomson, "We're Here for the Duration," *RAND Review* 26 (Summer 2002), www.rand.org.

47. Thomas L. Friedman, "Thinking About Iraq," *New York Times* (January 22, 2003), p. A23. Or as James Wolfensohn, the outgoing president of the World Bank, has put it, reflecting back on the meaning of the 9/11 attacks: ". . . there is no wall around the United States" [interviewed by Jim Lehrer, *The NewsHour with Jim Lehrer*, PBS (May 30, 2005)].

48. Anthony Lewis, "When We Could Believe," *New York Times* (June 12, 1987), p. A31.

49. Michael Ignatieff, "Nation-Building Lite," *New York Times Magazine* (July 28, 2002), p. 30.

50. Celia W. Dugger, "Discerning a New Course for World's Donor Nations," *New York Times* (April 18, 2005), p. A10, based on figures from the Organization for Economic Cooperation and Development.

51. George W. Bush, press release (July 17, 2001).

52. Transcript provided to the author by a Capitol Hill staffer in 1986.

53. Received by the author in 1988.

54. Interview with John Hughes, "Lunch with Cap," *Christian Science Monitor* (September 12, 1986), p. A12.

55. Daniel Patrick Moynihan, "Reagan's Doctrine and the Iran Issue," *New York Times* (December 21, 1986), p. E19.

56. Quoted by Colin Campbell, "Campaign Obscured Babbitt's Expertise in Foreign Policy," *Atlanta Constitution* (February 19, 1988), p. A6.

57. President Ronald Reagan, *Evening News with Peter Jennings*, ABC (May 31, 1988).

58. See Eqbal Ahmad and Richard J. Barnet, "A Reporter at Large: Bloody Games," *The New Yorker* (April 11, 1988), pp. 44–86; Steve Coll, *Ghost Wars* (New York: Penguin, 2004); and George Crile, *Charlie Wilson's War* (New York: Grove Press, 2003).

59. David D. Newsom, *Diplomacy and the American Democracy* (Bloomington: Indiana University Press, 1988), p. 217.

60. See Ralph K. White, *Fearful Warriors: A Psychological Profile of U.S.-Soviet Relations* (New York: Free Press, 1984).
61. John Mueller, "Simplicity and Spook: Terrorism and the Dynamics of Threat Exaggeration," *International Studies Perspectives* 6 (May 2005), pp. 208–234.
62. Quoted in Bernard Gwertzman, "A Citizen pays $43 for Aid, Schultz Says, and $35 for Hairdos," *New York Times* (February 25, 1983), pp. A1, A6.
63. I. M. Destler and Steven Kull, *Misreading the Public: The Myth of a New Isolationism* (Washington, DC: Brookings Institution, 1999).
64. Dugger, "U.N. Report Cites U.S. and Japan," p. A8.
65. The pets figure is from Susan Shepard, *Living on Earth*, National Public Radio (January 8, 2005).
66. "America, the Indifferent," *New York Times*.
67. Dugger, "U.N. Report Cites U.S. and Japan," p. A10. Retiring World Bank president James Wolfensohn believes that President Bush "has done much more than perhaps all of his predecessors in increasing the level of aid, in increasing the support, for example, for AIDS." [Interviewed by Lehrer, *The NewsHour with Jim Lehrer*, PBS (May 30, 2005)]. The data presented by Dugger reveal, however, that both Clinton and George W. Bush recorded overall aid levels —in contrast to just anti-AIDS funding— far below their predecessors.
68. "A First Step on African Aid," unsigned editorial, *New York Times* (June 14, 2005), p. A18; and Kristof, "Bleeding Hearts."
69. Powell, "No Country Left Behind," pp. 33, 35.
70. Celia W. Dugger, "Senate Rejects Bush Bid to Ease Delivery of Food to Poor Nations," *New York Times* (September 23, 2005), p. A9; Natasha C. Burley, "In Place Where the Hungry Are Fed, Farmers May Starve," *New York Times* (September 22, 2005), p. A3.
71. Unsigned editorial, "Raining Money," *New York Times* (January 4, 2005), p. A22.
72. Celia W. Dugger, "U.N. Proposes Doubling of Aid to Cut Poverty," *New York Times* (January 18, 2005), p. A6.
73. "America, the Indifferent," *New York Times*.
74. Steven R. Weisman, "Irate Over 'Stingy' Remark, U.S. Adds $20 Million to Disaster Aid," *New York Times* (December 29, 2004), p. A14; "Thousands Died in Africa Yesterday," *New York Times*, p. A12.
75. Sachs, *The NewsHour with Jim Lehrer*, PBS (January 17, 2005).
76. Cassidy, "Always with Us?" p. 77.
77. This figure is from "Thousands Died in Africa Yesterday," *New York Times*.
78. Dugger, "U.N. Report Cites U.S. and Japan," p. A10.
79. Cited by Joan Hoff Wilson, "Economic Foreign Policy," in Alexander DeConde, ed., *Encyclopedia of American Foreign Policy: Studies of the Principal Movements and Ideas*, vol. II (New York: Scribner's, 1978), p. 287.

As a general rule of thumb, approximately a $6,000 per capita GDP for a country is strongly associated with its chances for establishing a liberal democracy (see Fareed Zakaria, *The Future of Freedom: Liberal Democracy at Home and Abroad* (New York: norton, 2004), pp. 69–70.

80. Quoted by Ian J. Bickerton, "Foreign Aid," in DeConde, ibid., p. 375.

81. See Arend Lijphart, *Democracies* (Cambridge, MA: Harvard University Press, 1982), p. 5.

82. David Wise and Thomas B. Ross, *The Invisible Government* (New York: Vintage, 1974).

83. Quoted by Ann Hughey, "The Lessons of the Marshall Plan," *New York Times* (June 7, 1987), p. F4.

84. Gaddis Smith, "The Marshall Plan," in DeConde, *Encyclopedia of American Foreign Policy*, p. 544.

85. Bickerton, "Foreign Aid," p. 374.

86. Remarks to the author, Athens, Georgia (July 4, 1983).

87. Newsom, *Diplomacy and the American Democracy*, p. 178.

88. Bickerton, "Foreign Aid," p. 375.

89. Representative Stephen Solarz (D-NY), quoted on *Washington Week in Review*, PBS (March 14, 1986).

90. Cited by Cassidy, "Always with Us?" p. 75.

91. Quoted by Peter Osterlund, "Congress Tightens Foreign-Aid Screws," *Christian Science Monitor* (September 18, 1986), p. A12.

92. Both quotes from Kristof, "Bleeding Hearts."

93. Bickerton, "Foreign Aid," p. 378.

94. Cassidy, "Always with Us?" p. 75.

95. Joanne Omang, "$1.3 Billion More Sought in Foreign Aid Programs," *Washington Post* (December 31, 1986), p. A13.

96. Carl Rowan, "American Ignorance," *Atlanta Constitution* (November 4, 1979), p. A14.

97. Carl Rowan, "The Superpowers Learn a Costly Lesson," *Atlanta Constitution* (February 15, 1989), p. A15.

CHAPTER 7

Arrogance

AMERICA'S WAY OR THE HIGHWAY

There is a perception around the world that the United States has grown too big for its britches, that it has failed to live up to its noble rhetoric as a peace-loving power with lofty ideals, that it thinks its views are superior to those of other nations. "Why do they hate us?" Benjamin R. Barber has asked, posing the central question that has haunted Americans since the 9/11 attacks, with a growing sense that many people overseas actually found joy—Schadenfreude—in the suffering of the United States at the hands of terrorists. Barber's answer is "our hypocrisy": the "high moralism of our intentions conjoined with the harsh consequences of our deeds."[1]

What could be more emblematic of hypocrisy and the arrogance it reflects than the photographs of U.S. military intelligence interrogators humiliating Iraqi prisoners of war in Abu Ghraib, Iraq, in 2004; or the holding of some 680 prisoners at Guantánamo

Bay—caged, shackled, in orange prison jumpsuits, their beards often forcibly shorn as an act of humiliation—without the slightest nod to the Geneva Conventions, due process, or the right to legal counsel? More than 100 detainees have died in U.S. custody.[2] Reporting recently from Europe, two *New York Times* correspondents reached the conclusion that ". . . accusations of abuse at Guantánamo, as much as the war in Iraq, have become a symbol of what many see as America's dangerous drift away from the ideals that made it a moral beacon in the post-World War II era. There is a persistent and uneasy sense that the United States fundamentally changed after September 11, and not for the better."[3]

America's fixation on the terrorist threat, to the point of rejecting its fundamental values and sense of fair play, has alarmed allies and led people everywhere to brand the United States—however unfairly—as a hegemonic power intent on exercising its muscle without restraint. Reacting in instinctive anger and without waiting for verification, rioters throughout the Muslim world took to the streets in violent protests against the United States when *Newsweek* mistakenly reported in May 2005 that U.S. soldiers had desecrated the Holy Koran by flushing a copy down a toilet at Guantánamo Bay. (Further inquiries by the American military did uncover five cases, though, in which the Koran had been handled with disrespect by interrogators and guards at Guantánamo.[4])

The pictures of detainee abuse at Abu Ghrab and Guantánamo, coupled with the ongoing occupation of Iraq by U.S. troops and a widespread belief that Americans were continuing to torture Muslim prisoners, primed many people in countries like Afghanistan, Pakistan, and Indonesia to accept virtually any allegations that confirmed their suspicions about Americans being anti-Islamic. With the reports on the desecration of the Koran serving as lighted matches thrown into a dry forest, rallies and even rioting swept across Pakistan, Egypt, Indonesia, Malaysia, and the Middle East, killing at least seventeen individuals amidst the burning of American flags and the shouting of anti-U.S. slogans.

At an international conference in Oslo in 2003, I asked European lawmakers, bureaucrats, and scholars about their views on why the United States had lost so quickly the sympathy that Europeans felt toward them in the wake of the September 11th attacks.[5] After all, at the time of the terrorist attacks even the French newspaper *Le Monde*, which often relishes figuratively poking the United States in the eye, declared: "We are all Americans."[6] In Iran, where the United States is regularly decried as Satan, tens of thousands rallied spontaneously in the streets of Tehran to demonstrate their solidarity with the people of America.[7] Indeed, every Islamic country in the world condemned the attacks. The Europeans I talked with in Oslo in 2003 each responded in a similar fashion, though the conversations were held separately and they had not heard the replies of others. Each pointed, first, to the improper treatment of prisoners in Guantánamo (this was before the Abu Ghraib revelations) and, second, to America's unwillingness to consult and work more closely with the governments of Europe in resolving international disputes.

The United States has long had a special feeling about itself—an "exceptionalism." This is an understandable self-perception in light of the incredible bounty of natural resources and ample land the nation enjoys, along with its widely admired political and legal system; its mighty military establishment; its impressive scientific and medical achievements; the worldwide popularity of its movies, pop music, fashion, journalism, literature, even toothpaste; the irrepressible entrepreneurial spirit of its people; and its reputation as a successful melting pot of immigrants from most every country in the world—the most domestically "global" of all nations. Americans have much to be proud of, despite the troubling number of murders that occur in the United States each year (though declining in recent times), the unacceptable infant mortality rates (even poverty-stricken Cuba does better), and the deplorable rankings of students in science, math, and reading scores.

However, just as the high school bully is feared and disliked, so, too, is a major power if its words and deeds are seen as heavily coated with a veneer of hubris. Other nations are taken aback when they hear the president of the United States declare on the eve of the second Persian Gulf War: "I don't care what the international lawyers say, we are going to kick some ass."[8] They are put off when an active-duty U.S. Army general and deputy undersecretary of defense remarks in a public speech, referring to a Muslim fighter in Somalia: "I knew that my God was a real God, and his was an idol"[9] or when Secretary of State Condoleezza Rice declares that America wants to bring democracy to those who happened to have been born in the wrong place, an insensitive remark to people who cherish the land of their birth. Before she joined the second Bush administration, Rice declared in *Foreign Affairs* that America has "a special role in the world and should not adhere to every international convention and agreement that someone thinks to propose"—as if (for example) the global accords for the banning of land mines and cleaning up the environment, widely supported in the international community, had been advanced merely by "someone."[10] Rice was convinced that "the United States is the only guarantor of global peace and stability," just as before her, during the Clinton administration, Secretary of State

Madeleine Albright had insisted that America was "the indispensable nation. We stand tall. We see farther into the future."[11]

REMAKING THE WORLD
IN AMERICA'S IMAGE

One important manifestation of American arrogance in foreign affairs is the core concept that drives the foreign policy of the second Bush administration: a belief that the United States can remake the world in its own democratic image, beginning with the conversion of Iraq into a Western-style republic.[12] Once Iraq adopts a working representative form of governance, supposedly other nations in the Middle East and South Asia will follow suit, never mind their centuries of autocratic rule. This domino theory of democracy is just as simplistic as the earlier, if quite different, domino theory that drew America into Indochina in the 1960s, under the conviction that one country after another would fall to communism unless the armed forces of the United States set up a barricade to prevent the toppling.

In the nineteenth century, the idea of a manifest destiny spurred the westward expansion of early Americans in a march toward the Pacific Ocean. As newspaper editor John L. O'Sullivan intoned in 1845, it was the birthright of pioneers "to overspread and to possess the whole of the continent which Providence has given us."[13] At the beginning of the twentieth century, President William McKinley extended the idea to American foreign policy, especially with the Philippines in mind, but by implication any other overseas territories that might be susceptible to U.S. influence. Recall his proclamation that it was the duty of the United States in world affairs to "uplift and civilize and Christianize."[14] A McKinley-like brio has surfaced again in the second Bush administration, this time to advance Wilsonian democracy in the Middle East, South Asia, and beyond. In response, historian Arthur M. Schlesinger, Jr., proffers these cautionary words: "... history ... makes us—or should make us—understand the extreme difficulty, the intellectual peril, the moral arrogance of supposing that the future will yield itself so easily to us."[15]

COVERT ACTION, A STUDY IN ARROGANCE

Since the end of the Second World War, America's use of the CIA and covert action provides many examples of officials in Washington, DC, proudly believing—or at least hoping—they could channel the course of history in a direction more favorable to the United States through secret interventions abroad.[16] While a discussion of covert action could have easily fit into the chapters on executive dominance or unilateralism (again revealing the overlap between sins), I have placed it here because it so well illustrates foreign policy arrogance—a sense that the United States can alter the flow of history through a few well-crafted secret operations.

The legal authority for covert action—the use of propaganda, political, economic, and paramilitary operations against adversaries in such a manner as to conceal the hand of the perpetrator—stems originally from a catchall phrase in the National Security Act of 1947. Ambiguous language in the law permitted the CIA "to perform such other functions and duties related to intelligence affecting the national security" as the National Security Council might find necessary.

The early uses of covert action after the Second World War led to some encouraging successes, giving intelligence managers and policymakers the notion that this was an approach to world affairs that could advance the cause of democracy and America's other global security interests without the difficulties that accompany the noisy use of the U.S. Marine Corps and other overt instruments of military force. In the late 1940s and early 1950s, the CIA and its worldwide network of foreign agents (or "assets") succeeded in resisting communist political subversion in Western Europe (France, Greece, and Italy in particular) and the Middle East (Iran), as well as against Cuban-style—often Cuban-instigated—insurgencies in Latin America.

Notably stunning were its covert victories against political forces considered anathema to the United States in Iran in 1953 and, the next year, in Guatemala.[17] Both operations seemed to flow with the ease of a silk handkerchief from a magician's sleeve: abracadabra, the Commies were out and the U.S.-picked substitutes in. The new leaders were hardly democrats, but at least they were pro-U.S. and—the key criterion—would keep communists out of their government. As an added benefit, they could be counted on to sell their natural resources—from oil to bananas—to the United States at bargain rates. The CIA chalked up successes as well, at least over the short run, in Laos from 1962–68; in Portugal in 1975, when CIA political support to moderates blocked a Marxist electoral victory; and in Afghanistan against the Soviets from 1982–88. They later hunted down the Al Qaeda and Taliban in Afghanistan following the September 11, 2001 terrorist attacks.[18]

ABC—anybody but communists—became the rallying cry for administrations of both major political parties throughout the Cold

War, and the CIA was a primary instrument for carrying out this policy. It would be good to have more democracies in the world, but pro-U.S., authoritarian, anti-communism regimes would suffice, until conditions were riper for representative government.

The appeal of covert action was understandable. On the one hand, overt warfare was provocative and dangerous and, on the other hand, diplomacy was slow and frustrating. A "third option," covert action, might help rid the world of regimes hostile toward the United States without the public dustup that accompanies sending in the Marines, and with greater dispatch than the endless "jaw-jawing" of diplomats in Geneva. Washington officials began to see this secret use of American foreign policy, also known as the "quiet option" or "special activities," as a panacea to cure the spreading disease of Marxism in the world beyond the superpowers.

Of course, covert action would not work everywhere. It was too risky, for example, to apply much of this medicine (beyond propaganda activities) directly against the Soviet Union or China. Those powerful nations might retaliate. The battlefield for this subterranean Third World War would be the developing world, ill-equipped to strike back at the United States. As a member of the U.S. Senate observed in 1976, covert actions targeted chiefly "leaders of small, weak countries that could not possibly threaten the United States . . . no country was too small, no foreign leader too trifling, to escape our attention."[19]

The CIA's network of assets (agents), known by intelligence officers as "the infrastructure" or "the plumbing," contributed to the momentum within the U.S. government to favor the use of covert action. The assets, according to a CIA insider, sought to justify their existence on the CIA's payroll by often concocting various schemes just "to make themselves appear busy and worth their keep."[20]

The short, if impressive, list of the CIA's early accomplishments via covert action was soon overshadowed, however, by a much longer list of failures. Among them stood, most conspicuously, the Cuban Bay of Pigs fiasco in 1961. Bungled as well were assassination plots against foreign heads of state (including Cuba's Castro and Congo's Patrice Lumumba), along with such embarrassing missteps as attempts during the Cold War to topple the leaders of Indonesia and Chile (the latter democratically elected) and, from 1991 until the U.S.-led invasion in 2003, the feckless use of secret funds provided to the factious Iraqi National Congress in hopes of dislodging the Hussein regime.

THE ARROGANCE OF SHORT-TERM PLANNING

Even in the case of its "successes," the long-term contributions of covert action to the security interests of the United States and the cause of democracy are questionable. Certainly Iran is no close friend of America today. Indeed, its people remember the United States and the CIA (along with the British and its foreign intelligence service, MI6) as the reason so many of them suffered from 1953 to 1979 under an increasingly brutal regime. The CIA and MI6 selected the Shah of Iran to rule the nation and to keep a friendly hand on the pump dispensing crude oil at reasonable prices to the West. The Shah's main job was to be a courteous service station attendant, filling up gas tanks in the West. What he did inside his own country was an internal matter, of marginal interest to the United States—just as, today, Saudi Arabia plays a similar role at the gas pumps, never mind that leaders in Riyadh fund suicide bombers in the Middle East, or that most of the 9/11 hijackers came from Saudi Arabia.

Nor are Guatemala or Panama much closer to democracy than when the United States intervened in their affairs (the CIA and the U.S. military together, in the case of Panama in 1989). In fact, Guatemala slid backward, since its people elected the leader ousted by the CIA in 1954. Today, both nations are as poor and repressive as ever. Further, the first CIA intervention into Afghanistan—a success in the sense of helping to drive out the Soviet military—led to the establishment of an army of CIA-armed mujahedeen ("soldiers of god") guerrillas. Most of them would eventually join the Taliban regime, with its harshly antimodern views toward society. The Taliban would attempt, with considerable success, to return Afghanistan to the fourteenth century; and, for good measure, it provided a safe haven for Osama bin Laden and his nascent Al Qaeda terrorist organization.

After the 9/11 attacks, the American-led invasion of Afghanistan, spearheaded by the combined efforts of the CIA, military Special Forces, the U.S. Air Force, and anti-Taliban Afghanis in a "Northern Alliance," drove out the Taliban regime and the United States tried to nurture a democratic replacement. The viability of the new regime remains uncertain and, for all intents and purposes, it governs only in the capital city of Kabul. Independent and well-armed warlords control suzerainties in the hinterland, as they have for centuries in this troubled nation. As for the Stinger missiles and other advanced weapons provided to the mujahedeen by the CIA during the first invasion, large numbers were never returned to the Agency's inventory and remained in the hands of warlords. Some of the weapons, capable of bringing down U.S. military and commercial airlines, have been reputedly sold to Iran or given to various factions in the Middle East and South Asia, including jihadist warriors whose sole raison d'être is to fight against U.S. interests in Iraq, or wherever else they can.[21]

The Laos intervention in the 1960s, a source of great pride among CIA officers ("the war we won," claims a former director of central intelligence[22]), had a longer term downside, too. During the secret intervention, some four hundred CIA officers entered Laos to support Hmong (Meo) tribesmen in a struggle against a rising deluge—at first, seven thousand, and soon ten times that number—of communist fighters armed by the North Vietnamese. The two sides fought to a standoff. The CIA claimed victory, and indeed it was a remarkable effort. Yet when the United States decided to depart from Laos, the Hmong were left behind and were slaughtered by the communists, who then consolidated their power in the nation. A small percentage of the Hmong were able to escape to camps for displaced persons in Thailand; some eventually made their way to the United States as political refugees.

Laos was not the only place the United States abandoned secret allies during the Cold War after failed experiments to change the flow of history. Ukranian emigres were also left to await their deaths in Carpathian caves; and, in the final days of the war in Vietnam, the CIA's South Vietnamese assets were left behind, along with personnel files and dossiers that would identify them to North Vietnamese interrogators, leading to their execution or imprisonment.[23] In 1989, after supporting the mujahedeen for almost a decade, the United States walked away from them as well, alienating these forces and making them vulnerable to recruitment by Al Qaeda. Further, in

1991, the government of the United States (acting through CIA inter-mediaries) encouraged Kurds and Shiites to rise up against the Iraqi dictatorship; then U.S. troops, after securing the nation's oil fields, halted at the outskirts of Baghdad and stood by on the sidelines as Saddam Hussein ordered the murder of thousands of Kurds and Shiite rebels. Others who joined with the CIA in a variety of covert rebellions include the Khambas in Tibet, the Nationalist Chinese in Burma, the ever-suffering Kurds on and off throughout the Cold War, and the Bay of Pigs invaders—all "so many causes and peoples briefly taken up by the CIA and then tossed aside like broken toys."[24]

ASSASSINATION AND OTHER FOLLIES

Sometimes the arrogance of American foreign policy has been just plain ludicrous. According to a CIA operative, one operation designed to overthrow Fidel Castro envisioned

> spreading the word that the Second Coming of Christ was imminent and that Christ was against Castro, [who] was the anti-Christ. And you would spread this word around Cuba, and then on whatever date it was, that there would be a manifestation of this thing. And at that time—this is absolutely true—and at that time just over the horizon there would be an American submarine which would surface off of Cuba and send up some starshells. And this would be the manifestation of the Second Coming and Castro would be overthrown.[25]

Fortunately, upper echelon CIA authorities had the good sense to scotch this plan, known inside the Agency as Operation "Elimination by Illumination." Another CIA proposal during the Kennedy years envisioned the spoiling of Soviet-Cuban relations by lacing Cuban sugar bound from Havana to Moscow with an unpalatable chemical substance. President Kennedy rejected the scheme at the eleventh hour and the CIA scurried to confiscate the 14,125 bags of sugar before they were shipped to the Soviet Union.[26]

Other madcap strategems went forward, however, including efforts to impregnate Castro's cigars with chemical substances; spray his radio broadcasting studio with an LSD-like substance; and insert thallium salts (a strong depilatory) into his boots, thereby robbing the Cuban leader of his charismatic beard.[27] When these ploys failed, the CIA escalated its attacks to a more lethal threshold, dusting Castro's underwater diving suit with a fungus to induce the disease called Madura foot, attempting to place poison in his food, planting an explosive device in a coral reef where he swam, and hiring mobsters with Havana connections to kill him. Again, with a combination of luck and effective security forces (well-trained by the KGB), the Cuban leader lived on.

Another prime target for the CIA's "Health Alteration Committee" during the early 1960s was the Congolese leader Patrice Lumumba, who had visited Moscow one too many times in the view of leaders in Washington, DC. Using a State Department diplomatic pouch, the CIA's Special Operations Group forwarded to the Agency's chief of station (COS) in Congo an unusual set of diplomatic instructions, along with a pair of rubber gloves, a gauze mask, a hypodermic syringe, and a vial of lethal biological toxin. As the COS wryly testified to a congressional investigative committee years later, "I knew it wasn't for somebody to get his polio shot up to date." He personally preferred a more direct approach: the use of a high-powered, foreign-made rifle with a telescopic scope and silencer. Overruled, he planned an operation to inject the toxin into Lumumba's food or toothpaste. Before the COS could gain access to the Congo leader, a rival political faction reached him first and gunned him down in an internal power struggle.

At one point during the Cold War, an obstreperous Iraqi colonel with Soviet connections became a target of interest for the Health Alteration Committee. The Middle East division chief at CIA Headquarters recommended the colonel be disabled for several months by exposing him to an incapacitating chemical. "We do not consciously seek subject's permanent removal from the scene," read the chief's cable to the field. "We also do not object should this complication develop."[28]

To advance this approach for dealing with annoying heads of state and others—operations known within the CIA as "executive action," "termination with extreme prejudice," or "neutralization"—the Agency developed a storehouse of lethal weapons and substances, including enough shellfish toxin, cobra venom, and other poisons to kill the population of a small city. Today, the latest instrument for assassination is the unmanned aerial vehicle (UAV) or drone called the Predator, armed with Hellfire missiles. A new so-called thermobaric model of the Hellfire missile can fly around sharp corners and strike enemies hidden inside caves. "There are going to be some awfully surprised terrorists when the thermobaric Hellfire comes knocking," President Bush told the class of 2005 graduates at the U.S. Naval Academy.[29]

In 2003, an earlier version of the Hellfire missile fired from a Predator annihilated an automobile in the deserts of Yemen, killing six suspected terrorists (including an American citizen).

From time to time, the Predator has been known to strike the wrong individuals, such as a man in Afghanistan in 2002 who had the misfortune of being about as tall as Bin Laden (six feet five inches). The ethical, legal, and oversight questions raised by a possible indiscriminate use of this weapon in paramilitary covert actions are profound. Further, in 2003, the Pentagon created a Special Forces assassination team known as Task Force 121, with an assignment to hunt down and capture or kill Baathists (Sunni) insurgents in Iraq.[30] Neither the computer warriors who guide the Predator by remote control back in the United States nor the leaders and members of Task Force 121 are subject to close monitoring by congressional overseers or the White House.

Despite the mishaps of the assassination plots against Castro and Lumumba in the 1960s or errant Hellfire missiles launched in recent years, murder as a tool of American foreign policy remains a beguiling option—even though it was officially banned by an executive order signed by President Gerald R. Ford in 1976 and renewed by his successors. The language reads: "No person, employed by or acting on behalf of the United States Government, shall engage in, or conspire to engage in, assassination."[31] Presidents have found the order easy to sidestep, though, for it enjoys a waiver in times of war. Ordering air attacks against Libya for its involvement in global terrorism, President Ronald Reagan made it clear that he wanted the home of the nation's leader, Mu'ammar Gadhafi, hit by bombs in the raid. This was not considered a CIA assassination plot, but an overt military strike designed to kill a foreign head of state. Gadhafi happened to be away from home, but the bombs inadvertently struck his adopted daughter, as well as a French-operated hospital in the capital city. During the first Persian Gulf War (1990–91), the first

Bush administration ordered the bombing of Baghdad and Saddam Hussein's palaces. According to the director of central intelligence at the time, the Bush White House "lit a candle every night hoping Saddam Hussein would be killed in a bunker."[32]

In 1975, a Senate committee of inquiry concluded that the United States had become a "global Godfather," carrying out death plots around the world.[33] Now that President George W. Bush has declared some sixty nations as havens for terrorists, are Predators allowed to cruise around the globe, wreaking havoc from thirty thousand feet on suspected enemies of the United States in any one of these locations? Will Task Force 121 teams rove the planet with similar instructions—and the same limited accountability? It is not difficult to understand why other nations find these possibilities unsettling, and find the secret use of American power supremely overbearing.

Assassination as a foreign-policy tool raises additional direct problems for the United States. In the first place, as the record illustrates, such plots are not easily carried out. The multiple attempts against Fidel Castro failed. What if one had succeeded: would that have meant freedom in Cuba, or just another Castro in power—this time his brother, Raul? How many individuals must be killed before a regime takes on a coloration more to the liking of the United States? At what point do foreign regimes begin to retaliate against the United States by assassinating the American president, who lives in an open society and is more easily targeted? What kind of world would it be if countries killed each other's leaders? For many decades, Israel has pursued a policy of assassination against its enemies. The result: no change in its enemies, but many revenge murders against Israeli leaders.

A MORE DISCRIMINATING USE OF
COVERT ACTION

A retelling of this history of CIA covert actions and assassination plots is not meant to be a diatribe against the Central Intelligence Agency or its White House managers through the years. The CIA has done much good work to defend America's interests and, almost always, has acted not on its own but at the orders of various presidents of both parties. Moreover, as a CIA official insists, the people it supported in anti-communism covert actions during the Cold War "wanted to fight and would have anyway—we only helped them do what they wanted to do."[34] Nor is this retelling meant to suggest that covert action should be eliminated from the repertoire of American foreign policy. After all, it has had its successes, notably when the objectives have been limited (such as the broadcasts by Radio Free Europe during the period when that propaganda station was operated out of Munich by the CIA); when strong political opposition groups already exist within the target nation (the anti-Soviet warlords of Afghanistan in the 1980s); and, in the case of secret paramilitary operations, when aided and abetted by overt precision bombing from the air and elite Special Forces and indigenous allies on the ground (as in Afghanistan after 9/11).

Foreign dictators like Fidel Castro were certainly not princely fellows who should have been handled with white gloves during the Cold War. Former DCI John McCone explained the situation in the early Kennedy years:

Here was a man [Castro] who for a couple of years would seize every opportunity before a microphone or television to berate and criticize the United States in the most violent and unfair and incredible terms. Here was a man that was doing his utmost to use every channel of communication of every Latin American country to win them away from any of the principles that we stood for and drive them into communism. Here was a man that turned over the sacred soil of Cuba in 1962 to the Soviets to plant nuclear warhead short-range missiles, which could destroy every city east of the Mississippi. And before criticizing anything that was done, whether I knew of it or not—and I did not—I would think a little bit about the conditions of the time.[35]

The history of covert action does caution, however, against reliance on covert actions and assassinations to change the world—an arrogance spawned during the early stages of the Cold War by the successes in places like Iran in 1953 and Guatemala in 1954. No one owns a crystal ball, so the long-term consequences of covert action are difficult to predict. Still, is it not arrogant to dismiss in a cavalier fashion the possible negative results of American intervention abroad, whether secret or open? As a result of the excessive use of covert action during the Cold War, almost any disruptive event in the world has been blamed on the invisible hand of the United States and the CIA. A *New Yorker* cartoon once depicted island natives running away from an exploding volcano, crying "The CIA did it! The CIA did it!"

Today, critics continue to raise doubts, and reasonably so, about the wisdom of using the CIA and covert action to manipulate the media in fellow democracies, to intervene in free elections abroad, to tamper with open economic systems, or to kill suspected terrorists without trial or other forms of due process. When the government of China was charged with funneling secret funds into U.S. presidential elections during the 1990s, the American people were outraged. Yet, the United States has done this routinely in other countries over the years, such as the democracies of Chile and Italy. Why is this behavior acceptable for America, yet repugnant when carried out against the United States? The broader question is: who appointed the United States to shape the world according to its liking, whether through overt or covert means?

The CIA and covert action might be valuable, in certain extreme circumstances, as a shield for the United States against the likes of Al Qaeda and other immediate threats; yet, used indiscriminately, this approach to complex world affairs only lessens the nation's standing abroad. Concludes a U.S. Senator who in 1975 led a major inquiry into the uses of covert action: "If we have gained little from [covert action], what then have we lost?" His response: "our good name and reputation."[36]

A LITANY OF DISAPPOINTMENTS

The hidden side of American foreign policy is hardly the only place to look for haughty behavior by our nation in world affairs. Its overt policies have often exhibited a lordly attitude as well, such as President Lyndon Johnson's unnecessary dispatch of the U.S. Marines into the Dominican Republic in 1965. Among the most controversial examples of foreign policy arrogance has been the view of the second President Bush that the Geneva Conventions do not apply to America's capture of suspected terrorists. One of the most dubious spinoffs of this stance has been the use of "rendition," the secret and forcible transfer of terrorist suspects to other nations where they can be interrogated—read tortured—by foreign allies who have less concern about legal and moral ramifications.

In December of 2001, for instance, the CIA sent a Gulfstream V jet filled with hooded operatives to Stockholm, Sweden. Their mission was to take quick custody of two Egyptian prisoners held for the Agency by Swedish police officers.[37] At an airport in Stockholm, the two men (Ahmed Agiza and Muhammad Zery, suspected Islamic radicals) were stripped of all their clothing, physically probed, cuffed, hooded, tranquilized, and strapped to mattresses on the floor of the CIA aircraft. They were then flown to Cairo and turned over to Egyptian security personnel to undergo forms of interrogation prohibited for American intelligence officers inside or outside the United States (except on the popular Fox Network TV show 24). An inquiry into the case by the Swedish government led a parliamentary investigator, Mats Melin, to conclude that the rendition had violated the law of Sweden by subjecting the prisoners to "degrading and inhuman treatment." A lawyer for the Swedish Helsinki Committee for Human Rights, Anna Wigenmark, agreed that the operation was "against Swedish law and against international law."[38] The incident caused an uproar among Swedes, a nation known for its active support of international human rights.

The overmastering question reflected in this case is: can the United States absolve itself of improper practices, like harsh interrogations, simply by turning the dirty work over to an ally—in this instance Egypt (along with Israel, one of the top recipients of U.S. foreign aid)? Or by setting up CIA gulags around the world where Iraqi and Al Qaeda detainees can be held and interrogated away from the laws and ethical standards of the United States? Clearly not. Violations of the Geneva Conventions carried out by another nation at the behest of the United States remain the responsibility of the United States.

My conversations with foreigners living abroad, as well as with a good many who have traveled to America, indicate further concerns about how this nation is perceived by the rest of the world; so have my classroom discussions with U.S. students and professional colleagues.[39] Here are some illustrations:

- Foreigners are quick to observe that the American media pays little attention to what is occurring around the globe, other than to give a sense to viewers that there are some "crazies" out there who hate the United States and enjoy burning the American flag.
- Foreigners repeatedly note, too, that officials in Washington seem to have a philosophy of: "Let the rest of the world complain; we'll do what we want."
- Similarly, the statement from the second President Bush that "you are either with us or against us" in the war against terrorism left many with the impression that the United States failed to understand the nuances of international relations and the tangled ties between, say, the Europeans and nations in the Middle East.
- Many of those with a Middle Eastern heritage who admire the United States nonetheless lament the lingering presence of U.S. troops in Iraq and elsewhere in the region, finding this offensive to the holy places of Islam.
- Visitors from the Middle East raise questions, too, about the propensity of Americans to be full of patriotism, yet unable

to understand that Iraqis are patriotic as well and feel stung by the ongoing presence of an occupying army—even if it did come to "liberate" them.

- Anger stems, too, from the sometimes unseemly behavior of American forces abroad. Foreigners point to the show-off stunts of U.S. pilots, such as the Marine Corps EA-6B Prowler aircraft in 2000 that performed dangerous acrobatics too close to a ski lift near the resort town of Cavalese, Italy. The airplane sheared the cables, plunging the twenty occupants of a gondola to their deaths in the snowy valley below. The U.S. pilots got off lightly before a U.S. military tribunal.[40] Infuriating as well are the rapes of local women by American soldiers based overseas. However rare such cases may be, they cause understandable outrage and are long remembered by locals.

- Others note the incongruity of the United States spending billions on defense, yet expressing paranoia about the military buildup of other nations that seek to maintain their own defenses (such as China). In the same sense, it strikes foreigners as unfair for the United States and other nuclear powers to demand that no new nations have nuclear weapons, when those who already have them are so unwilling to reduce their arsenals to some reasonably small number—a nuclear arrogance. Or when America sells weapons around the world, then complains if other nations seek markets for their own weapons industry.

- Foreigners often mention America's support of dictators, during and after the Cold War, at the very time that officials in Washington espouse democracy around the globe. A key

contemporary illustration is Uzbekistan, a heinously repressive regime embraced by the United States for a few years after
the 9/11 attacks, because it provided a convenient airbase for
U.S. operations against insurgents in Iraq and Afghanistan.

- Some feel, as well, that it is pompous for the United States to
think it can "straighten out" Muslim extremism, rather than
relying on more moderate Muslims to do the job themselves.
They find this especially odd in light of the fact that Americans
largely ignored the Islamic world during the Clinton and Bush
administrations, until the 9/11 attacks. The American journalist Fareed Zakaria has pointed out that "if Muslims do not
take it upon themselves to stop their religion from falling prey
to medievalists, nothing any outsider can do will save
them."[41]

- A common expression of exasperation among foreigners is the
lack of interest Americans have in events beyond their own
borders, with the exception of battlefields where their soldiers
are engaged—especially their lack of foreign-language facility
and knowledge of the history and culture of other lands.

- On the world health front, others question the unwillingness
of U.S. pharmaceutical companies to assist in the war against
AIDS by providing low-cost—perhaps even free—generic
medicines to the extremely poor in Africa and elsewhere,
places where people are never going to be able to buy the necessary drugs at Western prices.

- A common criticism is directed toward the truculent rhetoric
of the Bush administration toward North Korea, with President Bush trashing the leader of that country publicly and

repeatedly with vituperative language that would be guaranteed to start a brawl in a Central Texas bar. Quiet diplomacy and working behind the scenes with other nations in the region is likely to produce better results than the public berating that, until recently, has been America's approach to the difficult problem of nuclear weapons in the hands of North Korea's enigmatic leadership.

- Some point to the Russian and Eastern Europe trip conducted by President Bush and Secretary of State Condoleezza Rice in 2005 as an example of overstepping the boundaries of international civility among major powers and fellow combatants against global terrorism. America's leaders lectured Russian President Vladimir Putin about democratic "backsliding" without noting the important steps toward democracy that Russia has taken, or realizing that democracy in Russia and Eastern Europe may take different forms than the U.S. model yet still be viable. Much has been made, for instance, of Putin's decision to appoint Russia's governors himself, rather than allow them to be elected; but, that is exactly how things are done in India, the world's largest democracy and one of the most impressive, given the enormous challenges of making democracy work in such a big and diverse nation. Russia has a long way to go to achieve a robust democracy but, again, the United States should work quietly to encourage that direction, not publicly embarrass an important ally and a Russian leader who faces dire domestic problems of counterterrorism, organized crime, and acutely factious politics.

- Above all, foreigners deplore the philosophy, which they find prevalent among Americans, that U.S. hegemony is a good thing, since the United States is wiser and more peace-loving than other great powers.

Some of these observations have merit, while others seem unfair. On the unfairness side, a few soldiers in every army throughout history have misbehaved and it is unreasonable to blame the United States for the misdeeds of a small number of individuals. Nonetheless, accused parties should be properly court-martialed, tried, convicted if guilty, and sentenced, not let off scot-free, as were the Marine pilots involved in the incident at Cavalese. The widespread abuse of military power at Abu Ghraib is, of course, a different matter, for that reflects an unacceptable permissiveness toward unsavory humiliation and interrogation techniques that seems to have permeated the U.S. defense establishment, with still no one yet held accountable at high levels of the military. Most U.S. soldiers stationed abroad, though, behave properly. Some have approached their jobs in a manner, and with the enthusiasm, of Peace Corps volunteers imbued with a strong sense of public service. In the latest war in Iraq, for instance, soldiers have built schools for girls who never before had a chance for formal education, served in the most trying conditions as temporary government officials in towns and villages until order can be restored, and done their best to befriend the people of Iraq in all walks of life.

Many of the negative observations one hears from foreigners and Americans alike deserve serious consideration, though. They have been repeated so often that surely the United States could benefit from considering changes in the way this nation relates to other countries, trying to align more with the hopes and expectations of friends abroad and thoughtful Americans at home.

AMERICA AS A GENTLE KNIGHT

Since the end of the Cold War, how seriously has the United States weighed the views of other nations? For example, to what extent have Americans tried to comprehend the forces fueling Islamic extremism, especially the fears in the developing world that the benefits of modernity are passing them by? The zealotry that led to the tragedy of September 11th cannot be tolerated, but some grievances in the Islamic world deserve more serious consideration by Americans. Did we really need to establish military bases in Saudi Arabia—so offensive to many Muslims, given the proximity of these installations to their holy shrines at Mecca and Medina? Why does the United States not resume a more balanced approach to peace negotiations in the Middle East, of the kind advanced by President Jimmy Carter during the Camp David Accords of 1978? Is it really necessary for U.S. security interests to stand alone, apart from friends and allies, in a refusal to sign treaties that prohibit the use of land mines, halt the international trade in small arms, clean up environmental pollution, limit greenhouse gas emissions, improve primary education in poor nations, and establish an International Criminal Court? Within America's international business community, must Wal-Mart insist on having its employees in Germany stand up every morning and sing the Wal-Mart song? As an employee has understandably complained, Germans are "uncomfortable about that in view of our history."[42] Even more problematic are the mere pennies a day that Wal-Mart and other Western corporations pay workers in many foreign lands—the downside of globalization.

Several U.S. foreign policy stances suggest a certain American egomania. What if, instead, the United States presented to the world a more humble demeanor, joining openly with others in a united search for world peace, tolerance, and prosperity? We could do worse that to adopt Louis J. Halle's image of medieval knighthood as a model for the conduct of U.S. foreign policy. "The national ideal of a supremely great power like the United States should be that of the gentle knight—exemplified in medieval literature by Lancelot, by Percival, by King Arthur," writes Hall. He continues:

> The gentle knight was strong, but his strength aroused neither fear nor resentment among the people because they knew it would be under the governance of moral responsibility and in the service of the general welfare. Precisely because he was strong, the gentle knight could afford to be modest, considerate, and courteous. His strength threatened only such outlaws as themselves constituted a threat to society. Consequently, his strength was not only his arm but in the regard of humankind. Where he went, his quiet voice represented legitimacy, speaking with its authority.[43]

During his second presidential campaign debate in 2000, George W. Bush for a moment seemed to understand the importance of humility as a hallmark for the world's mightiest military power. "The United States must be proud and confident of our values," he said, "but humble in how we treat nations that are figuring out how to chart their own course."[44] Sadly, the subsequent practice of American foreign policy has failed to lived up to this rhetoric.

NOTES

1. Benjamin R. Barber, *Fear's Empire: War, Terrorism, and Democracy* (New York: Norton, 2003), p. 21.
2. Thomas L. Friedman, "Just Shut It Down," *New York Times* (May 27, 2005), p. A23.

3. Somini Sengupta and Salman Masood, "Guantánamo Comes to Define U.S. to Muslims," *New York Times* (May 21, 2005), p. A6.

4. Salman Masood, "Reports of Mishandling Koran Bring Protest Worldwide," *New York Times* (May 28, 2005), p. A5.

5. Author's interviews, "Making Intelligence Accountable: Executive and Legislative Oversight of Intelligence Services," Oslo, September 18–20, 2003.

6. Jean-Marie Columbani, "We Are All Americans," *Le Monde* (September 12, 2001), p. 15.

7. Richard A. Clarke, *Against All Enemies: Inside America's War on Terror* (New York: Free Press, 2004), p. 285.

8. President George W. Bush, quoted by Richard A. Clarke, ibid., pp. 23–24.

9. Lt. Gen. William Boykin, quoted by Bob Herbert, "Shopping for War," *New York Times* (December 27, 2004), p. A21.

10. Condoleezza Rice, "Promoting the National Interest," *Foreign Affairs* 79 (January/February 2000), pp. 48–49.

11. The Rice quote is from ibid., p. 50; the Albright quote from Andrew J. Bacevich and Lawrence F. Kaplan, "Battle Wary," *New Republic* (March 25, 1998), p. 20.

12. President George W. Bush frequently praised the philosophy of foreign affairs found in the book by Natan Sharansky (with Ron Dermer), *The Case for Democracy: The Power of Freedom to Overcome Tyranny & Terror* (New York: Public Affairs, 2004), namely, that democracy can replace tyranny in Iraq and throughout the Middle East if the West has the will to promote it.

13. Quoted by Richard N. Current, Alexander DeConde, and Harris L. Dante, *United States History* (New York: Scott, Foresman, 1967), p. 234.

14. Quoted by Frances FitzGerald, "Reflections: Foreign Policy," *The New Yorker* (November 11, 1985), p. 112.

15. See Arthur M. Schlesinger, Jr., *War and the American Presidency* (New York: Norton, 2004), p. 140.

16. See William J. Daugherty, *Executive Secrets: Covert Action & the Presidency* (Lexington: University Press of Kentucky, 2004); Loch K. Johnson, *Secret Agencies: U.S. Intelligence in a Hostile World* (New Haven: Yale University Press, 1996); John Prados, *Presidents' Secret Wars*, rev. ed. (Chicago: Ivan R. Dees, 1996); Gregory F. Treverton, *Covert Action: The Limits of Intervention in the Postwar World* (New York: Basic Books, 1987). Of course, the United States is not the only nation to use covert action; most nations that can afford it find this "quiet option" beguiling [see Loch K. Johnson, "Bricks and Mortar for a Theory of Intelligence," *Comparative Strategy* 22 (Spring 2003), pp. 1–28].

17. See, respectively, Kermit Roosevelt, *Countercoup: The Struggle for the Control of Iran* (New York: McGraw-Hill, 1981); David Wise and Thomas Ross, *The Invisible Government* (New York: Random House, 1964).

18. See, respectively, William Colby and James McCargar, *Lost Victory: A First-hand Account of American's Sixteen-Year Involvement in Vietnam* (Chicago: Contemporary Books, 1989); William Colby and Peter Forbath, *Honorable Men: My Life in the CIA* (New York: Simon & Schuster, 1978), p. 368; Steve Coll, *Ghost Wars* (New York: Penguin, 2004).

19. Senator Frank Church, "Covert Action: Swampland of American Foreign Policy," *Bulletin of the Atomic Scientists* 32 (February 1976), p. 9.

20. Author's interview with senior CIA official in the Operations Directorate (January 21, 1976), Washington, DC; see Loch K. Johnson, *America's Secret Power: The CIA in a Democratic Society* (New York: Oxford University, 1989), pp. 66–70.

21. See Steve Coll, *Ghost Wars* (New York: Penguin, 2004); George Crile, *Charlie Wilson's War* (New York: Atlantic Monthly Press, 2003).

22. Richard Helms, with William Hood, *A Look over My Shoulder: A Life in the Central Intelligence Agency* (New York: Random House, 2003), p. 262.

23. See "The CIA Report the President Doesn't Want You to Read," *The Village Voice* (February 16 and 23, 1976), pp. 69–92; and Frank Snepp, *Decent Interval* (New York: Random House, 1979), pp. 573–580.

24. Ferdinand Mount, "Spook's Disease," *National Review* 32 (March 7, 1980), p. 300; see, also, Senate Select Committee to Study Governmental Operations with Respect to Intelligence Activities (the Church Committee), *Final Report*, 94th Cong., 2d Sess., Sen. Rept. No. 94-755 (Washington, DC: Government Printing Office, 1976).

25. See the Senate Select Committee to Study Governmental Operations with Respect to Intelligence Activities (the Church Committee), *Alleged Assassination Plots Involving Foreign Leaders*, 94th Cong., 2d. Sess. (Washington, DC: Government Printing Office, 1975), p. 181, note. The author served as assistant to the chairman on the Church Committee, 1975–76.

26. Tom Wicker, et al., "C.I.A. Operations: A Plot Scuttled," *New York Times* (April 25, 1966), p. A1.

27. For these facts about CIA assassination plots, see the Church Committee report on *Alleged Assassination Plots*.

28. Ibid., p. 181, note.

29. Elisabeth Bumiller, "Base Closing Will Be Fair, Bush Tells Naval Graduates," *New York Times* (May 28, 2005), p. A7.

30. Seymour M. Hersh, "Moving Targets," *The New Yorker* (December 15, 2003), pp. 48–55.

31. Executive Order 12333, Sec. 2.1 (1976).

32. Robert M. Gates, quoted by Walter Pincus, "Saddam Hussein's Death Is a Goal," *Washington Post* (February 15, 1998), p. A36.

33. Church Committee, *Alleged Assassination Plots*; Frank Church (D-ID), "Do We Still Plot Murders? Who Will Believe We Don't?" *Los Angeles Times* (June 14, 1983), pt. 2, p. 5.

34. Author's interview with CIA official (June 21, 1983), Washington, DC.

35. John McCone, press conference (June 6, 1975), Washington, DC (based on the author's notes at the time).

36. Church, "Do We Still Plot Murders?"

37. Craig Whitlock, "Swedish Report Sheds Light on 'Rendition,'" *Washington Post* (May 22, 2005), p. A1. For another troubling rendition case involving the CIA, the FBI, and a Canadian citizen, Maher Arar, born in Syria, see Scott Shane, "The Costs of Outsourcing Interrogation: A Canadian Muslim's Long Ordeal in Syria," *New York Times* (May 29, 2005), p. A11. Or for a case involving the CIA and a German citizen, Khaled el-Masri, see Don Van Matta, Jr., "Germans Looking into Complicity in Seizure by U.S.," *New York Times* (February 26, 2005), p. A1.

38. Whitlock, ibid.

39. As I was writing this book, I attended more than a dozen professional conferences (several overseas), where I spoke with foreign and American government officials, journalists, and scholars interested in issues of international affairs, and about how the United States is viewed in different nations. I also raised this question periodically to U.S. students on my own campus and others where I lectured, many of whom had traveled overseas. The questioning was by no means scientific, but it did elicit many thoughtful and revealing responses.

40. Chalmers Johnson, *Blowback* (New York: Henry Holt and Company, 2000), pp. 3–4.

41. Fareed Zakaria, "The Politics of Rage: Why Do They Hate Us?" *Newsweek*, Special Report (October 15, 2001), p. 27. See also his *The Future of Freedom: Illiberal Democracy at Home and Abroad* (New York: Norton, 2003).

42. Quoted by William J. Holstein, "Erasing the Image of the Ugly American," *New York Times*, "Inside the News" (October 23, 2005), p. 9.

43. Louis J. Halle, *The Elements of International Strategy: A Primer for the Nuclear Age* (Lanham, MD: University Press of America, 1984), p. 120.

44. Glenn Kessler, "Swell of Foreign Support Goes Flat," *Washington Post* (September 1, 2002), p. A1.

Conclusion:

Toward a More Worthy
Foreign Policy

THE SEVEN SINS AS A SYNDROME

The seven sins feed off one another, interacting to form a syndrome or pattern that leads to unfortunate distortions in the making of U.S. foreign policy. Ignorance among government analysts about language, history, and culture in the Middle East, Southwest Asia, and elsewhere produces alarming blind spots; and a lack of understanding among American citizens about foreign lands and how the United States conducts its affairs abroad—ignorance at the grassroots level—allows government officials too much leeway over foreign policy. In turn, too many contemporary lawmakers have displayed a tendency, as was the case before the war in Vietnam, to defer on matters of foreign policy to the executive branch; they become preoccupied with reelection pressures, such as

279

endless fund-raising and campaigning. Moreover, many members of Congress would just as soon place the blame on the executive branch if things go wrong overseas rather than bear responsibility themselves; they do not want to be a part of any crash landings, so they avoid the take offs, too.

The executive branch is happy to keep lawmakers and the public in the dark about foreign affairs, by stonewalling and slow-rolling on those occasions when Congress does request information and seeks to participate in the selection of policy options. For example, the White House resisted cooperation with the members of a special Joint Committee in establishing the facts about events that preceded the 9/11 terrorist attacks.[1] Then the White House refused to permit the panel authority to release information to the public about the relationship between Saudi Arabia and the terrorist hijackers, even though most of the terrorists came from that country. When the Congress recommended that another independent commission (the Kean Commission) further examine the 9/11 intelligence failure, the White House repeated the same pattern of resistance, stonewalling, and slow-rolling. A public that is provided truthful information about its government's foreign policies is apt to make responsible judgments; without that basic information— all too often kept sealed behind closed doors in Washington—the reactions of the people are no longer based on an empirical grounding of what has actually happened in the world.[2] Democracy rests on the foundation of an informed electorate and is greatly endangered when that foundation is allowed to erode.

Ignorance also clouds the public's understanding of the benefits to the United States that come from internationalism and globalization, and it encourages some forms of isolationism, such as an abandonment of international treaties and a reluctance to support foreign aid. Similarly, it retards the development of empathy among American citizens about the plight of the world's poor. Moreover, when the executive branch operates without adequate checks from the public and the Congress, it grows too strong and arrogant. Presidents and the foreign policy bureaucrats who serve them prefer unfettered movement in their operations overseas as well. Some presidents turn with undue haste to the use of the U.S. military and the secret intelligence agencies, toward whom Congress defers most of all,[3] to deal with problems abroad. They have been attracted, as well, to the ease of unilateral actions by the United States that require minimal negotiation and compromise with others. In tracing recent patterns of America's retreat from multilateral associations, David Skidmore has found that "the U.S. consistently seeks to shape or interpret international agreements so as to minimize constraints on its own freedom of action at home or abroad."[4]

The critique presented in this book suggests that American foreign policy works best when it avoids the seven sins and instead:

• Seeks to reduce ignorance through robust national debates about significant foreign policies, with full sharing of information (short of the most sensitive national secrets, like weapons blueprints and intelligence sources and methods) with Congress and the American people, coupled with steps to improve the foreign-language skills and knowledge about other nations at every level of society—from the general public to those who work within the bureaucracy;

- Encourages Congress and the executive branch to work together in a foreign-policy compact that taps into the combined wisdom of America's political institutions to address global challenges;
- Relies first and with more patience on the nation's intelligence officers to identify, and diplomats to resolve, international disputes, rather than rushing purblind into a military response;
- Works with other nations in a spirit of comity toward addressing global threats, not going it alone in the world;
- Eschews isolationist impulses by accepting a more cooperative relationship with the United Nations and other international organizations, and by appreciating the positive aspects of globalization while striving to reduce its harmful effects;[5]
- Cares about the plight of people in the developing world and mobilizing more effectively the combined resources of the United States and other affluent nations to close the widening gap between the rich and the poor around the globe; and,
- Exhibits a less prideful attitude toward the rest of the world.

Here are a set of baselines for judging the merits of specific foreign policy initiatives. The United States is more likely to succeed in the world—that is, achieve its goals, win friends abroad, and reduce the number and ferocity of its enemies—with these approaches than with policies that adhere to the contrary instincts embedded within the seven sins. Put simply, we need to think more about how we appear to the world.

In planning for the future of the United States, it is useful to look back over the record of the nation's foreign policies in the modern era, since the end of the Second World War. When have Americans shined, and when has their stock fallen with the rest of the world? When have we displayed thoughtfulness, knowledge, and concern about global affairs, rather than ignorance and disregard? When has America's government worked as the Constitution meant it to in foreign affairs, with all the branches actively engaged in debate, constructive criticism, and checking the excesses of the other branches? When has diplomacy been given a chance to succeed before the nation turned precipitously toward a military response, with all of the unintended consequences and "collateral damage" that accompany that blunt instrument? When has the United States rejected unilateralism in favor of consultation, shared decision-making, and mutual sacrifice with our allies? When have Americans pursued a restrained internationalism, treading their way between the Scylla of traditional isolationism and the Charybdis of compulsive interventionism? When have we displayed empathy toward the less advantaged nations of the world? When have we proceeded with a humble demeanor rather than hubris? The record suggests that the United States has often acted virtuously abroad since 1945, but all too often it has succumbed to the seven sins.

AN APPRAISAL OF AMERICAN
FOREIGN POLICY SINCE 1945

The Second World War brought the United States onto the world stage, however reluctantly, and center stage is where the nation has remained throughout the Cold War and into this new, uncertain age in which terrorism and the proliferation of WMDs have become the major immediate threats facing Americans, with pandemics and environmental degradation looming on the horizon. (It is useful to remember that other nations often have a far different set of concerns; AIDS leads the list in much of Africa, for instance, while Brazil grapples with domestic poverty and drug barons.[6]) Since 1991, the United States has assumed the mantle of the world's only superpower, but how well is the nation equipped to lead? Fate enjoys playing fresh tricks on humans; nevertheless, the results of previous foreign policy initiatives, as examined through the lens of the seven sins, can provide a sense of what the United States has done well in the past and when the nation has stumbled. Such an appraisal can provide at least a rough road map toward a better future.

America's relations abroad can be sorted according to four prominent approaches by which foreign policy is carried out: military, economic, diplomatic, and covert. From a much longer list of initiatives since the Second World War, only the most prominent foreign policies are examined here. Each is evaluated according to three criteria: some are deemed "good" if they largely rejected the seven sins, "bad" if they suffered in some important way from their influence, or "ugly" (America's most egregious ventures) if they were dominated by the influence of the sins. The guiding question is: from among the roll call of major foreign policies, which have stood out as *relative* paragons—all policies, made as they are by mere mortals, have flaws—and which have been less reputable?

A sifting of this kind obviously requires subjective judgments. If one were assured, for example, that a ballistic missile defense (BMD) could truly intercept and destroy incoming missiles, then a case could be made for President Reagan's Star Wars proposal and its subsequent iterations. Yet, if one were convinced that BMD is bad physics, too expensive, and at any rate unable to prevent a nuclear attack (which might come by way of a bomb sneaked across a U.S. border in a suitcase or entering inside a container box on a freighter in an American harbor), then this initiative would hold little attraction. Even if the physics seemed plausible, one would still have to evaluate the wisdom of a missile shield in light of its potential as a stimulus for an arms race, pushing Russia and China toward the development of a new generation of penetrating missiles and decoys as their way of maintaining a credible deterrent posture of their own.

How one feels about America's various foreign policies over the years will depend upon one's ethical perspectives as well, along with the degree of threat one perceives, one's basic ideological perspective on the world, and one's estimation about the likely short- and long-term effects of a policy. For example, on the ethical front, some policies—let us say, assassination plots—may be considered so anathema to American values that they should never be countenanced (a purist or Kantian view of foreign-policy ethics, in the manner of the German philosopher Immanuel Kant, 1724–1804, who proclaimed that one should "do no evil"). Even with assassination, though, others may see a higher moral objective that might require the use of this extreme option, perhaps the killing of Adolf Hitler in 1938 in hopes of preventing the Holocaust; or Saddam Hussein in 1991, to curb his use of WMDs against Israel or elsewhere (a consequentialist's view, in which the consequences of a policy—that is, its ends—are of more importance than the means one employs).[7]

How mad or "roguish" one thinks the enemy is can also play a role in these judgments.[8] If to the observer a threat to U.S. interests appears acutely dangerous, he or she may be drawn to policies of a more extreme nature employing a military component—perhaps preventive war or even a preemptive strike. For those who see the enemy through a more benign lens, as someone with whom one can negotiate differences, then intelligence gathering and diplomatic initiatives may override covert action and military operations.

Some observers of American foreign policy, just like some practitioners, peer at the globe through an ideological prism. A bleak zero-sum outlook might encourage a tough-minded foreign policy based on military strength maximized for use against an implacable enemy. In contrast, some individuals are more pragmatic; they are prepared to experiment with a range of approaches, including arms-control accords and altruistic programs of economic and technical assistance—initiatives that a rigid "realist" or "neorealist" might consider "soft" and naive.

Estimates of a foreign policy's short- and long-range effects can matter as well, though the effects can be hard to gauge.[9] Some policies may have all the earmarks of success over the short run, but may turn out to have been ill-judged and with unfortunate consequences over the long run. Deciding not to carry the first Persian Gulf War to Baghdad may have appeared prudent to the first Bush administration in 1991, because it avoided additional U.S. casualties and prevented Iraq from becoming a power vacuum (which would perhaps make it tempting to Iran). But what if Saddam Hussein had gone on to build a nuclear bomb and dropped it on Tel Aviv, or sold (or given) it to Al Qaeda for use against the United States? These are the kinds of scenarios, lacking confirmation through reliable intelligence, that contributed to the decision of the second Bush administration to attack Iraq again in 2003.

Providing Stinger missiles to the Afghan mujahedeen seemed like a good idea to the Reagan administration and it did help drive the Soviets out of Afghanistan; but was that nation any better off, or any friendlier toward the United States, under the fundamentalist rule of the Taliban (patrons of Al Qaeda)? Clearly not. And what has happened to many of the sophisticated weapons provided by the CIA to the mujahedeen? They were sold to the highest bidder, including Islamic fundamentalists in Iran—far from the intended purpose of the original covert action. This temporal element makes the evaluation of foreign policies tricky. In a critique, does one look at the immediate results, or weigh whether policymakers could have done a better job at anticipating the longer term negative effects? In the Stinger missile example, one is inclined to give the CIA full marks because the operation had the immediate desired effect of helping drive the Soviets out of Afghanistan. Nonetheless, the ultimate dispensation of the advanced weaponry, the rise of the Taliban regime, and the use of Afghanistan as a haven for Al Qaeda are deeply troubling long-range consequences of the original covert intervention.

Foreign policy is complex and difficult to evaluate—even after the fact, let alone before. Still, it is worth trying because an evaluation may draw out some lessons that can help craft better policies. The seven sins do not lead ineluctably to failed results, as the Nixon administration's secret negotiations with China—executive branch dominance over foreign policy—remind us; but they often are to blame and America's greatest successes in the world have usually been achieved when the nation's leaders rejected their temptations.

A FOREIGN POLICY HONOR ROLL

Only half of America's major foreign policies since 1945 that involved the military merit high marks, while the United States posted a number of significant international economic successes. This favorable judgment of economic initiatives is stained, though, by the fact that the United States has become the world's largest net debtor nation, with all the long-term fiscal risks posed by that reality. The current trade deficit amounts to about $1 trillion overall—ten times greater than just a decade ago. In 2005, the United States scored a record deficit of $726 billion in goods and services with the rest of the world.[10] In place of the trade surplus in agriculture that America boasted in the 1950s, even this sector recorded an alarming deficit in 2005.[11]

All but two of the diplomatic initiatives, but less than half of the foreign policies that resorted to covert operations, are judged meritorious. From among those foreign policies on the honor roll, a few are singled out as "most notable"—recipients of an "A" grade (see Figure 1).[12]

Good Military Policies

In the military domain, the containment doctrine that guided America through the Cold War, along with the supporting deterrence doctrine of mutually assured destruction (MAD), win high marks. This bold stance taken by the Truman administration—backed by the Congress, with lawmakers playing a role in shaping the doctrines—put the communists on notice that their avowed quest for world domination would meet stiff resistance from the democracies, led by the United States.[13] Another initiative from

FIGURE 1
The Honor Roll of American Foreign Policy, 1945–2005*

MILITARY

CONTAINMENT (1947–91)

DETERRENCE/MAD (1947–)

NATIONAL SECURITY ACT (1947)

Berlin Airlift (1948)

KOREAN WAR (1950–53)

Ike's No-Go in Vietnam (1954)

Berlin Confrontations (1960, 1961)

CUBAN MISSILE CRISIS (1962)

WAR POWERS RESOLUTION (1973)

GOLDWATER-NICHOLS ACT (1986)

First Persian Gulf War (1991)

Balkan Peacekeeping (1993–99)

War Against Al Qaeda and the Taliban (2001–02)

ECONOMIC

TRUMAN DOCTRINE (1947)

MARSHALL PLAN (1947)

Point Four (1949)

Food for Peace (1954)

Alliance for Progress (1961)

Trade Expansion Act (1962)

Opening to China (1972)

Caribbean Basin Initiative (1982)

North American Free Trade Agreement (1994)

DIPLOMATIC

UNITED NATIONS CHARTER (1945)

NATO (1947)
International Atomic Energy Agency (1957)

PEACE CORPS (1961)

Camp David Accords on the Middle East (1978)

Test Ban Treaty (1963)

Détente and Middle East Shuttle Diplomacy (1969–74)

HUMAN RIGHTS (1977–)

Panama Canal Treaties (1978)

Intermediate-Range Nuclear Force (INF) Treaty (1978)

START I and START II (1991, 1993)

*The most notable successes appear in capitalized, bold type.

NON-PROLIFERATION TREATY (1969)   Chemical Weapons Convention,
                                     CWC (1993)

Rapprochement to China (1972)   Dayton Accords on the Balkans
                                     (1995)

SALT I and SALT II (1972, 1979)

Anti-Ballistic Missile (ABM) Treaty (1972)

___

COVERT

___

EARLY COVERT ACTIONS   Intelligence Oversight
IN EUROPE (1945–53)   Act (1980)

DEVELOPMENT OF U-2 SPY   Boland Amendments for
PLANE (1956–60)   Nicaragua (1983–85)

DEVELOPMENT OF SPY   Iran-contra Investigations
SATELLITES (1960–)   (1987)

HUGHES-RYAN   Covert Action in Afghanistan
AMENDMENT (1974)   (1983–89)

ASSASSINATION   COVERT ACTION IN
PROHIBITION (1976)   AFGHANISTAN (2001–02)

ESTABLISHMENT OF
INTELLIGENCE OVERSIGHT
PANELS IN CONGRESS (1976, 1977)

1947, the National Security Act, was a lasting effort to bring about better military coordination through the creation of a modern department of defense and to set up a more sophisticated intelligence capability, with the CIA as the cornerstone. Unfortunately, President Truman ended up trading away a strong director of central intelligence (DCI) in exchange for the military's endorsement of consolidation; however, the National Security Act still stands as a bold measure to improve America's security posture.[14] The determination displayed by the Congress and the president together during the Korean War, at a time when international communism seemed in an especially aggressive phase of expansion, and during the Cuban missile crisis when the Soviet Union attempted the provocative placement of nuclear weapons into the Western Hemisphere, stand as the most vivid manifestations of America's commitment to containment.[15]

The Cuban missile crisis was an outstanding example of foreign policy crisis management by the United States, including consultation with individuals outside the narrow confines of the National Security Council. The Korean War and the missile crisis also enjoyed the support of an anti-communist consensus in the country. Even with this advantage, however, public opinion turned against the conflict in Korea as casualties mounted with no end to the war in sight. While these two initiatives draw praise here for stopping communist expansion and for their impressive crisis management, both suffered from a lack of meaningful consultation with lawmakers in the lead-up to decision.

Noteworthy, too, was the opposition of the Truman and Kennedy administrations to dangerous Soviet challenges to containment in Berlin. President Truman ordered an airlift in 1948 to break a Soviet blockade against Western access to the divided city; and President Kennedy faced tank-to-tank confrontations with the Soviets twice in Berlin: in 1961 and even more perilously in 1962.[16] These displays of force occurred only after extensive diplomatic efforts had failed.

During the Eisenhower administration, one of the president's most conspicuous foreign policy successes was the avoidance of a military confrontation with communist troops in Vietnam. Urged by some advisers to come to the rescue of besieged French troops at Dien Bien Phu in 1954—even to use nuclear weapons if necessary—Eisenhower prudently consulted with congressional leaders and, accepting their counsel over the advice of his own secretary of state John Foster Dulles, the president declined to enter the distant fray.[17]

The War Powers Resolution makes the list of "most notable" among the military-related policy successes. This controversial law qualifies, despite its flaws, because lawmakers at last proved willing—even overriding a presidential veto—to take responsibility for becoming a partner with the executive branch in decisions over the use of the war power. The law insisted on presidential reporting to Congress on the entry of U.S. troops into a foreign "zone of hostility"; and it required the chief executive to bring the military home within a maximum of ninety-two days, unless granted an extension by the Congress. Even though the Resolution has proved less successful than reformers hoped,[18] it continues to stand as a warning to presidents that congressional authorization is necessary before the engagement of the United States in offensive warfare. The Goldwater-Nichols Act of 1986 is of special significance, too, since it accelerated U.S. military consolidation and efficiency, helping to overcome debilitating service rivalries.

To its credit, the first Bush administration drove Iraq out of Kuwait's sovereign territory in the first Persian Gulf War in 1991. President George H. W. Bush requested authority from Congress to carry out the military operation and received a formal vote of support in both chambers. Regrettably, though, the president's approach to war-making was marred by a thinly veiled threat that he would use military force against Iraq, regardless of what lawmakers decided; and, on the congressional side, such an important undertaking warranted more than just four days of formal debate—although that period of time substantially surpassed what lawmakers would devote in 2003 to an appraisal of the need for another war against Iraq.

President Clinton successfully led a NATO coalition to restore peace in the war-torn Balkans, with full congressional and allied consultation and support; and President George W. Bush forcefully guided America's retaliation against Al Qaeda terrorists responsible for the 9/11 attacks and the Taliban regime in Afghanistan that harbored them. Neither event yielded perfect results and the Balkans, as well as Afghanistan, remain beset with internal tensions and periodic violence; nevertheless, both cases displayed the virtues of Congress and the president working together and with other nations—though again congressional debate was, in both instances, far more anemic than citizens deserved.

Good Economic Policies

For some observers and practitioners of American foreign policy, global economic opportunities should be preeminent on any listing of international objectives. "It's no longer American foreign policy," observed a chairman of the Senate Foreign Relations Committee. "It's American foreign *economic* policy."[19] The senator meant to convey the extent to which, in his view, international economic issues had displaced more traditional national security and diplomatic issues on the agenda of U.S. foreign policy. Despite their significance, however, major economic policies have been pursued less frequently than any other policy category, although these initiatives have often reaped substantial benefits to the United States and its trading partners.

Each of the economic policies presented in Figure 1 sought to improve international peace through better commercial relationships, along with economic and technical assistance to the fledgling economies of the developing world. Again, none is perfect, yet each tried to raise the tide of prosperity around the globe and, for the most part, each reflected a healthy, bipartisan working relationship between Congress and the executive branch. Most notable are two proposals that followed on the heels of the Second World War: the Truman Doctrine and the Marshall Plan, both advanced in 1947.

The Truman Doctrine, a policy of providing military and economic assistance to countries resisting "totalitarian aggression," provided vital aid to the beleaguered nations of the northern Mediterranean tier, Greece and Turkey, helping them to avert Soviet domination.[20] President Truman expanded America's opposition to communism by providing economic aid through the Marshall Plan to sixteen countries of Western Europe. This initiative encouraged reconstruction and helped to stabilize the region against Soviet inroads. Though neither were acts of pure altruism (the United States stood to gain from a more stable Greece and Turkey, along with a growing market in Europe), they epitomized the value of an economic helping hand for defeating what George Marshall knew to be freedom's greatest foes: poverty and the accompanying sense of desperation that provide fertile soil for the seeds of communism, terrorism, and other radical movements.[21]

The Point Four Program, announced in Truman's inaugural address of 1949, carried economic containment into the developing world by providing technical assistance and private investment for developing nations vulnerable to communist blandishments. Although a relatively small program compared to the massive infusion of funds into Europe through the Marshall Plan, Point Four had several ambitious goals: the eradication of disease, the building of roads and hydroelectric power, educational improvements, and increases in food supply for the world's poorest nations.[22] During the Eisenhower years, the Food for Peace program (known also as PL-480, after the public law that created it in 1954) became America's chief means for channeling food aid to poor nations, as well as for granting emergency and disaster relief—another illustration of Congress and the executive branch working hand in hand to shape effective policy.[23]

The Kennedy administration undertook an ambitious approach to trade policy, which had been largely dormant for the past three decades with the exception of a few innovative agreements established under the leadership of Cordell Hull, America's longest serving secretary of state (1933–44). In his announcement of an Alliance for Progress in 1961, President Kennedy pledged a commitment to the economic growth and democratization of Latin America. The United States spearheaded an effort to infuse into this region public and private capital—a Marshall Plan for Latin America and yet another attempt to counter the lure of communism in the developing world. With the Trade Expansion Act of 1962, President Kennedy worked with Congress to embrace a broad cutback in U.S. tariffs on imports, as a way of stimulating world trade by encouraging reciprocal reductions—a marked liberalization of trade policy.[24]

In 1972, the Nixon administration advanced the boldest global economic initiative by the United States since the Kennedy years by opening up trade relations with the land of a billion consumers: the People's Republic of China. In a hedge against the concern that Marxist influence might sprout close to the United States, President Reagan targeted the Caribbean Basin for a special economic initiative in 1982. The agreement allowed for permanent tariff-free and reduced-tariff entry into the United States for almost all of the products coming from the twenty-four countries of the region. The first President Bush and President Clinton also concentrated on the Western Hemisphere in their proposal for the North American Free Trade Agreement (NAFTA) of 1994, for which they both share credit with lawmakers for passage of the proposal through Congress.

Good Diplomatic Policies

In this analysis, diplomatic policies refer to noneconomic agreements entered into with other countries by the United States in hopes of resolving ongoing disputes or building collective security arrangements. Preeminent here are arms-control accords and defense alliances (in contrast to the actual use or threat of force examined above). Almost all of the major diplomatic initiatives have been useful, for they have attempted to build bridges of cooperation among nations while guarding America's own interests. Most noteworthy are: the establishment of the United Nations Charter in 1945 and the North Atlantic Treaty Organization (NATO) in 1947; creation of the Peace Corps in 1961; the signing of the Non-Proliferation Treaty in 1969; and various accords to enhance global human rights, a centerpiece for foreign policy during the Carter administration.

The United Nations, imperfect as it is, remains an important forum for an array of international activities designed to enhance peace and improve life on the planet. NATO became not only the backbone of the Western alliance against the communist regimes, but also a means for nurturing trade and good will among Canada, the United States, and fourteen other members in Western Europe— an impressive feat of diplomatic negotiations that involved a major role for Congress and facilitated no doubt by the looming shadow of the Red Army across the Elbe.[25] The Peace Corps presents American foreign policy at its idealistic best, with citizen-ambassadors garnering much affection for the United States abroad.[26]

Several important arms-control negotiations occurred during the post-WWII period, including the Test Ban Treaty of 1963; the Anti-Ballistic Missile (ABM) Treaty of 1972; the Strategic Arms Limitation Treaties (SALT) of 1972 and 1979; the Intermediate-Range Nuclear Forces (INF) Treaty of 1987; the Strategic Arms Reduction Treaties (START) of 1991 and 1993; and the Chemical Weapons Convention of 1993. The Nuclear Non-Proliferation Treaty of 1969, though, deserves special praise because its efforts to slow the arms race between the superpowers set the stage for the significant reductions in arms that would follow.[27] The Eisenhower administration's support in 1957 for the establishment of an International Atomic Energy Agency (IAEA) assisted the goal of bringing some accountability over the worldwide dissemination of nuclear technology, and provided an international forum for efforts to curb the proliferation of nuclear weapons. All of these pacts, though, still have left the United States and Russia today with far too many nuclear weapons—more than seven thousand operational warheads in the Russian and over five thousand in the U.S. arsenals—with many of the weapons still on hair-trigger alert even though the Cold War is long over.[28]

Also on the diplomatic front, one of America's most remarkable secretaries of state, Henry Kissinger, led the Nixon administration into rapprochement with China, smoothed the troubled waters of the Middle East with his famous shuttle diplomacy, and encouraged détente with the Soviet Union. Kissinger's short suit was working with lawmakers. President Carter substantially advanced peace in the world with the Panama Canal Treaties (1978) and the Middle East summit at Camp David (1978). Moreover, his human rights diplomacy, though selective and often displaying more rhetoric than achievement, espoused laudable objectives and served as a stimulus to the rising democratic impulse that would soon sweep across much of the world. Finally, in 1995, the Clinton administration brokered the Dayton Accords that helped to advance peace in the Balkans.

Good Covert Policies

The United States has the most elaborate intelligence establishment in the world or, for that matter, in all of history. The major purpose of this loose confederation of sixteen agencies is to spy overseas and provide insights for U.S. policymakers about world events and conditions. Almost immediately in the wake of the Second World War, however, the Truman administration gave the CIA a more aggressive mission as well: covert action, the secret manipulation of events abroad in an effort to move history in a direction more favorable to the United States. This hidden side of American foreign policy has scored some successes, along with a raft of questionable outcomes.

The covert actions that immediately followed the Second World War attempted to counter Soviet covert influence in Greece and other European nations. These operations were complemented by many similar, if less well-known, subterranean struggles in Asia, Africa, and Latin America. The communists tested the West's mettle in struggles for control over labor unions, political parties, and the media in a wide range of countries (such as Italy and France), finding the CIA and other Western intelligence services prepared to protect democracy's interests during this crucial early stage of the Cold War. Equally important, the Eisenhower and subsequent administrations invested heavily in spy planes (beginning in 1956) and satellites (1959), necessary to maintain America's awareness of Soviet and Chinese military capabilities and activities—the first line of defense in support of deterrence and the containment doctrine.

Additional measures related to covert operations attract high praise.[29] The Hughes-Ryan Act (1974) acknowledged the need for closer supervision of the CIA by requiring presidential approval (a "finding" by the president) for all important covert actions, accompanied by reports to the two new intelligence oversight committees established in the Senate (1976) and the House (1977). This law and the new committees prepared the way for further steps toward improved intelligence accountability, as vital to democracy as the warnings the intelligence agencies try to provide about foreign and domestic dangers. Among other steps significant to intelligence accountability was passage of the Intelligence Oversight Act of 1980 that required prior notice to the Congress of all important intelligence activities.

Of special importance, too, was an executive order signed by President Ford in 1976 that banned assassination plots against foreign leaders and removed the United States from playing the odious role of an international hit man. Some ambiguity exists, though, about when assassinations might be used in today's struggle against global terrorism. While Al Qaeda's leaders have been targeted for capture or death, it remains impermissible under the executive order to target foreign heads of state—unless the White House can make the case to lawmakers that these leaders, too, are involved in terrorism. In 1991, the first President Bush waived the executive order so he could target the leader of Iraq, Saddam Hussein. President Clinton waived the order, as well, to allow attacks against the Al Qaeda leader, Osama bin Laden. So did the second President Bush with respect to Bin Laden during the war against Al Qaeda that began in earnest after the 9/11 attacks, as well as for Saddam Hussein during the war against Iraq in 2003. At the end of that year, U.S. troops managed to capture Saddam alive, extracting him from a hole in the ground where he was hiding near his place of birth in Iraq.

Worthy of mention, as well, are the series of Boland Amendments (1983–85) designed to halt covert actions in Nicaragua opposed by a majority of the Congress; and the thorough investigations in 1987 by Congress, as well as an executive branch panel (the Tower Commission), into the wrongdoing of the Reagan administration in flaunting the Boland laws. The CIA interventions in Afghanistan, twice, were also significant, especially after 9/11.

AMERICA OFF COURSE

The United States has been most apt to embrace the seven sins when pursuing military and covert operations. The candidates for the "bad" and the "ugly" categories of foreign policy, presented in Figure 2, include thirteen military and fourteen covert policies, a pair of diplomatic initiatives, and a single—though singularly troubling—economic circumstance. The "ugly" designation in the figure points to those policies that have been particularly guilty of succumbing to one or more of the seven sins.

Bad Military Policies

The Formosa (1955) and Middle East Resolutions (1957), declarations of intent by President Eisenhower to curb communist expansion both in Taiwan and the Middle East, were examples of

FIGURE 2
American Foreign Policy Off Course, 1945–2005*

MILITARY

Formosa Resolution (1955)	Grenada Invasion (1983)
Middle East Resolution (1957)	Ballistic Missile Defense (1983–)
VIETNAM WAR BUILDUP (1965–68)	
CAMBODIAN INCURSION (1970)	Libyan Air Attack (1986)
Mayaguez rescue in Cambodia (1975)	Lebanon Peacekeeping (1989)
Carter Doctrine (1979)	**PANAMA INVASION** (1989)
Iran hostage rescue (1980)	**SECOND PERSIAN GULF WAR** (2003–)

ECONOMIC

World's Largest Debtor Nation (Over the Years)

DIPLOMATIC

SEATO (1954)	ABM Treaty Reinterpretation (1987)
	ABM Treaty Abrogation (2001)

COVERT

Iran Coup (1953)	*PUEBLO* **CAPTURE** (1968)
Guatemala Coup (1954)	Iran Weapons Sales (1986)
ASSASSINATION PLOTS (1959–61)	**CONTRA SCANDAL** (1986–87)
U-2 SHOOT DOWN (1960)	Iraq Covert Actions (1994–2003)
BAY OF PIGS (1961)	9/11 Intelligence Failure (2001)
Laos Paramilitary War (1962–68)	**IRAQI WMD INTELLIGENCE FAILURE** (2002)
CHILE COVERT ACTIONS (1963–73)	**INDISCRIMINATE PREDATOR/ HELLFIRE ATTACKS** (2002–05)

*"Ugly" initiatives appear in capitalized, bold type.

risky military posturing in regions of the world where the United States had little leverage. Further, they attempted by executive fiat to commit this nation to perilous military positions without detailed authority from, or even serious debate in, the Congress. In these instances, President Eisenhower and his headstrong Secretary of State Dulles abandoned the bipartisan and consultative approach to foreign policy that had been the hallmark of success for the Marshall Plan and NATO. The Korean War ("Truman's War") was an earlier example of this presidential usurpation of the war powers, but at least that intervention was militarily feasible and required urgent attention. Therefore, Korea makes the list of good military policies, despite Truman's regrettable aggrandizement of war-making authority; Eisenhower's resolutions, though, were neither militarily sound nor constitutionally defensible.[30]

The military missions ordered in 1975 by President Ford in Cambodia to rescue the crew of the merchant ship *Mayaguez*, and in 1980 by President Carter to rescue hostages in the U.S. embassy in Iran, both failed. The first mission was devoid of adequate intelligence, lacked urgency, and led to the deaths of forty-one U.S. military personnel; the second collapsed from the poor execution of what seemed like a workable plan.[31] In each instance, diplomacy would have been the more prudent course, as Carter's Secretary of State Cyrus Vance advocated in the second crisis (although the president chose to reject his advice). The Carter Doctrine, a label given to President Carter's declaration in 1979 that the United States would counter with military force any Soviet move toward the Persian Gulf, smacked of a hubris reminiscent of the Eisenhower Resolutions in both its brashness and lack of congressional endorsement.

In its use of the military in Lebanon (1983), in Grenada (1983), and in Libya (1986), the Reagan administration placed U.S. forces in harm's way for no compelling reason. Lebanon led to the deaths of more than two hundred Marines, with no effect on the local civil war; and Grenada was a dubious exercise in muscle flexing. The Libyan attack, purportedly launched to deter future terrorism by Mu'ammar Gadhafi, did nothing to deter a subsequent Libyan intelligence operation that destroyed a Pan Am commercial airliner in flight over Lockerbie, Scotland, in 1988.

As for ballistic missile defense programs (beginning in 1983), the physics remain deeply suspect. In an important test of the missile defense system in December 2004, the interceptor rocket failed to launch, ignoring its lift-off command and shutting down. The problem was "an unknown anomaly," according to the department of defense.[32] Most of the earlier tests, under highly controlled and unrealistic conditions, proved ineffectual, too. The Defense Department has already spent $130 billion on the program, and plans to invest another $53 billion over the next five years. This projected sum could be tapered down, allowing some research to continue but with the bulk better invested in diplomatic and economic initiatives to ameliorate conditions of poverty in the world that increase the danger of terrorism and the use of WMDs against the United States in the first place. A group of forty-nine retired generals and admirals have already counseled the second Bush administration on the wisdom of using most of this funding instead on low-tech antiterror defenses, especially to make America's harbors, borders, and nuclear weapons depots more secure.[33]

Ugly Military Policies

The "ugly" military category is reserved for policies deeply flawed by the influence of one or (usually) more of the seven sins. Leading examples are President Johnson's escalation of the war in Vietnam (1965–68), President Nixon's continuation of that war and its expansion into Cambodia (1970), the first President Bush's invasion of Panama (1989), and the second President Bush's invasion of Iraq (2003). Criticism of these wars, or any other American war, is certainly not leveled at our men and women in uniform, many of whom lost their lives in service to their country. For example, the humanitarian acts bravely carried out by U.S. soldiers during the second war in Iraq amidst the dangers of enemy fire—from their rebuilding of sewer lines and water pipes to the protection in local civilians from insurgents in Iraq and their leadership for village councils—have done much to win friends abroad for the United States and deserve the deepest appreciation and respect of all Americans. Instead, the criticism here is directed toward the policy-makers in Washington who launched the wars in the first place.

The Vietnam conflict—the darkest stain on the ledger of modern American foreign policy—resulted in more than fifty-eight thousand American deaths, three hundred thousand additional U.S. casualties, and an estimated three million fatalities among all participants;[34] the Cambodian incursion catalyzed one of the most disruptive periods of civil unrest in the United States, with massive protests in the streets and on college campuses; and the main result of the Panamanian invasion was the jailing of a pathetic drug-dealing general, Manuel Noriega (Panama's leader at the time), who is now confined to a jail in Miami, with no discernable improvement in the life of Panama and no interruption in the flow of drugs through Central America to the United States.

As an illustration, consider the seven sins in relationship to the war in Vietnam. The United States knew precious little (sin number 1) about Vietnam outside of Saigon, including an inaccurate understanding of communist strength in the hinterland.[35] Presidents played the Vietnam War cards close to their vest without much congressional involvement (sin number 2). The surrender of power began in 1964 when lawmakers gave President Johnson a blank check in Indochina by way of the Gulf of Tonkin Resolution, after the White House misled them into believing that an American destroyer had come under attack by the North Vietnamese in the Gulf. The Pentagon dominated the war years from 1964 to 1973 (sin number 3), as Presidents Johnson and Nixon relied on the generals and rejected reports from intelligence officers and diplomats estimating that the war could not be won. The U.S. war-fighting benefited from the loyal support of troops from Australia, New Zealand, South Korea, and a few other nations but the war depended chiefly on the half-million troops sent to Vietnam by the United States and was primarily a unilateral enterprise (sin number 4), with the other major democracies standing on the sidelines.

The Vietnam War was hardly an example of isolationism (sin number 5). On the contrary, sins 1 through 4 trumped number 5. Here was a case of hyperinterventionism, with America far from home for no strong reason of national interest beyond the domino theory, which by 1964 had become suspect since nationalism had proven a powerful force of resistance against communist efforts to topple dominos. Lack of empathy (sin number 6) was a factor, though, as the United States used napalm, powerful incendiary bombs dropped from an altitude of thirty thousand feet, Agent Orange defoliates, and search-and-destroy missions that often failed to discriminate between friends and enemies or soldiers and civilians—leveling villages in order to save them. And what could be more arrogant (sin number 7) than to think the United States could use the muscle of B-52 Stratofortress bombers, F-4 Phantom jets, M48 tanks, and 105mm howitzers to quell a civil war in the remote jungles of Indochina?

The second President Bush responded appropriately to the 9/11 attacks with a counteroffensive against Al Qaeda and the Taliban regime in Afghanistan. Unwisely, however, Congress provided (all too hastily) open-ended authority for the war against terrorism around the world, allowing the U.S. military and the CIA to hunt down terrorists wherever they might be hiding—supposedly in some sixty countries. Here was a prescription for an indiscriminate use of force, setting the stage for the launching of Hellfire missiles mounted on pilotless aircraft against anyone suspected of being a terrorist. More questionable than the war against terrorists, though, was the second Persian Gulf War. Lawmakers yielded quickly, without meaningful debate or independent inquiry, to the tenuous argument of the second Bush administration in 2003 that war was necessary—an argument based on questionable intelligence sources never admitted to Congress or the American people by the White House or the director of central intelligence. The U.S.-led invasion force discovered neither WMDs nor significant ties to Al Qaeda in Iraq, but did manage to engulf U.S. troops in a guerrilla war of attrition with questionable prospects for democracy in a nation decimated by insurgent rockets, suicide bombers, and longstanding ethnic enmities.

"The whole Iraq situation has brought back memories of the big stick—American power as used in Nicaragua or Chile during the cold war," laments a former Brazilian foreign minister, Luiz Felipe Lampreia. "The problem is the perception that Bush uses immense power in an egotistical way."[36] Scholars of the war in Iraq worried that it carried "with it the cost of an expanding breach with our NATO partners and the demise of a re-energized Atlantic Alliance. If this becomes the ground truth, success in Iraq will be a pyrrhic victory and a strategic blunder of immeasurable consequence."[37] In the view of the American historian Günter Bischof, the Bush administration "managed to do more damage to transatlantic relations in three years than his predecessors had done in the aggregate over more than half a century as they tried to build a relatively harmonious relationship."[38]

Bad Economic Policies

While the economic initiatives of the United States since 1945 have been laudable for the most part, the record is marred by a worrisome international indebtedness that stems from a combination of arrogance that America can spend wildly and ignorance that it will have no negative repercussions. The cycle is pernicious: the United States runs up debts with wars in Iraq and Afghanistan, and at the same time spends more on buying goods from abroad than selling American products to other countries. In the meantime, the military spending is exacerbated by a weakened tax base, eroded by sweeping tax cuts during the second Bush administration that wrecked the balanced budget left by the Clinton administration. The United States then borrows money to continue the spending necessary to fight its wars, as well as to prop up the dollar among international currencies. America's taxpayers must shell out for interest on these loans, thereby further increasing the national debt. China and Japan have provided the United States considerable amounts of capital by investing in U.S. Treasury securities, essentially "lending us money so we can buy their goods."[39] This is not a sound arrangement and, if allowed to continue much longer, it will soon qualify for the "ugly" designation—indeed, potentially the most damaging among all of America's foreign policies.

Bad Diplomatic Policies

The diplomatic initiatives in the "bad" category are the Southeast Asian Treaty Organization (SEATO) of 1954, the Anti-Ballistic Missile (ABM) Treaty reinterpretation of 1987 to allow development of the ballistic missile defense system, and the unilateral abrogation of the ABM Treaty in 2001 by the second Bush administration. The SEATO arrangement conveyed unrealistic expectations about America's ability to defend the nations of Southeast Asia, setting the stage for the debacle in Vietnam. The ABM reinterpretation, as well as the subsequent abrogation of the treaty, stand as blatant examples of executive branch arrogation of power. In the first case, through sleight of hand the Department of State sought to alter a solemnly approved pact. Fortunately, the Senate had the intestinal fortitude to stand up and block the attempt to weaken its treaty powers. In the second case, the Congress capitulated. President George W. Bush dissolved the ABM Treaty, a bothersome hindrance that threatened to block further development of his proposed missile shield, without so much as a how-do-you-do to U.S. lawmakers or to Russia (the cosignatory of the treaty).

Bad Covert Policies

The "bad" covert actions include the coups that took place in Iran (1953) and in Guatemala (1954); the paramilitary war against communists in Laos (1962–68); secret weapons sales in Iran (1986); and, most recently, coup attempts in Iraq (during the Clinton and both Bush administrations). Quite to the contrary, some observers will view these operations as marvelous successes, yielding pro-U.S. leaders in Iran and Guatemala in the fifties, a standoff with the Laotian communists in the sixties, freeing hostages with Iran's help in the eighties, and bringing pressure to bear on the Iraqi regime in the nineties.

Yet the United States could have had acceptable relations with the existing leaders of Iran and Guatemala anyway (both democratically elected), without the calumny that accompanied the covert interventions and led to brutal dictatorships. Moreover, the war in Laos accomplished little, while bringing about the decimation of the local Hmong tribesmen who helped the CIA. And even if President Reagan thought he needed to trade weapons for influence in Iran to gain its help in releasing captive Americans in Lebanon (he would hardly have been the first president to barter for hostage releases), his chosen approach was an inappropriate defiance of Congress and the law. Had he quietly informed lawmakers of his dilemma, most likely they would have supported some form of secret negotiations and bartering with Iran and, as a result, at least the Iranian part of the Iran-contra scandal could have been avoided. The covert actions against Iraq prior to the 2003 invasion were abject failures by all accounts. They consumed large amounts of money to aid dissident factions that proved incapable of cooperating among themselves, let alone overthrowing Saddam Hussein.

Finally, the inability of the intelligence agencies to warn the nation about the 9/11 attacks led to one of the greatest tragedies in the history of the United States. Had the CIA developed a better ring of agents in Afghanistan, it might have been able to penetrate Al Qaeda. Still, the 9/11 failure escapes the "ugly" category in this case, because at least the CIA did offer warnings to high government officials as far back as 1995 that enemies of the United States might resort to "aerial terrorism," that is, hijacking and flying commercial airlines into skyscrapers.[40] Despite repeated warnings to this effect over the next six years, officials did little to improve airport security, warn pilots, or even notify the Department of Transportation about the threat of aerial terrorism.[41] Moreover, lawmakers on the oversight committees—now resolute in criticizing the CIA for not developing a better espionage capability in the Middle East and South Asia—did little from 1995–2001 to push the intelligence agencies in that direction, earning for themselves a share of the culpability for America's lack of preparedness to thwart the terrorist attacks.

Ugly Covert Policies

The "bad" covert actions pale in comparison, however, to the botched, embarrassing excesses of the assassination plots against Fidel Castro and other foreign leaders (1959–61); the provocative flight of a U-2 over Russian territory, shot down on the eve of a U.S.-Soviet summit (1960); the Bay of Pigs fiasco (1961); the secret attacks against the democratically elected Chilean President Salvador Allende during the Nixon years; another unnecessarily provocative espionage operation, this time in the coastal waters of North Korea, that led to the capture of the U.S. spy ship *Pueblo* (1968); the extraconstitutional means adopted by the Reagan administration in 1985–86, when the NSC staff secretly bypassed existing laws to support the contras during the Nicaraguan civil war; and the use since 2002 of the airborne drone, the Predator— the most lethal of all the CIA's covert action instruments—to launch Hellfire missiles at unconfirmed terrorist suspects in Afghanistan and Yemen.[42]

Garnering special attention is the failure of the intelligence agencies to accurately assess Iraq's WMD program during the Clinton years and the early years of the second Bush administration. Again, the CIA had poor sources (human intelligence, or "humint") in Iraq. The Agency had to rely chiefly on a dubious German source with the codename "Curveball," an Al Qaeda operative by the name of Ibn al-Shaykh al-Libi who turned out to be a fabricator, satellite photography (often of little use in this age, when rogue nations have learned to construct nuclear weapons in underground caverns), and extrapolations based on the state of the Iraqi WMD program when America had boots on the ground there in 1991. A National Intelligence Estimate that predicted in October 2002 that the Iraqi regime was apt to have WMDs proved wrong, as U.S. troops and various civilian inspectors discovered when they entered Iraq in 2003.

Worse still, in the months leading up to the U.S.-led invasion of Iraq, the director of central intelligence, George J. Tenet, seems to have become more a member of the president's team than a neutral conveyor of factual information to the White House. In his zeal to support the administration's inclination toward war against Iraq,

Tenet went far beyond the evidence and proclaimed to the president that the probability of Iraqi WMDs was a certainty—a "slam dunk," in his words[43]—rather than a hunch based on Saddam's reckless pursuit of WMDs ten years prior. The intelligence director violated the cardinal rule of his profession: to remain objective and detached from policy.[44]

Here, then, are examples of the CIA at its worst, though with respect to covert actions the Agency acted with presidential approval for the most part (or, in the case of the Iran-contra affair, with inappropriate NSC staff approval). The Iran-contra operations displayed the most extreme arrogance in modern American foreign policy, with the Reagan administration bypassing the Congress altogether. "If a White House can decide that a law passed by Congress [the Boland Amendments prohibiting covert action in Nicaragua] is inconvenient, and simply set out to circumvent it," concluded a Washington, DC, correspondent, "then our constitutional system is finished."[45] At least during Lyndon Johnson's secret build-up of the war in Vietnam, lawmakers on the Armed Services and the Appropriations Committees knew about the president's actions, although they kept this information from their colleagues and the public.

CASTING OFF THE SEVEN SINS

The United States has been at its best in the conduct of foreign policy when it has eschewed the seven sins—when it has acted with the support of an informed public and Congress; when it has tried to help others develop their own economies, at the same time establishing markets for itself; when it has used its intelligence agencies responsibly to gather information about threats and opportunities abroad, not to engage in unnecessary covert actions; and when the executive and legislative branches have worked together in a spirit of comity to fashion initiatives that enjoy widespread support in the country. The Truman Doctrine and Marshall Plan are illustrations of when the United States was all square to the wind, assisting others to find their economic legs instead of attempting secretly to overthrow or murder leaders in poor countries, or sending troops overseas to settle civil wars or change governments—situations that the indigenous populations must sort out for themselves.

Sometimes the United States will have to intervene abroad with force, as with the efforts during the Clinton years to halt the brutal "ethnic cleansing" in the Balkans; but, even then, the nation must be prudent enough, as the first Bush and the Clinton administrations usually understood, to join with others in a NATO, UN, or other multilateral response. Such interventions also warrant the involvement of Congress, with full debate on the subject and a formal vote on whether authority—well-defined—should be granted to the president for the use of military force. Occasionally, secret foreign policy has been useful, as with Nixon's opening to China and various "back-channel" arms negotiations and human rights interventions. For the most part, though, secret activities have led to terrible mistakes, as the Bay of Pigs disaster and President Johnson's escalation of the war in Vietnam underscore.

Proponents of solutions to international disagreements based on U.S. military force may balk at the notion of entering into collaborative endeavors with other nations around the world. Fascinated by America's great arsenal of weapons and the possibility of quick results through the use of force—not to mention the popular allure, potential heroism, and thrill of danger that accompanies war-fighting—they are unable to imagine the advantages of a foreign policy in which the United States exhibits tolerance for the views of others and the kind of patience that got us through the tightest straits of the Cold War. Proponents of military solutions criticize as too "soft" a foreign policy that turns to the use of force only after thorough debate on Capitol Hill, detailed (not open-ended) authorizations from lawmakers, and serious dialogue with our allies; that understands the inevitability of religious and ethnic conflicts for decades to come around the world, which for the most part must be resolved by indigenous factions themselves and seldom by the United States; that relies primarily on diplomacy as the most vital instrument in America's relations with other countries; and that exhibits caution over the risks of using military power or secret CIA operations, along with skepticism about their possibilities for success.

"Our conduct should be principled and just," wrote Harvard University law professor Roger Fisher almost two decades ago, in an essay that criticized CIA assassination plots and unsavory operations in Chile. "Conduct that is wrong for others is wrong for us," he continued.

> When we choose our weapons, let's choose ones we are good at using—like the Marshall Plan—not ones that we are bad at—like the Bay of Pigs. To join some adversaries in the grotesque world of poison dart-guns and covert operations is to give up the most powerful weapons we have: idealism, morality, due process of law, and belief in the freedom of others to disagree, including the right of other countries to disagree with ours.[46]

An America that is a strong but empathetic power, a friend and partner, a nation that lives up to its high ideals and professed principle, and is an integral part of the community of civilized nations dedicated to solving the problems that stalk the planet—here is the hope of our allies, and the dread of our enemies.

The record of this nation's successes and failures over the years should remind Americans of the dangers that stem from an ignorance about the rest of the world; of the need to demand openness and debate as the nation shapes its foreign policies, instead of relying on the instincts of a president or vice president, or the schemes of unelected bureaucrats; of the importance of rejecting a rush to military options to resolve complicated international disputes that require patient diplomacy; of repudiating unilateralism and isolationism; of becoming more compassionate about the conditions of squalor and disease that afflict much of the world; and, above all, of adopting a more humble demeanor in our relations with other nations. When the United States adopts these approaches to foreign affairs, we are more likely to succeed in our objectives abroad; when they are forgotten or dismissed, failure awaits us.

NOTES

1. See Loch K. Johnson, "Accountability and America's Secret Foreign Policy: Keeping a Legislative Eye on the Central Intelligence Agency," *Foreign Policy Analysis* 1 (March 2005), pp. 99–120.
2. Richard A. Brody and Catherine R. Shapiro, "A Reconsideration of the Rally Phenomenon in Public Opinion," in *Political Behavior Annual*, 2nd ed. (Boulder, CO: Westview Press), pp. 77–102; see, also, Richard Sobel, *The Impact of Public Opinion on U.S. Foreign Policy Since Vietnam* (New York: Oxford University Press, 2001). On the increases in government secrecy, see OpenTheGovernment.org, "Secrecy Report Card 2005."

3. Loch K. Johnson, "Presidents, Lawmakers, and Spies: Intelligence Accountability in the United States," *Presidential Studies Quarterly* 34 (December 2004), pp. 828–837.

4. David Skidmore, "Understanding the Unilateralist Turn in U.S. Foreign Policy," *Foreign Policy Analysis* 1 (July 2005), p. 219.

5. See Thomas L. Friedman, *The World Is Flat* (New York: Farrar, Straus and Giroux, 2005).

6. See Roger Cohen, "An Obsession the World Doesn't Share," *New York Times* (December 5, 2004), sec. 4, p. 1.

7. For a discussion of these ethical perspectives, see Joseph S. Nye, Jr., *Nuclear Ethics* (New York: Free Press, 1986).

8. See Loch K. Johnson, "Operational Codes and the Prediction of Leadership Behavior," in Margaret G. Herman, ed., *A Psychological Examination of Political Man* (New York: Free Press, 1977), pp. 80–119.

9. Henry Kissinger offers this summation of the approach taken by British foreign ministers, quoting British Foreign Secretary Sir Edward Grey on the successes of nineteenth-century British diplomats, who were guided by "what seemed to them to be the immediate interest of this country, without making elaborate calculations for the future" [Henry Kissinger, *Diplomacy* (New York: Simon & Schuster, 1994), pp. 95–96]. My thanks to Professor Michael J. Glennon for bringing this quote to my attention. There is something to be said, though, for looking beyond one's nose, to the extent that this is possible.

10. Press release, U.S. Department of Commerce (February 10, 2006).

11. Ibid.

12. A few initiatives that some readers might anticipate finding on the honor roll are absent. For example, the Reagan administration often receives credit for bringing the Cold War to an end. Certainly the end of the Cold War was a great event and no doubt the administration's burgeoning military budget gave the Kremlin pause, since the Soviet Union would have had to tighten belts even more to match the spending. However, the end of the Cold War, anticipated by few, is much more complicated than that. It relied ultimately on the accelerating collapse of the Soviet economy from its own inefficiencies and, above all, on bold leadership exercised by the Soviet President Mikhail S. Gorbachev. [See Robert Kaiser, *Why Gorbachev Happened* (New York: Simon & Schuster, 1992.] The Soviet president was willing to bring the Cold War to an end so he could focus on the restructuring of his own economy. Much to Gorbachev's surprise, the process lurched beyond his control and brought about a more democratic regime in Russia. At the same time, while the Reagan military build-up helped the U.S. weapons manufacturers reap enormous profits (several of whom are based in the president's home state, California), it tore America's safety net for the poor and undermined other social programs at home—negative domestic consequences of America's foreign policy.

13. See John Lewis Gaddis, *Strategies of Containment: A Critical Appraisal of Postwar American National Security Policy* (New York: Oxford University Press, 1982). Again underlining the complexity of U.S. foreign policy, neither the containment doctrine nor most any other aspect of America's external relations is purely good, bad, or ugly. For example, containment helped with the Cold War but also spawned many of the ugly initiatives presented in this chapter, including the covert actions in Iran and Guatemala in the 1950s, the Vietnam War in the 1960s, and the Iran-contra scandal in the 1980s. On balance, though, the beneficial features of the containment doctrine outweigh its negative aspects—especially since none of the bad or ugly initiatives *had* to flow from a belief in containment, but rather were excesses of that doctrine.

14. Loch K. Johnson, "Truman's Dream Deferred," *American Journal of Intelligence* 23 (Autumn/Winter 2005), pp. 6–15.

15. David S. McLellan, *The Cold War in Transition* (New York: Macmillan, 1966); Graham Allison and Philip Zelikow, *Essence of Decision: Explaining the Cuban Missile Crisis*, 2nd ed. (New York: Addison Wesley Longman, 1999); James G. Blight, Joseph S. Nye, Jr., and David A. Welch, "The Cuban Missile Crisis Revisited," *Foreign Affairs* 66 (Fall 1987), pp. 170–188; John Lewis Gaddis, *We Now Know: Rethinking Cold War History* (New York: Oxford University Press, 1997).

16. Amos Yoder, *The Conduct of American Foreign Policy Since World War II* (New York: Pergamon, 1986); Martin J. Hillenbrand, *Fragments of Our Time* (Athens: University of Georgia Press, 1998).

17. See Chambers M. Roberts, "The Day We Didn't Go to War," *The Reporter* (September 14, 1954), pp. 31–35; Stephen E. Ambrose, *Eisenhower: The President* (New York: Simon & Schuster, 1984), p. 184; Fred I. Greenstein and John P. Burke, "The Dynamics of Presidential Reality Testing: Evidence from Two Vietnam Decisions," *Political Science Quarterly* 104 (Winter 1989–1990), pp. 557–580.

18. See, for instance, Louis Fisher, *Congressional Abdication on War and Spending* (College Station: Texas A&M University Press, 2000).

19. Remarks to the author, Senator Frank Church (D-ID), Washington, DC (August 28, 1980), original emphasis. Another senator, Daniel Patrick Moynihan (D-NY), observed that "political economy is the name of the next task [in foreign policy], not geopolitics" ["Reagan's Doctrine and the Iran Issue," *New York Times* (December 21, 1986), p. E19].

20. Howard Jones, *"A New Kind of War": America's Global Strategy and the Truman Doctrine in Greece* (New York: Oxford University Press, 1989).

21. Forrest C. Pogue, *George C. Marshall: Statesman, 1945–1959* (New York: Viking, 1987).

22. See Jonathan B. Bingham, *Shirt-Sleeve Diplomacy: Point 4 in Action* (New York: John Day, 1953).

23. McLellan, *The Cold War in Transition*.
24. Richard Reeves, *President Kennedy: Profile of Power* (New York: Simon & Schuster, 1993).
25. Don Cook, *Forging the Alliance, NATO, 1945–1950* (New York: Arbor House/William Morrow, 1989).
26. For a moving account of one young Peace Corps volunteer in Africa, see Mike Tidwell, *The Ponds of Kalambayi* (New York: Lyons & Burford, 1990).
27. Strobe Talbott, *Deadly Gambits* (New York: Random House, 1984).
28. See David E. Sanger, "Who Scares the Rest?" *New York Times* (May 8, 2005), p. A4.
29. One covert action of significance in the latter stages of the Cold War would qualify for the honor roll but remains classified [author's interviews with CIA officials, Washington, DC (June 28, 1996)].
30. See Arthur M. Schlesinger, Jr., *The Imperial Presidency* (Boston: Houghton Mifflin, 1973).
31. See Richard J. Barnet, *Real Security* (New York: Simon & Schuster, 1981); and, on Iran, author's conversations with President Carter's vice president, Walter Mondale, Minneapolis, Minnesota (April 21, 2000).
32. David Stout and John H. Cushman, Jr., "Defense Missile for U.S. System Fails to Launch," *New York Times* (December 16, 2004), p. A1.
33. "The Naked Shield," unsigned editorial, *New York Times* (December 16, 2004), p. A34.
34. Stanley Karnow, *Vietnam: A History* (New York: Viking, 1983); Stanley I. Kutler, ed., *Encyclopedia of the Vietnam War* (New York: Scribners, 1976); Neil Sheehan, *A Bright Shining Lie* (New York: Random House, 1988).
35. James C. Thomson, Jr., "How Could Vietnam Happen? An Autopsy," *Atlantic Monthly* (April 1968), p. 52.
36. Cohen, "An Obsession the World Doesn't Share," sec. 4, p. 6.
37. Jacek Kugler, Ronald L. Tammen, and Brian Efird, "Integrating Theory and Policy: Global Implications of the War in Iraq," *International Studies Review* 6 (October 2004), p. 179.
38. "American Empire and Its Discontents: The United States and Europe Today," in Michael Gehler, Günter Bischof, Ludger Kühnhardt, and Rolf Steininger, eds., *Towards a European Constitution: A Historical and Political Comparison with the United States* (Wien: Böhlau Verlag, 2005), p. 197.
39. "As the Dollar Declines," unsigned editorial, *New York Times* (November 13, 2004), p. A30. According to the Congressional Budget Office, the Bush administration budget would increase the federal deficit by more than $1.2 trillion over the next decade (see Edmund L. Andrews, "Bush Plan Would Raise Deficit by $1.2 Trillion, Budget Office Says," *New York Times* [March 4, 2006], p. A28).

40. Loch K. Johnson, "The Aspin-Brown Intelligence Inquiry: Behind the Doors of a Blue Ribbon Commission," *Studies in Intelligence* 48 (Winter 2004), pp. 1–20.
41. See *The 9/11 Commission Report: Final Report of the National Commission on Terrorist Attacks upon the United States* (New York: Norton, 2004).
42. Loch K. Johnson, *America's Secret Power: The CIA in a Democratic Society* (New York: Oxford University Press, 1989); and *Bombs, Bugs, Drugs, and Thugs: Intelligence and America's Quest for Security* (New York: New York University Press, 2000). This is not to say the Predator is without merit; it has been a valuable intelligence-gathering device throughout the wars in Afghanistan and Iraq in 2001–.
43. Quoted by Bob Woodward, *Plan of Attack* (New York: Simon & Schuster, 2004), p. 438.
44. See Loch K. Johnson, "A Framework for Strengthening U.S. Intelligence," *Yale Journal of International Affairs* 1 (Winter/Spring 2006), pp. 116–131.
45. Elizabeth Drew, "Letter from Washington," *The New Yorker* (March 3, 1987), p. 111; see, also, William S. Cohen and George J. Mitchell, *Men of Zeal: A Candid Inside Story of the Iran-Contra Hearings* (New York: Viking, 1988); and Laurence H. Tribe, "Reagan Ignites a Constitutional Crisis," *New York Times* (May 20, 1987), p. A30.
46. Roger Fisher, "The Fatal Flaw in Our Spy System," *Boston Globe* (February 1, 1976), p. A9.

INDEX